THE INVESTOR'S GUIDE TO

TECHNICAL ANALYSIS

INVESTOR'S GUIDE TO

TECHNICAL ANALYSIS

Predicting Price Action in the Markets

Elli Gifford

FT
PITMAN
PUBLISHING

PITMAN PUBLISHING
128 Long Acre, London WC2E 9AN

A Division of Pearson Professional Limited

First published in Great Britain 1995

British Library Cataloguing in Publication Data
A CIP catalogue record from this book can be obtained
from the British Library.

ISBN 0 273 61068 6

3 5 7 9 10 8 6 4 2

Typeset by PanTek Arts, Maidstone, Kent
Printed and bound in Great Britain by
Biddles Ltd, Guildford and King's Lynn

*The Publishers' policy is to use paper manufactured
from sustainable forests.*

CONTENTS

ACKNOWLEDGEMENTS

I am grateful to the following for their contributions: Investment Research of Cambridge Ltd, 28 Panton Street, Cambridge CB2 1DH, Tel 01223 356251, Fax 01223 329805; Neural Network Investment Forecasting Ltd, Steeple House, Percy Street, Coventry, CV1 3BY, Tel 01203 222228, Fax 01203 223728; Chart Analysis Ltd, 7 Swallow Street, London, W1R 7HD, Tel 0171 734 7174, Fax 0171 439 4966; Deliberations, IRIS Ltd, P O Box 182, Adelaide Street Station, Toronto, Ont. MSC 2JI, Canada; Synergy Software, Britannic House, 20 Dunstable Road, Luton, LU1 1ED, Tel 01582 424282, Fax 01582 48274, Reuters Ltd, 85 Fleet Street, London, EC4P 4AJ, Tel 0171 250 1122 and Chartwell, Tollit and Harvey Ltd., Lyon Way, Greenford, Middlesex UB6 0BN, Tel 0181 578 6861, Fax 0181 575 8253.

INTRODUCTION

Technical analysis was once likened to the reading of tea leaves but that time has long passed; now it is a subject which has attracted the attention of academics ranging from mathematicians to rocket scientists. Vast sums of money are traded on financial exchanges using signals generated from the computerisation of its techniques. Indeed, significant work is being done in the field of neural networks where computers are being 'taught' to recognise past market movements and predict future ones. This book is not for that market, it has the private investor and the market student in mind. It goes back to the beginning and covers in detail the basic concepts, giving its readers a real understanding of the psychology of markets and a firm grasp of the methods used to interpret them.

Technical analysis is the analysis of price behaviour in financial markets, as against the analysis of the underlying assets represented by that price. It addresses the fact that a share price not only reflects the value placed on it by those in the market, but also the hopes and fears of those buying and selling it. As a consequence, over-enthusiasm, or panic, can cause prices to move well away from their value, sometimes for protracted periods. As price and value often differ analysis of the balance sheet alone is unlikely to enable an investor to time his market commitments as well as he otherwise might. The techniques employed in technical analysis monitor patterns as they build on charts and, using past experience as a guide, allow users to determine what the price is most likely to do next.

The book starts with a mention of Charles Dow who, at the turn of the century, recognised that the buying and selling activity of investors has as much to do with price movements as the value of the shares themselves. This approach allows examination of how support and resistance function, trends form and the significance of new highs and lows. Whilst technical analytical techniques have advanced very considerably since Dow, the logic of his Theory is still at the core of the subject today. Whereas some assume the subject to be rule-based (and, to a certain extent, it is) this book addresses it primarily from the perspective of market psychology, noting the effects of fear and greed in particular, and thus stresses the need for flexibility in interpretation, together with its use in the formulation of a discipline.

Chapter 2 discusses the different types of charts used: the construction of daily, weekly, and monthly bar charts; point and figure charts; and the 'new' candlestick charts ('new' only to Western investors – they have been in use in

Japan for many centuries). Also addressed are the two different forms of scaling – arithmetic or semi-logarithmic – and their appropriate uses.

Chapters 3 to 7 go into detailed analysis of market trends and chart patterns. Aspects covered are how trends are formed and the roles of inclined support and resistance; the importance of a break in the trend; and trend reversal. Methods of defining trends include trend lines and channels, moving averages (and the choice of their periodicities), stop and reverse points and speedlines. The psychology behind pattern development is investigated and individual patterns (such as rectangles, triangles, heads and shoulders, double tops, flags and so on), and price predictions from them, are looked at in detail. Additionally, warning signals coming from one period of trading – such as key reversals – are examined and Chapter 7 is devoted to a brief look at short-term formations in Japanese candlestick charts.

Chapter 8 moves on to the technical analysis of the stock market itself and covers the use of market indices; the relationship between interest rates, bonds and equities; stock market cycles and the use of breadth indicators to establish the significance of a move in an index. Also addressed is the measurement of the performance of an individual share against that of the market, and the confirmatory role of volume.

All the most basic concepts of technical analysis have now been addressed and Chapter 9 goes on to discuss the fine-tuning of market commitments by the use of technical indicators designed to measure overextended price moves. These indicators highlight situations when a price move has 'gone too far' and is vulnerable to reversal. Broadly speaking, they are constructed in a manner which, by comparing today's price with a price scored previously, calculates the speed at which price change is occurring. Once that speed slackens slightly, particularly if the indicator is giving historically 'overbought' or 'oversold' readings, warning signals through. Many such indicators have been developed and the most popular ones – Momentum, Rate of Change, Welles Wilder's Relative Strength Index, Coppock, Moving Average Convergence/ Divergence, Williams' Percentage R and George Lane's Stochastics (and others) – are covered here.

By the time Chapter 10 is reached the reader should have a good understanding of the basic techniques in use in technical analysis today. What he or she may not have, however, is a grasp of how to pull these techniques all together effectively. This chapter, using a considerable number of practical examples from real market situations, addresses this problem and, starting with the long-term picture and breaking it down to the very near term charts, goes through a logical analysis of all the signals coming through. Trends, patterns, predictions are analysed and, using the timing devices discussed earlier, the matter of how to come to an investment decision and when to act is addressed. Indeed, two examples of making an investment and then monitoring its progress are shown in great detail. The last chapter is devoted to a basic description of cyclical analysis and, in particular, how it was applied by the famous technicians, Dow, Elliott and Gann.

It can be seen that technical analysis now covers considerable territory but is in many ways still simplistic. This is an advantage since it means the novice can benefit from his first acquaintance with it; the structure of the book should assist in this endeavour. As time passes experiments will tell whether the new user wants to plot his own charts by hand – to increase the 'feel' for the market – or run programs on his computer; whether he feels happier defining the trendlines himself, or wishes to rely on moving averages or other calculated values; whether he wishes to concentrate on strongly trending prices or investigate potential reversal situations. In time the techniques discussed here should allow him to build an investment discipline which should greatly enhance his confidence in taking decisions and his enjoyment of investing in the market.

1

THE BASIC PRINCIPLES

- The Dow Theory upon which many of the modern techniques are based
- How investor anticipation is responsible for the stockmarkets discounting future events – except 'Acts of God'
- The reasons patterns build and repeat in markets time and time again
- How technical analysts adopt the role of market psychologist, anticipating the effect of the actions of buyers and sellers on price
- How fear and greed can cause apparently illogical price moves; and how markets can become overstretched and stay so for a very long time.

Charles Dow was an economist who edited the *Wall Street Journal* at the end of the last century and it was he who recognised that it was the action of people in the market-place that caused price to change, rather than economic news itself. He constructed the now-famous Dow Jones Industrial Average and noted that it consistently stopped going up and started going down before the Journal carried evidence the economic boom was over. Equally, it stopped going down and started to rise before it was clear the recession had ended. It is now the received wisdom that stock markets discount future events. The price is thus largely dependent on the hopes and fears of investors taking decisions in anticipation of their judgement proving correct when results come out: it is the summation of the collective interpretation of all known factors at any one time. This allows acceptance of the basic premise of technical analysis – that, although long-term trends form due to fundamental valuations, price change on a shorter-term basis is heavily dependent on shifts in sentiment among the players in the market. To this extent technical analysts are market psychologists, watching the actions of investors and noting the effects of those actions on the price.

In normal, everyday circumstances the pattern building in the price chart will probably look like that in Figure 1.1.

Prices are backing and filling between two levels – 280p and 350p. Each time the price rallies to the upper level buyers become less aggressive, unwilling to pay more than they have had to do previously. This causes the rise to run out of steam. The balance of the market argument now favours the sellers and prices sink back. But once the lower region is approached, sellers become less anxious and buyers, looking to buy at levels which have served them well

Pattern building in price chart

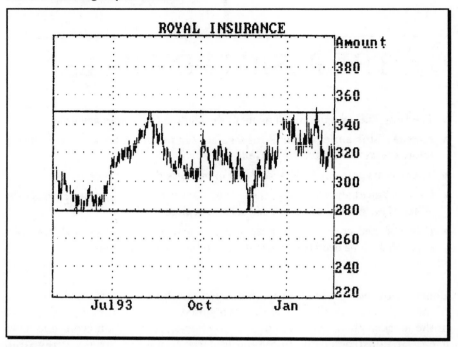

Figure 1.1

Chart by Reuters Technical Analysis

The price action building in this chart is typical of what happens most of the time – no significant change is seen from day to day. A market argument is underway, confined by 'support' around the lows and 'resistance' around the highs. Support is effective at previous lows as people recall prices bouncing from that level before and they buy, looking forward to a similar rise. The highs are in an area where rises are resisted; nervous holders who failed to get out previously and then saw prices fall are tempted to sell now.

before, return to the market. This interaction between buyers and sellers is a normal, everyday occurrence which, statisticians will tell you, happens the vast majority of the time. Technicians call the price area where falls are arrested, 'support' and the region where the rallies reverse, 'resistance'.

However, whilst such gentle market activity may occur most of the time, it certainly does not always prove the order of the day. Indeed, there are a considerable number of occasions when prices move in a much more aggressive manner – such as the sharp fall in prices seen in Figure 1.2.

The trading prior to the fall can be said to be a balanced argument, with neither the buyers nor the sellers sticking their necks out and taking a strong view. The fall was occasioned by the sellers suddenly becoming very much more aggressive and the buyers either withdrawing or, in the circumstances, becoming very much less sanguine. This change in attitude could have been

Sharp fall in prices once a market argument is over

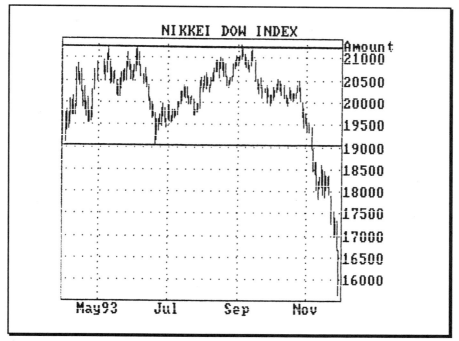

Figure 1.2

Chart by Reuters Technical Analysis

When a market argument is 'won' the move is often sharp as people who had been buying in the support region rush to close their position. Once the initial falls are over, any corrective rallies are likely to be defeated with ease as the previous support area is approached.

caused by a particular piece of news, or it could have come about because sentiment had, unaccountably, shifted. Either way, sellers won the previous market argument and caused the fall.

It is the interaction between buyers and sellers and the recognition of support and resistance that causes trends to form. This is because, once resistance is cleared, it becomes support and, likewise, once support is broken, it reverses its role and becomes resistance. The chart of BAT Industries in Figure 1.3 is a good example of this.

At the beginning of the period resistance is being consistently encountered around 300p. Once this was cleared, prices went to 390p before profit-taking caused them to retrace to 290p where support came into play. The reason falls are arrested at a previous resistance level is that, to traders who saw them rise (by 90p, or over 30 per cent, in the example) from that point before, they now look cheap; they buy in adequate quantities to stem the decline and reverse it. The same thing happened in 1993; the mid-1992 highs, previously resistance, now offer support, and so, by this step-and-repeat performance, this uptrend

Support and resistance

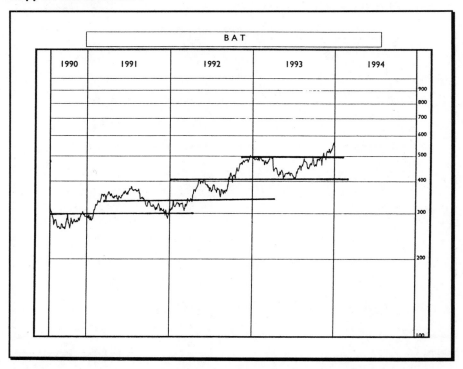

Figure 1.3   Chart by Investment Research of Cambridge Ltd: Design by NNIF

Once resistance is cleared it subsequently becomes support (and vice versa). The 'stepping stones' so formed allow trends to develop.

formed. In a downtrend the opposite occurs; following a similar psychology, broken support subsequently becomes resistance as traders, who failed to get rid of their holdings as the support gave way, use rallies to make sales as the previous support area (now resistance) is approached. Sometimes support and resistance areas can remain effective for years – investors have long memories, particulary where money is concerned.

Having recognised that it is the people in the market that cause prices to move when they do, the technician acknowledges that he needs to consider what they are most likely to do next. Much will depend on how they feel. If prices are moving in their direction and they are feeling confident and happy that the position they have adopted is the right one, then it is probable only dramatic news – a real surprise – that will cause them to take another view. But, say, after very considerable analysis, a broker has come to the conclusion that a share which had been falling for many months has now got to a price where it is very cheap. All bad news the analyst can imagine has been discounted in the price and, in his view, prospects for the company's recovery are good. This market analyst is very experienced and he has done his research in a methodical manner and made recommendations to his clients to buy, or bought on their behalf. It is at this stage there is a good possibility the most negative of all emotions – fear – will creep in. Why should it do so? Because, despite his scientific approach, he recognises there is a danger prices may not move in the direction he believes justified. After all, as can be seen in Figure 1.4 – the market has been taken by surprise before.

Prices attempting to recover in a downtrend

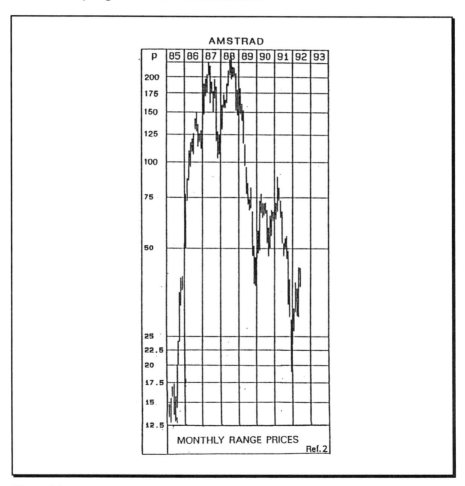

Figure 1.4   *Source:* Investment Research of Cambridge Ltd –

Once an investment has been made even experienced investors will feel some fear in case bad news takes the market by surprise.

In the latter part of 1990 and early 1991, it can be seen that confidence was returning to the market and the price of Amstrad shares was rising. However, by mid-1991 the rise had been reversed and, by the end of the year, prices were in new low ground. On this occasion the market had been taken by surprise: first, by the chairman suddenly selling a large line of stock and, secondly, by results which were far from market expectations. Until such time as some news comes out to confirm his belief the shares are now due for recovery, the analyst will suffer some fear at least.

Fear is a surprisingly prevalent emotion, even among professional market participants, since it is not only those in a losing position who suffer from it. Odd as it may seem, it is apparent when traders are not only making profits but when they are making more money than they had anticipated. On this occasion it comes out in the question, what should they do?

Say a fund manager had bought Babcock (see Figure 1.5) in June, anticipating a 40 per cent rise by the year-end; and this rise has not only come through,

Babcock International Group

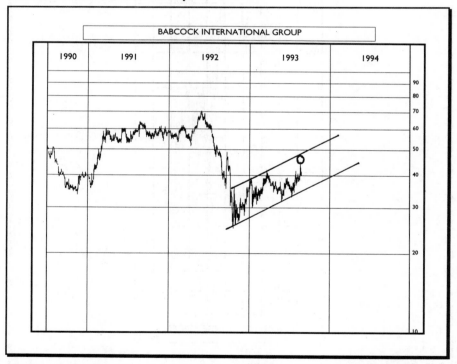

Figure 1.5   Chart by Investment Research of Cambridge Ltd: Design by NNIF

Sudden price moves can cause anxiety even when profits are being made. The projected price for the year-end has been fulfilled prematurely – should profits be booked?

but has done so in two months, rather than the six months originally anticipated. There is a certain amount of danger in any action he might take. If he
says thank you very much to the market and takes his profit, he is at risk of
underperforming against competing fund managers who might not follow this
course if the share maintains its extraordinary rise. Additionally, what does he
do if, subsequent to his booking his profits, news comes out that justifies the
market's new valuation on the shares in question? Does he go back into the
market and, if so, at what price? On the other hand, he may maintain his holding, even if he cannot fundamentally justify the new price range. This leaves
him in a position to benefit from the strongly rising trend but it also leaves him
open to the risk the market may recognise its overvaluation, and suddenly
reverse. He is then in the position of wishing he had sold at his targeted price
when he had the chance which, as can been seen from looking at Figure 1.6,
happened here. Whatever the level of sophistication and experience of the
market player, fear is an element that cannot be ignored.

Babcock International Group

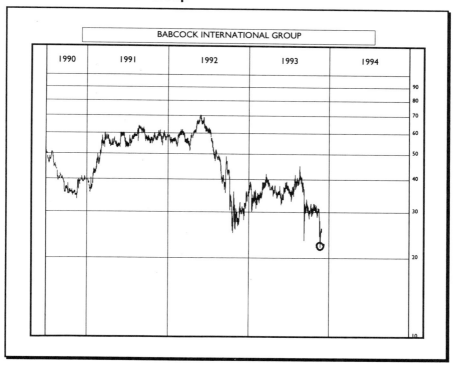

Figure 1.6   Chart by Investment Research of Cambridge Ltd: Design by NNIF

A danger of not taking a sudden profit is that the move could be reversed.

The other, equally dangerous, emotion is, of course, greed. The following chart (Figure 1.7) is a particularly popular one used to emphasise this point. In fact, my company published it on several occasions before the crash in 1987, warning that the greed factor could push prices to such extremes that a sharp market reversal, as seen in 1929, was almost inevitable.

The chart shows the Dow Jones Industrial Average (as a representation of Wall Street) plotted over two time periods, 1912-1929 and 1970-1987. The patterns traced are extraordinarily similar – indeed, they correlate well statistically. During the early part of the history over both time periods prices moved very broadly sideways, enjoying mild bull and bear markets over a rough four-year cycle. Then, in 1924 and 1982 respectively, they cleared their earlier highs (100 and 1000) and started rising strongly; and continued to do so – for five years.

Dow Jones Industrial Average; 1912 – 1929 and 1970 – 1987

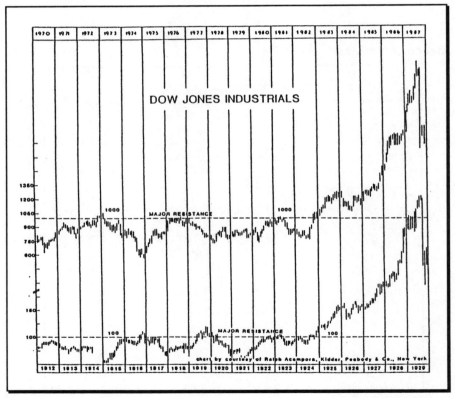

Figure 1.7   *Source:* Kidder Peabody

Technical analysts believe people will react in the same way in a given set of circumstances as they did in the past thus causing a similar price move.

One of Dow's most important observations – which has become a key part of his Theory today – was that if the Averages hit new historic highs (or lows) further significant gains (or falls) were called for. This was because investors were forced to consider seriously whether or not the economic expansion was so great that higher prices than had ever been paid before were justified. He reasoned that if the conclusion was a positive one then circumstances had likely changed enough for even more substantial rises to come through. This certainly happened on both occasions here.

Dow's recognition of the importance of new highs and lows led him to develop a second market average – the Dow Railroads Average. He reasoned that if new highs were of such significance, then some form of confirmation that they truly reflected a conscious reappraisal by investors, rather than perhaps an aberration in the calculation of the Industrials Average, was necessary.

Dow argued that if industrial stocks were set to enjoy greater profitability, then so should railroad stocks, since their traffic would greatly increase as the demand for goods grew across the continent. Thus, strong gains would only be signalled when both Averages moved into new high ground – the move by one had been 'confirmed' by the other. This – the Principle of Confirmation – is an extremely important aspect of technical analysis today; much of the interpretation of signals from market background indicators and studies registering momentum and overbought/oversold market conditions is based upon it and its opposite – Divergence. It will be addressed at considerable length later.

It is interesting to note that the earlier highs were, on these two occasions, round numbers – 100 and 1,000. Every shopkeeper recognises the significance of these and purposely prices items at £9.95 (and so on) so as to avoid the danger of the customer reconsidering his purchase. Old price extremes and round numbers are often responsible for halting price moves and their importance is at the heart of technical analysis today. Indeed, the round numbers in question are not only the tens and one hundreds, figures such as 5, 50, 500 and 2, 20 and 200 etc. all assume the same role. Anything that is likely to force a consumer or producer to reconsider a purchase or a sale is a potential area where a price move may halt.

A glance at the previous price history shows these rises to be unusual phenomena but, what is perhaps even more surprising, both the rises and the subsequent falls were extraordinarily similar in extent. This may be considered particularly odd when it is revealed that the 1929 fall was heralding even more serious weakness, whilst the collapse of 1987 can now be seen to have been only a sharp correction to a sustained rise. What does all this mean? It means that whilst the collapse in 1929 was heralding the recognition of an horrendous depression, the falls of 1987 merely adjusted some temporary overheating in the stock market; both were caused by the greed of the traders trying to preserve profits already made.

This forces us to recognise something very important; prices can at times reflect almost solely the emotions of the people in the market-place. This is the one thing the two market periods had in common – large quantities of people making large amounts of money. For many it was the only game in town. Once prices start moving this dramatically attention becomes focused on prices alone. Fundamentals are forgotten and markets become extremely 'overbought' or 'oversold' and, the faster the price movement, the longer such conditions can prevail.

All would recognise that it was an extraordinary period, that it could not last for ever but equally, each would feel it was an opportunity not to be missed. For the professional fund manager, the danger of going liquid was too great – his consequent underperformance would drop him to the bottom of the league tables immediately. For the private investor, recognising this was a one-off chance in a lifetime to make a large return, the temptation to continue to go along for the ride was too much. Despite the vast changes that had occurred in the world over the 50 years in question, the reactions of the market players remained the same. They 'stayed for the ride', determined that, at the first sign of trouble, they would get out and, not being greedy, they would 'leave the last 10 per cent for the next guy'. The longer the rise lasted, the more nervous the investors became so that, by the time that first sign of trouble emerged, everyone's mental stoploss was triggered and the resultant collapses are now history.

It is not possible to explain scientifically why the rises and subsequent reactions were so similar in extent. Suffice it to say that a rise of that nature would have attracted a large number of investors who, as it went on, would become increasingly nervous about protecting their profits. The consequent emotional build-up against the excessively frothy market background would almost inevitably lead to a fall, triggered by their panic to sell, whose extent bore a direct relationship to the rise. Although this particular example is exceptional, time and again market patterns repeat themselves and it is upon this well-tried observation that technical analysis is based.

Figures 1.8 and 1.9 showing charts of Copper and Sterling/Dollar serve to make the point that, not only do patterns repeat themselves, individual markets adopt their own characteristics and retain them over time. The most probable explanation is that people trading particular markets have their own reasons for doing so and they continue to trade in a similar manner. Hence, the same patterns repeat themselves in the same way. It is rare to find a market whose character changes completely and, if it occurs, it will almost certainly be due to a shift in the perception of what that market represents – and thus, who trades it, how and why. In other words, the personalities of the traders will stamp themselves on how the price behaves and, if their constitution changes, this will become immediately apparent on the chart.

Two similar uptrends in copper prices

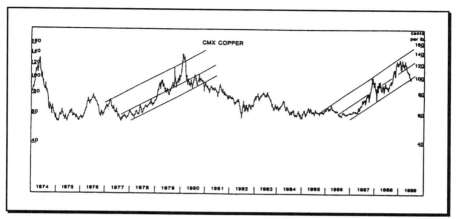

Figure 1.8
Source: Investment Research of Cambridge Ltd

Markets adopt particular characteristics and repeat similar price moves time and again.

Trends in the Pound

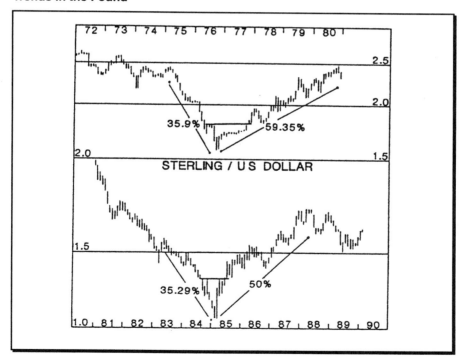

Figure 1.9
Source: Investment Research of Cambridge Ltd

Over the two different periods prices enjoyed similar declines, similar reversal patterns and similar uptrends.

Long-term charts of gold, platinum and copper

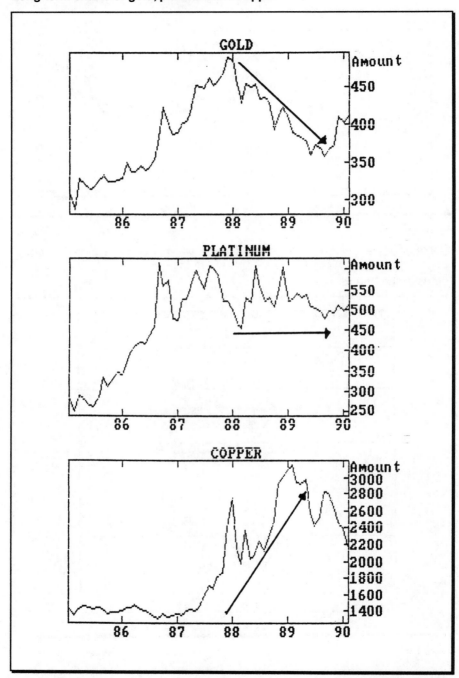

Figure 1.10

Figure 1.10 shows long-term charts of gold, platinum and copper. Until the mid-1980s, platinum correlated very well with gold but this relationship disappeared between 1987 and 1989. This was because previously platinum had been considered a precious metal but then its industrial demand increased since it was being used in catalytic converters in cars. During the latter part of the period, although precious metals were falling, base metals – as can be seen from the copper chart – were rising. As a consequence platinum, caught between the two influences, moved broadly sideways. But such examples are rare. Against different market backgrounds – bull and bear markets and phases of uncertainty – the dynamics of the trading may alter, but not the basic characteristics of the market itself.

The basic tenet of technical analysis is that it is the people in the market-place, taking into account all known fundamental facts and their reactions to them, that make the prices and that involvement in the market can increase emotions. Emotional reactions grow as large price changes get underway and heightened emotions, particularly fear and greed, cause people, spurred by the subconscious impetus of the crowd, to act less rationally than they otherwise might. They can be tempted into paying more for a share than they would wish, or taking less as a panic sell-off occurs.

Once these prices are plotted as charts they form patterns and trends which reflect the activity of the people in the market-place. When patterns build in a similar manner to how they have in the past it is highly probable people will react in the same way as they did previously and, consequently, the outcome in terms of price move is likely to be similar in extent.

This chapter started by mentioning Charles Dow who can be credited with recognising the effect of people on price. His research became known as the Dow Theory and, although this Theory in its pure form is not much in use today, its essence forms the basis on which modern analytical techniques are built. Throughout the rest of this book reference to Dow tenets will be made, but this chapter finishes with his first 'law' – perhaps the most succinct. It states what, once thought about, is obvious: 'Prices Discount Everything – Except Acts of God'. If all perceptions as to value are built into the price, then only a complete surprise will cause a price move which is so sudden it implies earlier judgements were 'wrong'. Acts of God which come to mind are sudden frosts which damage the coffee crop or, as in 1993, dramatic floods in the Mid-West of the USA which washed out fields of grain.

Figure 1.10 (opposite)

Traders stamp their personalities on markets; if their constitution changes, so will the trading characteristics of the price. Once industrial demand for platinum grew, its performance became less like that of gold and more like that of copper; in that gold was falling and copper rising at the time, platinum effectively traded sideways.

However, the chart in Figure 1.11 provides as nice an example of a market taken by surprise as any; 9 April 1992 was a general election in the United Kingdom. The polls suggested the chances of a Conservative victory were slim and the stock market had been falling steadily during the campaign. Late in the afternoon on the 9th prices rallied, a move generally judged to be caused by futures traders closing out short positions before they went home to vote. By the time the market opened on 10 April results had started coming in and a

Averages Discount Everything (Except Acts of God)

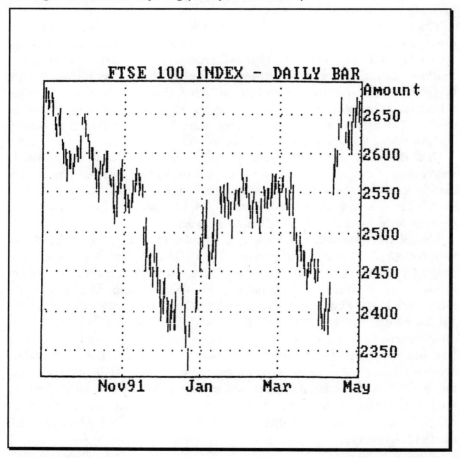

Figure 1.11   *Chart* by Reuters Technical Analysis

Dow stated 'The Averages Discount Everything – Except Acts of God'. On 9 April 1992 the Conservatives were not expected to be returned to Parliament with a majority – the 100 point rise on the 10th proves a win was not factored into the price.

Tory victory was very much more likely. People scrambled to buy back shares they had sold and the market opened 100 points up. Perhaps not a traditional 'Act of God', but it was proof that a Tory victory had not been factored into the price.

2

CHARTS AND THEIR CONSTRUCTION

- Charts can be constructed for any regular time period – minute to minute, hourly, daily, weekly; and there are plots, which basically ignore time factors, such as tick or point and figure charts. The same rules of interpretation apply to all
- There are two main forms of scaling – linear and semi-logarithmic – and they have different uses and effects
- It is essential that the data used to construct charts is accurate, consistent and logical in its choice. It is probable that the most frequently used and most important price series is the daily one – with its close being recognised by more people than any other price
- The different time periodicities can all be plotted in a similar manner; the most popular methods are lines, bars, point and figure and candlesticks.

The basic working tools of a technical analyst are charts, hence the synonymously used titles, 'chartist' or even 'technical chart analyst'. Some, however, would argue they are not the same at all. Perhaps the real difference is that at its simplest, this form of analysis is the 'reading' of price charts. At a more advanced level price charts are accompanied by moving averages, indicators and so on, and the interpretation is not dependent on the price chart alone. Further sophistication is possible; techniques previously in the realm of physics are applied to price series and the results used to generate technical trading signals.

I am not aware of an official definition of 'chartist' versus 'technical analyst' and, whilst I have no personal objection to being referred to as a chartist, there is clear evidence that others definitely prefer the title technical analyst. In 1985 the UK professional association – The Association of Chart and Technical Analysts – became The Society of Technical Analysts Ltd and the membership has grown very significantly since.

It is my view that the techniques used are there for the purpose of refining market timing and, as this is a highly personal thing, what suits one investor will not get the confident support of another. Certainly, each must build his own discipline and I would argue it matters not what the subject is called so much as how successfully its methods are implemented. Either way, the vast majority of practitioners use price charts in some way and so this chapter goes back to basics and addresses their construction.

Until relatively recently it would be the automatic assumption that a technician needed to understand in fine detail how to construct a chart so he could plot it by hand and keep it up to date. This is no longer the case since computers and relevant software are now well within the average investor's budget. Many would argue that, in a way, this is a shame since the need to hand-plot charts had a very useful by-product – a 'feel' for the market. But others believe this facet can be compensated for by the increase in efficiency computers and automatic data updating provide. As has been said previously, analysis and the methods employed are an extremely personal choice; each person engaged in the subject must experiment and find what attitudes and techniques work for him best. But whatever choices are made it is essential to understand the construction of the charts – the pictures upon which investment decisions are to be based.

The structure of charts is relatively flexible. Decisions need to be made as to their frequency of plot: tick-by-tick for floor traders; 5 minute, 15 minute, half-hourly and so on for day traders; and hourly, daily, weekly and monthly for 'position' traders (anyone who is likely to hold his position overnight or longer). Stock market investors traditionally are more interested in the longer-term bull and bear markets and nowadays would probably use daily or weekly charts to take their decisions, monthly charts to double-check the longer-term trend was favourable and a shorter-term chart, daily, or quite possibly hourly, to time their market commitment. This is, of course, open to personal choice but, whatever the decision, the charts are constructed in the same way and their strengths and weaknesses are addressed here.

Also, it should be mentioned that, although many traditional techniques are derived from daily bar charting, the same methods of analysis are used, whatever the periodicity chosen. Patterns form in tick charts that have the same near term significance as those that form in daily charts where their resolution is likely to be more enduring. In addition, trend reversal on a daily chart is analysed in the same manner as a reversal on a weekly chart although, of course, the significance of such a reversal can have a very different import.

Apart from deciding what periodicity of data is important, a decision as to what kind of scale to use needs to be made. Charts differ in appearance significantly when plotted on an arithmetic scale as against a logarithmic scale. For some uses one is more appropriate than another. Normally speaking, arithmetic (or linear) price and timescales are used to get the most sensitive view of what a price is doing. They are very adaptable and the user can make his own choice about how he sees the price change occurring. But often the logarithmic (or, more specifically, the semi-logarithmic) approach – where price change shows in percentage terms – is more appropriate. It adds a necessary discipline, particularly in long-term analyis. Additionally, there are many users of point and figure charts around who believe that time is irrelevant in chart plotting; action in the market is all that counts. The structure to these charts is entirely different. And last, but not least, the Japanese candle charts are, to the Westerner, unusual in construction – but visually very effective for the chart analyst.

The arithmetic, or linear, chart grid shown in Figure 2.1 is straightfoward in the extreme. This particular example has a millimetre-based grid, with each little box a millimetre square. Every fifth line, both horizontally and vertically, is printed in heavier type, with every tenth heavier still. This makes reading off the scale very much easier. This sort of paper is designed primarily for daily charts as most major markets enjoy a five-day trading week. So, reading across the X axis (the horizontal time axis) the first millimetre square after the heavier line will represent Monday's trading and the next square Tuesday's – and so on. It is the convention to leave a square blank if it is an official holiday and no trading occurs. The Y axis is used for the price scale; the benefit of this kind of grid is the price differences between the horizontal lines can be varied so that the plot shows up clearly.

A line chart is the simplest plot of all. The example in Figure 2.2 is a daily chart where the closing price of each day is plotted with a line joining it to the close of the previous day. It is an accepted convention that the closing price is the most important of the day. The whole of the Dow Theory is based on closing prices (of the Dow Jones Averages) and it has become a well-accepted method of plotting the progress of a market or a share. Indeed, most moving averages and technical indicators are calculated on the close and many trading systems give their signals on this basis.

In the modern world where 24-hour markets exist, the analyst has to make his own choice as to what figure to use. For instance, in the currency markets where trading continues day and night some use three separate charts – to represent the closes in Tokyo, London and New York – whilst others take the decision to use the open in Tokyo as the 'open' and the close in New York as the 'close'. Others, recognising that the busiest period is the afternoon in Europe when New York is also open, use the London close. The important thing is to decide which point is the most useful to you and then remain consistent.

The line chart in Figure 2.3 shows an even more simplistic picture. It is the same price series as in the previous example but some of the 'noise' has been cut out as it is plotted just once a week instead of five times; this allows coverage of more back history in the same space. The convention is to take the Friday's close as it is argued this is bound to be the most important of the week since anyone slightly concerned about their investment might be inclined to close their position before the markets closed for the weekend.

Arithmetic chart grid

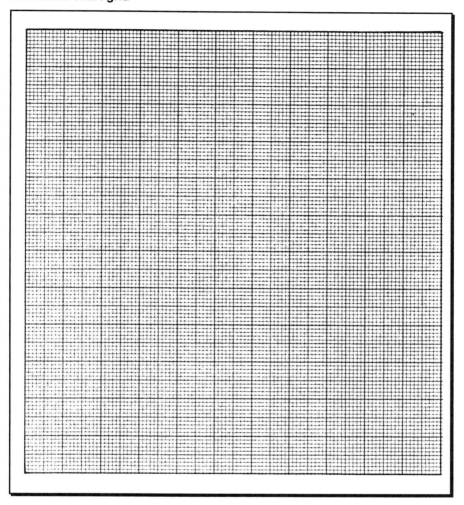

Figure 2.1   *Source:* Chartwell

Arithmetic (or linear) grids are very flexible and are used to obtain the most sensitive view of what the price is doing. This design is particularly useful for daily charts since the heavier lines denote the start and end of the five-day trading week.

The High/Low/Close chart (see Figure 2.4) is just that – a plot that gives the closing price as a horizontal bar across a vertical line that joins the highest price of the day (or of whatever period is chosen) to the lowest. These charts are also known as bar charts or daily/weekly (etc.) range and close charts. Anyone with a good intraday computer screen service can find this data easily,

Line chart

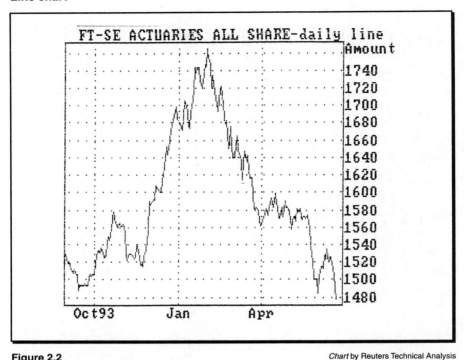

Figure 2.2   *Chart* by Reuters Technical Analysis

The line chart – which joins one closing price to the next – is simplicity itself. Its impact can send an immediate message.

as can those who download it from a database service. Most computer packages provide communications software which can access several of these suppliers. But if you are relying on newspapers, the data is less easy to come by. The *Financial Times* gives closing prices only on UK shares but the *Wall Street Journal* gives the highs and lows on the larger issues.

The relationship between where the price closes and where it was trading through the period can be very important. In a strongly rising market – particularly during the early stages of the trend – the close is likely to be near the high, suggesting the buying power has not yet been exhausted. When it ceases to be in this position, the first signs the trend may be tiring slightly start to come through. The opposite is true in a downtrend. In a broadly sideways trend, often called a 'congestion' or 'consolidation' area, the close is likely to be roughly in the middle of the range. Once prices have broken up from a congestion area it is often referred to as a region of accumulation since it can be seen in retrospect that the balance of the argument favoured the buyers who

Weekly line chart

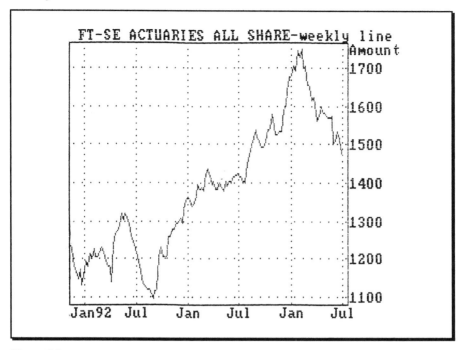

Figure 2.3   *Chart* by Reuters Technical Analysis

The weekly line chart cuts out the fine detail and allows coverage of more of the price history.

were accumulating shares – if prices break down the area is referred to as one of distribution.

The position of the close relative to the range can give some very stark signals. This is particularly so if, say, on an intraday basis, prices break up through resistance, or down through support, but close near the opposite end of the range. This strongly suggests the attempt to make the breakout has been abandoned, at least for now. This is another reason why many people take their signals on the close only.

The daily range chart in Figure 2.4 is a European convention, reflecting the fact that, until relatively recently, opening prices were not readily available. But in the United States the Open/High/Low/Close chart has long been used in the futures markets. As can be seen from Figure 2.5 the vertical bar showing the range remains the same but the open price is plotted to the left of it, and the close to the right. As long as the user is happy that the opening price is representative of the market as a whole at that time (in thinly-traded issues this may not be the case), the relationship between the open, high, low and close

High/Low/Close chart

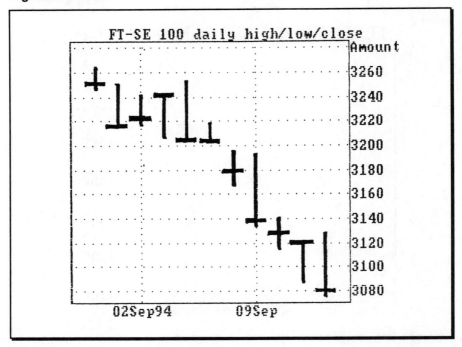

Figure 2.4

Chart by Reuters Technical Analysis

The daily high/low/close chart is a European convention as, until recently, official opening prices were unavailable.

can give some very useful signals. Whilst the close would normally be considered the most important price of the day, a lot more can be read into the chart if the open is present too. A price which opens up on the previous close, but then closes below it, is reinforcing the suspicion you may get from the high/low/close chart that it is not ready to make the breakout yet.

Figure 2.6 shows a weekly open/high/low/close chart following the normal convention of Monday's opening price being used for the open and Friday's closing price for the close. The logic is the same as that for Friday's close being used if only one price per week is to be plotted; nervous traders may close their positions before the weekend but, if all is still well, once the markets reopen they will reinstate them on Monday. Indeed, this reasoning leads to the 'Tuesday Rule' which states that, in a bull market, prices will resume their rise on Monday as everyone re-enters the market after a bullish weekend press, but buying will dry up on Tuesday and prices will react.

Daily Open/High/Low/Close chart

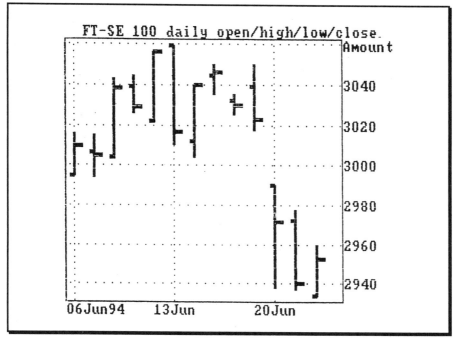

Figure 2.5

Chart by Reuters Technical Analysis

The US futures markets' convention shows the daily range as a vertical bar with the opening price shown as a tick to its left and the close as a tick to the right.

It may come as no surprise to statistically-minded readers that tests have shown the opening on Monday is no more significant than that of any other day of the week, the Friday close is no more important than any other close and prices are just as likely to see a reaction in a bull market on a Monday, Wednesday, Thursday or Friday as they are on a Tuesday. However, these myths persist and, in that a choice for a weekly plot needs to be made, the Monday-to-Friday week is as good as any. Indeed, as Monday has to be the first trading day and Friday the last, logically it has to be better.

All the examples in this chapter so far have been plotted on flexible, arithmetic grids. This flexibility is of prime importance for short-term trading as it can be used to show the price change as clearly as possible. However, for longer-term analysis, the semi-logarithmic (or ratio) grid is very popular and, I believe, better.

Weekly Open/High/Low/Close chart

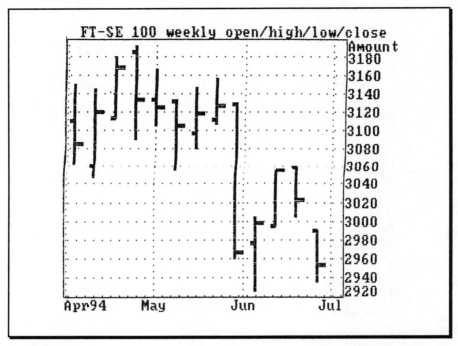

Figure 2.6   *Chart* by Reuters Technical Analysis

A weekly range chart will show Monday's open and Friday's close either side of the bar
representing the high and low for the week.

Figure 2.7 shows an example of a one-cycle logarithmic scale, a conventional choice. The grid is called semi-logarithmic since the X axis remains arithmetic, to allow time to be plotted at a constant rate. The scale is mathematically constructed along the same lines as a slide-rule. Down the left-hand side of the grid are small numbers from 1 to 10 which are multipliers. On the right-hand side is the scale itself and it is constructed by taking a price which is lower than any in the price series to be plotted (and which is easily divisible by 2, 2.5, 4, 5 or 10 if the chart is to be hand-plotted) and putting this on the bottom scale line. The next price is placed on the heavier horizontal grid line which has the multiplier 2 against it and is the result of multiplying the base scale price by 2. The next price is the base price multiplied by 3, and so on.

It is immediately apparent that these main horizontal grid lines are not evenly spaced – the distance between them gets narrower the further up the page you go. This forces the chart plot to visually emphasise price change in percentage terms. If you measure the physical distance on the price scale

Semi-logarithmic grid

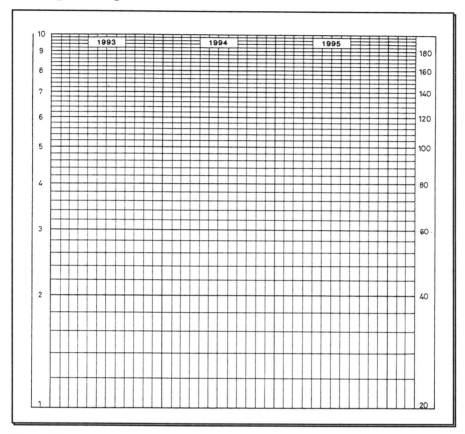

Figure 2.7

Source: Chartwell

A semi-logarithmic scale is constructed by using multipliers (on the left) against the base scale price (20 here). It has the effect of showing price change in percentage terms – the physical distance between 20 and 40 is identical to that from 40 to 80 – they are both moves of 100 per cent.

between 20 and 40 you will find it is identical to the distance between 40 and 80 – they both represent price changes of 100 per cent.

The two charts in Figure 2.8 show the very different appearance of the price series when plotted on the arithmetic and logarithmic grids. Although the rise is a sharp one in both cases, the trend channel still defines the price movements well on the log grid, but on the arithmetic grid the move has become almost parabolic and difficult to follow.

Arithmetic and logarithmic grids

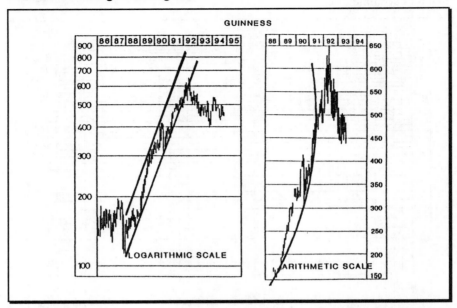

Figure 2.8   *Source:* Investment Research of Cambridge Ltd

Trends differ greatly on a semi-logarithmic and arithmetic grid in the longer term. A parallel uptrend on the former can become virtually parabolic on the latter.

    The ability to make comparisons between one market and another is one of the great strengths of the logarithmic grid; another is the fact that the structure of the scale allows current price history to be put in proper perspective when comparing it with the past. This forces a firm discipline on the observer as he cannot be tempted to alter the scale to make a favourite investment look more interesting than it is.

    Figure 2.9 shows how the logarithmic grid explains the nature of a share. The chart of Marks and Spencer shows a strong, steady performance whilst that of Next shows a very different story. The price movements are much more dramatic, both on the downside and the up. You can tell at a glance that Next, in recent years, would have been a much better performer, but the serious falls seen at the end of the 1980s serve to remind you of how high volatility can work against you too. Indeed, Next's movements have been so large they not only fill the full log cycle (scaled 40-400), but also the grid has been extended by adding part of another cycle below the original one to encompass the whole history.

    Whilst the user of line or bar charts has a choice between arithmetic or logarithmic grids, point and figure charts are usually plotted on arithmetic scale

Logarithmic scale showing direct comparison of two price series

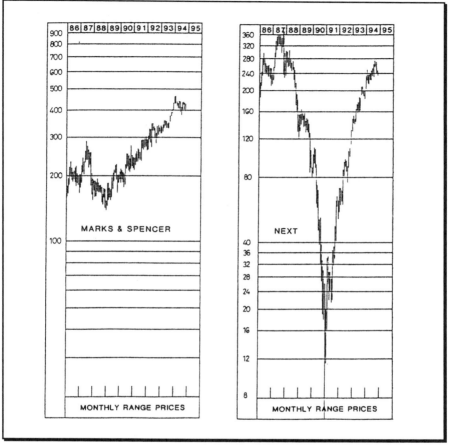

Figure 2.9

Source: Investment Research of Cambridge Ltd

The logarithmic scale allows direct comparison of two price series; both these shares are in the same sector but it can clearly be seen that Next is very much more volatile than Marks and Spencer.

alone. These charts form similar patterns and trends to other charts but they are very different in their construction. The first, and major, difference is that they have no timescale. The point and figure chartist will argue that it is the energy of the market argument that is important; if the price stays the same, or moves only a fraction, then no note need be made.

Conventionally, rising prices are shown as a column of crosses, whilst falling prices are represented by a column of zeros, although some computer systems use crosses only and show rising prices in one colour and falling prices in another (see Figure 2.10). Notations to show the passage of time often appear; the first time the chart is plotted in January a 1 appears in the chart instead of the nought or cross, and a note of the year is made below the column. When the chart is plotted for the first time in February a 2 substitutes for the plot, and so on.

Line and point and figure chart compared

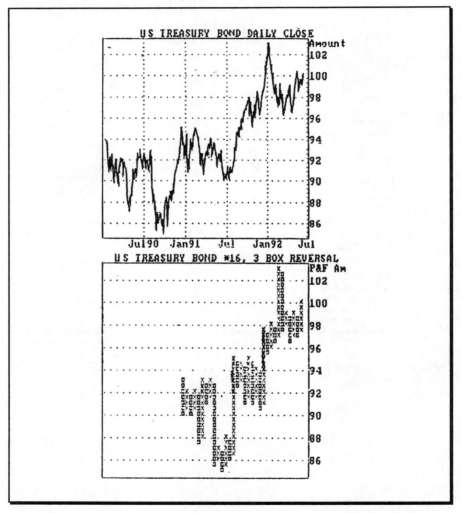

Figure 2.10   *Chart* by Reuters Technical Analysis

Point and figure charts form similar patterns to other plots, even though their construction ignores the passage of time.

The chart grid chosen for plotting point and figure charts has somewhat larger squares than that usually used for line or bar charts to accommodate the noughts and crosses. The price scale is constructed slightly differently too, since each square is given an absolute value, so blunting the sensitivity of the chart and allowing support and resistance areas to stand out boldly. Thus, if each box is worth 1p, the column of noughts will only extend if a price falls from 120p to 119p or less – no plot will be made if the decline only goes to 119.5p. The choice of box size is up to the user but normally it would represent about 1 per cent of the price of the share being plotted.

The next decision to take concerns the reversal factor. This is the amount by which the price has to change direction before you stop plotting in one column and move over to the column on the right. The original point and figure charts were one-box reversal charts and these are perhaps the most difficult to construct until you get the hang of it. If you are using a 1p box size and have a price series which goes 120, 118, 116, 117, 115, 114, 113, 112, 113, 111, 110, 112 the column of noughts would continue to extend from 120 down to 116 and then you would move one column to the right and up one square to plot 117. Then, to plot the fall to 115 you would stay in the same column and place two noughts below the cross representing the small rally to 117; this is the area that can cause confusion because, as the squares below 117 were empty, there was room for the noughts. As a consequence you find some columns have both a cross and a nought (or noughts) or a nought and a cross (or crosses) in them. This only happens with a one-box reversal, the most sensitive kind of point and figure chart, and the one that makes the most sense of the point and figure count – the method of predicting price moves once a congestion area has been abandoned.

Assuming the price series continued as follows: 113, 114, 115, 114, 115, 116, 116.5, 116, 117, 115, 114.5, 114, 115, 116, 117, 117.5, 118 and you were constructing a less sensitive, three-box reversal point and figure chart, the original column of noughts would continue to extend until you reached the 110 low as you need a rally of at least 3p before the plot moves over. The reversal into the next column would be plotted when the rally extended to 113 – three boxes above the 110 low.

Figure 2.11 shows this price series plotted as both a one-box and a three-box reversal chart. It can be seen that the three-box reversal condenses the activity, allowing more price history to be plotted in the same amount of space. The most common reversal factors are one, three and five, with the three-box reversal the most popular since it allows a certain amount of sensitivity, while still showing a useful amount of back history for perspective. However, short-term traders still use the one-box since it shows up near term support and resistance levels more clearly.

The construction of the candle or candlestick chart has been left till last. Since these charts have been in use for many centuries in Japan this may seem illogical. However, it is only relatively recently they have been brought to the

One-box and three-box reversal

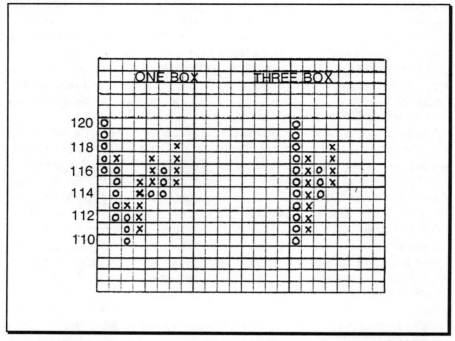

Figure 2.11
Source: Investment Research of Cambridge Ltd

The most sensitively scaled point and figure chart, the one-box reversal, allows both noughts and crosses to appear in the same column. The three-box reversal is more compact and one of the most popular choices.

attention of Western analysts. Much of the credit for this can be given Steve Nison who carried out an excellent study of the techniques involved before publishing his very popular book 'Japanese Candlestick Charting Techniques' in 1991. Prior to this I had seen these charts and had understood them to be called candle charts. Since they look like candles I had considered the title logical. I was confused by Steve's reference to 'candlesticks' until I learned that, although in the United Kingdom we put candles in candlesticks, in the United States candlesticks go into candlestick holders. The candlestick title has stuck.

The candlestick chart uses the open, high, low and close. Traditionally, in the West, the open would be plotted as a tick on the left of the vertical bar and the close as a tick to the right of the bar. As Figure 2.12 shows, the candlestick is drawn by extending both the open and close ticks across the bar and joining the extremes with vertical lines, so that a rectangle forms.

The terminology is different too; the part of the bar that extends above the rectangle is called the 'upper shadow'and the part that extends below is called

Candlestick chart

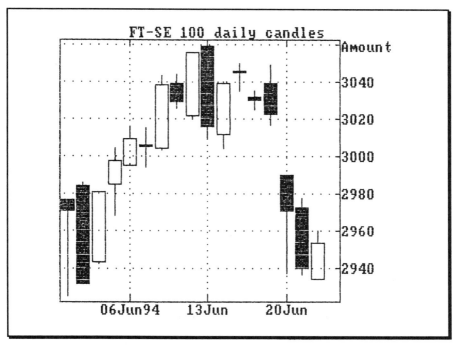

Figure 2.12   *Chart by Reuters Technical Analysis*

Open/High/Low/Close data gives a clear message when plotted as a candlestick chart. The black rectangles show the price closing lower than the open and vice versa for the white ones. These rectangles are called real bodies and the lines extending above and below them are called the upper and lower shadows.

the 'lower shadow'. The rectangle itself is called the 'real body'. The real body shows as white if the close is above the open and as black if the close is below the open. If the open and close are the same, the candlestick plot will look the same as a high/low/close bar chart – this is called a 'doji' and can give extremely important signals. The use of the light and dark colouring technique is what gives the candlestick charts such visual impact.

This brings to an end the discussion of chart construction. All the different types of charts can be plotted on either arithmetic or logarithmic grids and all can apply to different timescales. We are now in a position to address the interpretation of these charts; basically the methods employed to 'read' these charts are the same, with some fine differences as far as point and figure and candlesticks are concerned, with the import of the interpretation becoming larger the longer the periodicity of the plot.

3

TREND DEFINITION – TRENDLINES AND CHANNELS

- Why and how trends form
- Many trends of differing periodicity exist at any one time. They can last for many years, several months, a matter of weeks or only a few minutes. They can all be defined in a similar manner – and put into context
- Trends head in three main directions – up, down and sideways. All are equally important
- Trendlines – offering inclined support and resistance – are traditionally drawn to the right of rising or falling prices. They should, conventionally, have three points of contact as a minimum. But a breach of a trendline alone does not signal its automatic reversal
- Fanlines – trends adopt different angles at different times and the lines defining them become fanlines. Frequently three need to be broken prior to the trend finally being reversed
- Parallel trend channels frequently form, encompassing the vast majority of data points; these tramlines identify overextension when the price approaches them
- 'A Trend Continues Until It Stops': it is only reversed when the last rally peak in a downtrend or last reaction low in an uptrend is breached conclusively. The action of the price is of primary importance, but an accompanying increase in volume is an important confirmation of such a move.

Without doubt, exceptionally long-term trends exist and in stock market prices these point upwards. But within those long-term trends there are phases of strength followed by periods when quite substantial contra-trend moves come through. These we refer to generally as bull and bear markets and, for the stock market investor, they are his main concern. Dow called them 'primary' trends and estimated that they lasted for a year or more. In general terms post-war experience suggests this is still true although the past decade or so has shown that the upward phase can last very much longer than this.

The primary trends themselves see contra-trend moves referred to as 'reactions' or 'corrections'; Dow called them 'secondaries' and he estimated these might last between three weeks and three months and accomplish a retracement of between one-third and two-thirds (frequently 50 per cent) of the previous move. Later, when we look at the bull market in NFC we will see those reactions accomplish roughly 25 per cent, 50 per cent and 25 per cent of the previous upthrust; these are normal corrections to look for too.

These trends would be made up of minor trends with which Dow did not concern himself but they are the trends the short-term traders use. Dow drew a nice analogy: he likened the primary trend to the tide, the secondary to the waves and the minor trends to the ripples. Whilst he was, as always, referring to the closing prices of the Dow Averages, the basic principles of trend definition and monitoring are nowadays applied to individual share prices as well as the market as a whole. Conventionally they also apply to highs and lows (not just closes) and to trends of any length – whatever is most useful for each particular chart user.

This chapter takes a general look at trend definition, with emphasis being placed on the normal attitude of the stock market investor whose aim is to buy relatively low and sell reasonably high and, as far as possible, avoid undue risk. An analysis of the stock market as a whole is dealt with in a later chapter.

Much of a market analyst's time will be spent monitoring the health of trends and checking whether or not they may prove vunerable to reversal. The trends that cause the most excitement are those that go up or down but there is also the third sort, the sideways movement, and this can be equally important.

A bull market is identified by a series of rising peaks and troughs and a bear market can be defined as a series of declining peaks and troughs as shown in Figure 3.1. In that a straight line can always be drawn between two points, a third point of contact should come in to confirm a trendline. More precisely, as long as each rally gains new highs and each reaction holds over the previous reaction low, the uptrend remains in place. The opposite leaves a downtrend intact; each renewed fall finds new lows, whilst each contra-trend rally stops short of the previous rally peak. When this is no longer the case, warning signals come through – the trend could soon be reversed. Although, as was seen in Chapter 1, each reaction in an uptrend 'should' find support on the previous rally peak, the Dow Theory states that the actual reversal is only signalled when the previous reaction low in an uptrend (or the earlier rally peak in a downtrend) is broken. A glance at the daily range chart of Siebe (Figure 3.2) shows why this qualification is critical.

Siebe prices started rising in 1990 and the early stage of the uptrend conformed to the definition in that each rally made new highs and each reaction held over the previous reaction low. Then, in July 1992, the first warning of possible trend reversal came through; the strongly rising uptrend line was broken, but the price held over the previous reaction low seen in November 1991. Prices rallied but failed to clear the May rally peak, a second alert. However, it transpired that this was merely a period of consolidation and in December new highs were gained and the uptrend (defined by the parallel

Uptrends and downtrends

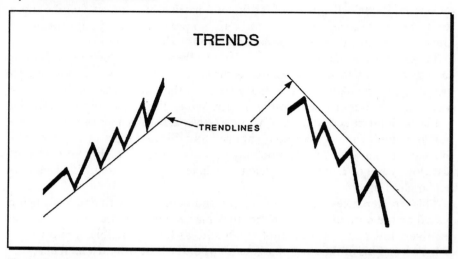

Figure 3.1   *Source:* Investment Research of Cambridge Ltd

An uptrend is a series of rising peaks and troughs and a downtrend is the opposite. In that a straight line can be drawn through any two points, a third point of contact is useful confirmation the trendline is a valid one.

trend channel) continued, albeit at a steadier pace. It is not at all unusual to find that the original speed at which a new trend moves is not maintained and this is why it is important to recognise that a trend reversal is not signalled by the break of the trendline alone.

However, once the last reaction low in an uptrend is broken, falls can be significant. The chart of Spring Ram (Figure 3.3) shows a strong uptrend which was broken in March 1992. Nevertheless, prices held over the December 1991 reaction low and, edging back into the uptrend, moved into new high ground. But the rise was not maintained; prices fell and conclusively broke both reaction lows. The subsequent falls were large, and there is no doubt the trend had been reversed – it was a clear signal for investors to get out. In this example the trend was easy to define and its reversal was signalled clearly. But often definition of where the trend lies is less obvious. This is addressed in more detail in the trend monitoring example below; but users will have to be prepared to adopt a consistently flexible approach.

Before going into greater detail on how to define where a trend lies, it would be appropriate to stress the rationale behind why a trend forms. Long-term trends form as more evidence comes through of changing fundamental factors affecting the market in question. If the news shows an improving background, people become more optimistic and are prepared to buy, pushing the price

Siebe daily range chart 1990 – 1993

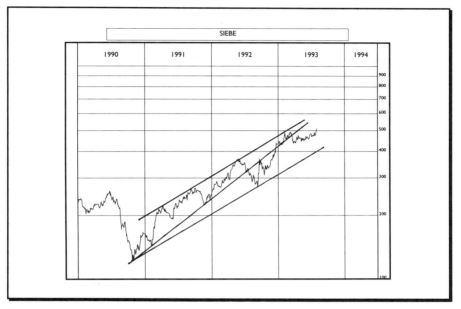

Figure 3.2　　　　　　　　　　　Chart by Investment Research of Cambridge Ltd: Design by NNIF

A trend continues until it is reversed; reversal occurs when the last reaction low in an uptrend, or the last rally peak in a downtrend, is broken. Thus, although the trendline on Siebe was broken in mid-1992, as prices held over the last reaction low the trend was not reversed. Indeed, it continued, albeit at a slower pace. Once the reaction low was seen, the trend channel could be put in place to define the newly-angled trend.

higher. The price will stop rising and start to fall if the perception is that the rise has gone too far and profit-taking sets in. Prices fall back until they reach a level where they look cheap. Buyers become attracted to the shares, the decline is reversed and the uptrend carries values higher yet.

An example of this was seen in BAT Industries in Chapter 1 but the chart in Figure 3.4 shows that it is not only in share prices that perceptions of value allow trends to form.

I use this particular example of a developing trend because it is something with which everyone identifies. In the steamy property market of the mid-1980s house prices in Cambridge were under considerable upward pressure due both to the general property boom and the fact that the area was one of fast development. It enabled a neighbour of mine to sell a small, inconvenient house for what seemed to him an excellent price of £138,500 – coincidentally the average price for detached houses in Cambridge that month. That house came onto the market some months later at just over £120,000 and at that time

Spring Ram – trend reversal

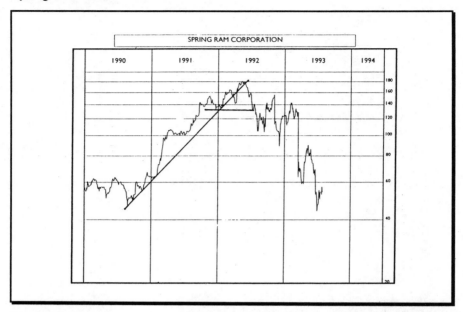

Figure 3.3   Chart by Investment Research of Cambridge Ltd: Design by NNIF

The uptrend line, extending from September 1990, had a considerable number of points of contact when it was broken in early 1992. This was an alarming development; although new highs were subsequently achieved, they were not maintained and the last reaction low was broken soon thereafter. The trend was then reversed and the falls were large.

I happened to overhear a conversation between two people who were looking at the details and saying 'it's really pretty, and so cheap'. As can be seen from the chart, at no time prior to 1988 would £120,000 for a house in that area have appeared cheap – it was only considered good value because it had previously sold for more. People adapt to rising (and falling) prices and their value judgements change accordingly.

We have already looked at trend lines and trend channels but they deserve going into in a little more detail so they can be drawn in confidently in the right place. In that a straight line can be drawn between any two prices, before you place great reliance on a trendline it really should have three points of contact at least. However, in the early stages of a new trend this is unlikely to be possible so a tentative trend needs to be drawn in and adjusted accordingly later.

As Figure 3.5 shows in November 1990 NFC prices broke their downtrend and cleared the minor rally peak scored in September. However, the major hurdle at that time looked to be the 140p barrier which had reversed the rises seen in May and July. Thus the trend was broken but there was no conclusive evidence it had been reversed.

Price trends

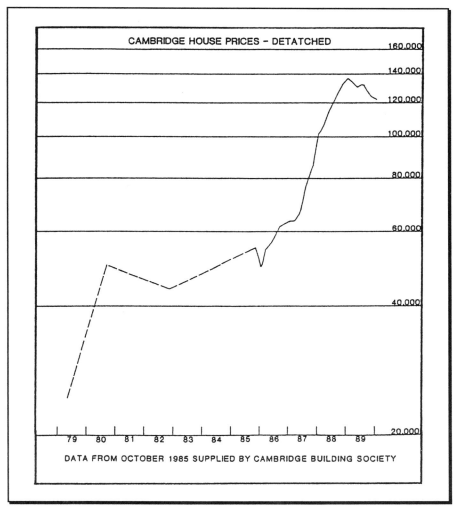

CAMBRIDGE HOUSE PRICES - DETATCHED

DATA FROM OCTOBER 1985 SUPPLIED BY CAMBRIDGE BUILDING SOCIETY

Figure 3.4   *Source:* Cambridge Building Society

Trends in price form in all financial assets. This chart shows the average for house prices in Central Cambridge during the 1980s. In early 1990 a house selling for £120,000 was described by a would-be buyer as 'cheap'. Why? Because in 1988 it had sold for £138,500. At any time prior to 1988, £120,000 would have been expensive. Trends form because perceptions of value change.

What happened next was an interesting, and quite frequent, phenomenon (see Figure 3.6). Prices fell back, but found support from the back of the broken downtrend. In the same way as horizontal support and resistance, once broken, reverse their roles and become resistance and support respectively, the

Break in a trendline

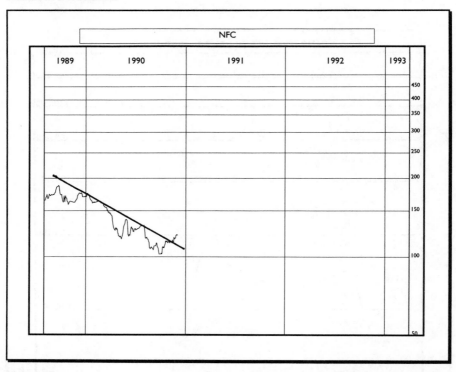

Figure 3.5   Chart by Investment Research of Cambridge Ltd: Design by NNIF

The break in a trendline warns of its possible reversal. In this case, clearance of the May rally peak at 140p was required to effect this.

inclined support and resistance offered by trendlines behaves in the same way once breached. A glance back at Figure 3.3 will show that resistance in the region of the original uptrend was partially responsible for Spring Ram's trend reversal. This action, following the breach of the trendline, was the second clue the trend might be reversed. The reaction held over the October lows – the next hint of imminent trend reversal – and suddenly the rise accelerated. The rally peak seen in November was taken out and a base formed; conclusive trend reversal had been signalled.

At this stage an attempt to define the uptrend needs to be made. In this example there are two possibilities. The first is a shallow trend, established by joining the October and January lows. Prices have risen rapidly away from it to such a degree it serves no useful purpose at this stage. The next, more sharply angled, line can be drawn in from the January low after the first bout of con-solidation occurs and prices move into new high ground (see Figure 3.7).

Broken trendline offering support

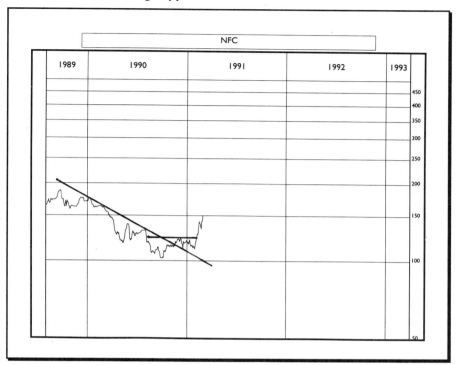

Figure 3.6   Chart by Investment Research of Cambridge Ltd: Design by NNIF

*The rally petered out at 130p, leaving this level as critical resistance now requiring clear-
ance if the downtrend was to be reversed. In February 1991 this occurred, but not before
prices had sunk back and tested the back of the broken downtrend for support – which
proved effective. Previous inclined resistance from trends reverses its role and becomes
support, and broken inclined support will become resistance too.*

This sharply-rising trendline contained price action until December 1991
when it was breached. Could it be argued the bull market was over? No,
because prices held over the previous reaction low and resumed their rise,
quickly moving into new high ground to confirm the continued bull trend.

The terms 'uptrend' and 'bull market' (and 'downtrend' and 'bear market')
are sometimes used synonymously and this is a mistake the nature of which
becomes apparent as we watch this chart develop. Indeed, it becomes patently
obvious that, despite broken trendlines, the bull market remains in place. Once
again the January low could be joined to the most recent reaction low and so it
went on. Each successive trendline was at a less acute angle and each time
prices rose they found resistance as the back of the earlier trendline was

Two posible uptrends

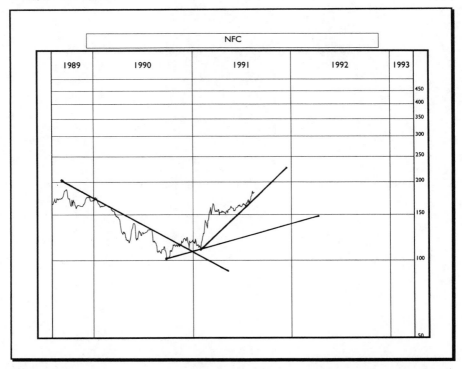

Figure 3.7   Chart by Investment Research of Cambridge Ltd: Design by NNIF

Two possible uptrends can be drawn at this point. The slow one, joining the October and January lows and, once new highs were scored in August, that joining the January low to several lows in July.

approached. It is entirely normal to see trends become shallower as the bull market ages and a series of fanlines such as these often forms. Indeed, it is a frequent observation that once the third fanline is broken, the price extreme has likely been seen (see Figure 3.8).

This is not the first time the number three has been mentioned; it is an important number in technical analysis and it will crop up again. In that each of these trendlines only has two points of contact, they are as much use in defining where resistance is likely to come into play subsequent to their being broken as they are in indicating the area of potential inclined support.

By November 1991, however, we were in a position to put a trend channel in place. It is the convention to draw trendlines to the right of the price action – beneath rising lows or above falling peaks. But trend channels are different in that their role is to encompass not only reaction lows in an uptrend, but the

Fanlines

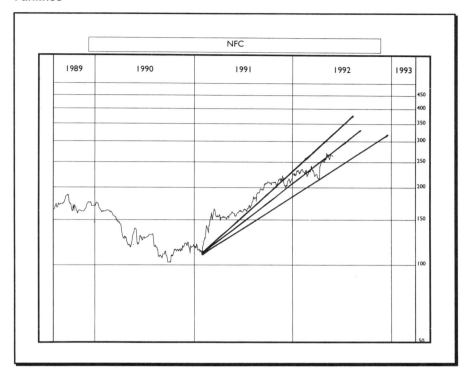

Figure 3.8   Chart by Investment Research of Cambridge Ltd: Design by NNIF

As a trend progresses it will frequently lose pace before it eventually reverses. Each time a line defining it is broken, providing the last reaction low is not breached, another can be drawn. This leaves the chart covered by a series of fanlines which, once broken, provide resistance to renewed bouts of strength. It is often noted that by the time the third fanline has been broken, the actual highs have been seen.

vast majority of the price observations including, in particular, the rallies' highs. I often find that you get more points of contact on the upper parallel line (sometimes called the return line) than you do on the lower line and this can tell you where the 'true' trend lies.

Figure 3.9 shows the same price history as Figure 3.8 but the trend channel has been defined instead of the fanned trendlines. It can be seen that, by joining the earlier highs, it was possible to drop a parallel line down to the most recent reaction lows. The lower line stemmed the March–April fall whilst the upper parallel thwarted the April–May rise. This is a good example of a logarithmic scale at its best. Not only has it allowed the channel's clear definition – a frequent occurrence on a log scale – but as it shows price change in

Trend channel defined

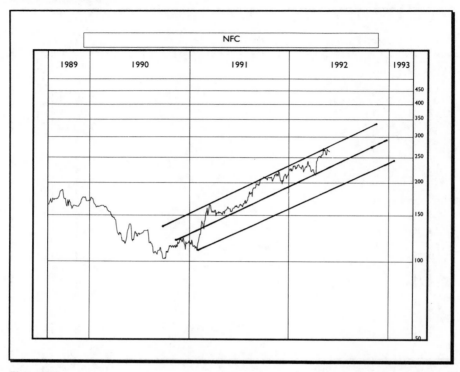

Figure 3.9   Chart by Investment Research of Cambridge Ltd: Design by NNIF

Parallel trend channels are a frequent phenomenon on logarithmic charts and often best define where the true trend lies. Once the first two rally peaks have come in, the tentative trend channel can be put in place.

percentage terms it highlights the fact that as the trend develops it loses some of its upward thrust and as the rallies run out of steam the angle of the trend channel becomes less acute; it gives the appearance of 'keeling' over.

Once the upper trend channel was broken in July, and prices tested support from the lower parallel trend channel reaching back to the January low, rallies failed to re-enter it. However, support has held prices over the April 1992 reaction low and so, as yet, the trend has not been reversed – its most recent phase has become sideways. It serves as a good example of why it could prove dangerous to assume a trend break signals a trend reversal (see Figure 3.10).

The trendlines and channels referred to so far have been constructed with an old-fashioned ruler and pencil and are none the worse for that. Indeed, despite the proliferation of computerised charts it is common to find traders printing off the chart to draw in their trends. But sometimes

The trend has become sideways

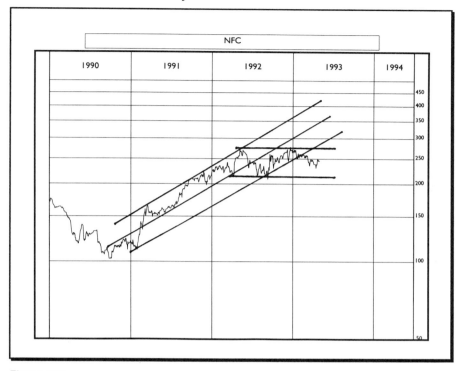

Figure 3.10   Chart by Investment Research of Cambridge Ltd: Design by NNIF

Once the upper half of the trend channel, which lasted 18 months, was broken it offered consistent inclined resistance to subsequent rallies. A lower parallel extending back to the January 1991 low was breached in early 1993 and since then the trend has been sideways.

there is confusion as to where the lines should be placed – not all trends develop as clearly as the above examples – and one software package I use helps out here considerably.

The trend channel in Figure 3.11 shows the 'line of best fit' running through the core of the trend and the two outer lines are parallel to it. The core line is the linear regression line (calculated using the least squares method) and the parallels are called confidence limits. They are set at 50 per cent which means that the price is 50 per cent likely to remain within the parallels displayed. A statistician will tell you that when prices move outside these parallels there is a probability there will be a movement back towards the core of the trend. A technical analyst would say price moves were overextended and support and resistance in the area of the trend channel had proved effective.

Computer - generated trend channel

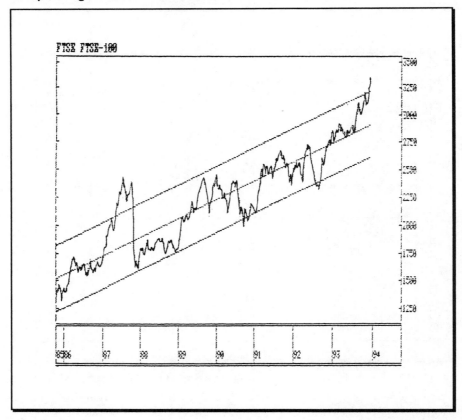

Figure 3.11   *Chart* by Synergy Software's Technical Analyst

Synergy Software's 'Technical Analyst' has a program called Correlation which determines where the trend for the period in question lies.

Parallel trend channels occur surprisingly often in a library of logarithmically-scaled charts and they persist for a very long time. Figure 3.12 shows the Dow Jones Industrial Average rising in a strong trend from the 1982 lows to the mid-1987 highs – when the channel is breached on the upside.

Bearing in mind the fact that this is a logarithmic grid and the rise has not only lasted for nearly six years but also prices have trebled, this action should be read as a sign that this move is unsustainable; at some stage this phase of the rise will reverse. In this case the reversal came through dramatically, in the crash of October 1987. However, although the lower parallel to the long-term uptrend channel contained the fall, the earlier pace was never regained; but prices clung to the trendline until the 1990 short bear market set in. Thereafter a new, more gently-angled uptrend formed.

Parallel trend channels

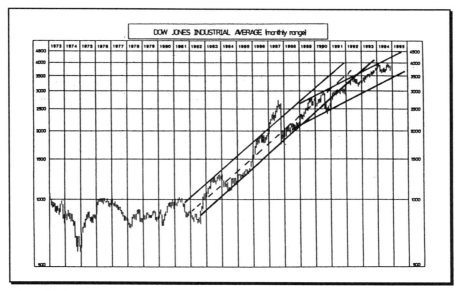

Figure 3.12

Source: Investment Research of Cambridge Ltd

Parallel trend channels can last for a long time. When uptrends have been in place for a considerable period and they are breached on the upside, as happened here in 1987, it is unlikely the new pace will be sustained for long. But the upper parallel, having been cleared, may reverse its original role and become support, at least temporarily. When this support gives way prices are indicated to fall to the trend's core line at least, quite possibly to the lower trend channel line, as happened here. Although the original channel in this example contained prices for many months, it has now been abandoned and prices are rising at a gentler pace.

Historical charts are of no immediate use to the short-term trader but this example certainly serves to show how useful it can be to keep an eye on where long-term support and resistance could come in; it may well not be apparent on shorter-term charts.

Technical analysis is based on price action primarily, but not alone. It would be wrong to discuss trend definition without acknowledging the role volume (the number of shares traded) plays. Dow believed 'volume goes with trend'. During an uptrend strong days should be accompanied by high volume and on days when prices react volume should contract; the opposite should occur in a downtrend.

The chart of Barclays (see Figure 3.13) shows the daily range price chart, with volume plotted as a set of vertical bars across the foot of the page. It can be seen that during the early stage of the chart a strong uptrend is being enjoyed, accompanied by good rises in volume when prices accelerate. In mid-

Daily range price chart with trend and volume

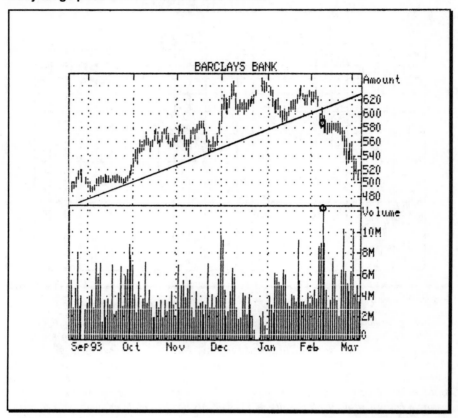

Figure 3.13   *Chart* by Reuters Technical Analysis

In an uptrend, volume should expand on strong days and contract as prices react. The importance of a break in trend is confirmed if volume increases. Once prices are in a down-trend, volume will generally increase on weak days and diminish as rallies come through.

February, however, the situation changed. First the uptrend line was broken against high volume but, for two days, the last reaction low offered support. Then, on the Wednesday, prices fell through that support; a serious breach, confirmed by the even higher volume. As can be seen, the subsequent fall in price was large and volume reversed its behaviour; it grew on weak days, and was poor on days prices tried to rally.

Generally speaking, volume levels are a good way of measuring the significance of a price move, and not only in trend analysis – the subject will be readdressed when we come to pattern analysis later. As will the 3 per cent rule; this is the requirement that prices need to clear the support or resistance point by a factor of 3 per cent (on a closing basis) before the significance of the breakout, and the reversal to the trend, is confirmed. However, it would not be appropriate to apply it here; the Barclays chart is a short-term, traders' tool and the 3 per cent rule is only used in long-term analysis for determining the main bull and bear trends. The trader operates on a higher risk basis and would not be prepared to give up such a large move. A colleague once suggested that an alternative to this rule is the use of a thick pencil lead, whatever timescale is used.

This book is an introduction to technical analysis and concentrates on the mainstream principles which have been derived primarily from line and bar charting techniques. However, both point and figure and candlestick charts have made a very considerable contribution to the subject and so, when methods of interpretation differ radically, mention is made. As far as trend definition is concerned, similar methods to those used on bar charts can be applied to candles. But users of point and figure charts, where the time factor is ignored, can use a different approach.

As far as the sensitive one-box reversal point and figure charts are concerned, little attempt to draw trendlines seems to be made. The patterns and their counts for short-term trading are all-important. But the methods of identifying trends on the very popular, more condensed, three-box reversal charts fall into two camps. Figure 3.14 shows the two attitudes. The first trendline, the one that shadows the price more closely, is drawn in a conventional manner below the 1990-91 lows; prices remain above it, test it around 400-405 in late 1992, and finally breach it in early 1994 – when the long-term trends on bar and line charts went too.

The alternative approach is to adopt a line which rises at an angle of 45° from the lows. The 45° angle is not peculiar to point and figure charts, it is used in Gann's TimeXPrice analysis too. But the justification for its use here is unclear. This is particularly so since the co-ordinates of the boxes used are not specified. With the point and figure chart employing no time factor on the x axis, the actual size of the box is obviously significant if the breach of a line travelling at a particular angle is to be considered important. However, despite the lack of any psychologically-significant rationale behind its use, it is a popular methodology and, at the time of writing, places the trendline in an interesting position. Whilst the first trendline on the point and figure chart of the S&P Composite in Figure 3.14 has been broken, the 45° line has not; this suggests it is either going to give a rather late bearish signal, or its indication that the bull market is still intact will have been proven correct by the time this book is in print.

This brings us to the point where the fine differences between long- and short-term trend analysis should be addressed. Throughout the text it has been stressed that the same principles apply and, with one or two exceptions such as the 3 per cent rule, this is the case. However, all price movements must be

Three-box reversal chart: two methods of identifying trends

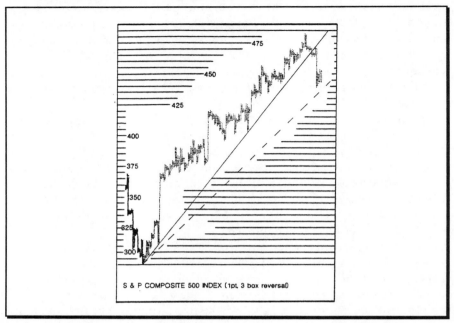

S & P COMPOSITE 500 INDEX (1pt, 3 box reversal)

Figure 3.14   *Chart* by Chart Analysis Ltd

The three-box reversal point and figure chart can be tracked in two ways. Chart Analysis Ltd (whose chart this is) advocate a line drawn through the rising lows. Others use a line at 45° (dashed here) from the low point itself, although the results of using this method must depend on the actual size of the boxes used.

placed in proper perspective before their significance can be judged. We have already mentioned the need to keep an eye on the very long-term charts to see where historic support and resistance from persistent trends, or old highs and lows, may come into play and for this purpose the stock market investor can find no better data than the monthly range. We have also looked at the long-term chart of the Dow Jones Industrial Average in Figure 3.11 but the same use can be made of monthly range plots on individual shares themselves.

The monthly range of Shell Transport and Trading in Figure 3.15 is on a logarithmic scale and this is no accident. We discussed the use of scaling earlier and although some analysts, mainly in the field of commodities and futures in general, argue in favour of using arithmetic scales for all charts, it is the convention to use the ratio grid for long-term analysis and I could not agree with this more. Although the benefits of this form of scaling have

Monthly range of Shell Transport and Trading

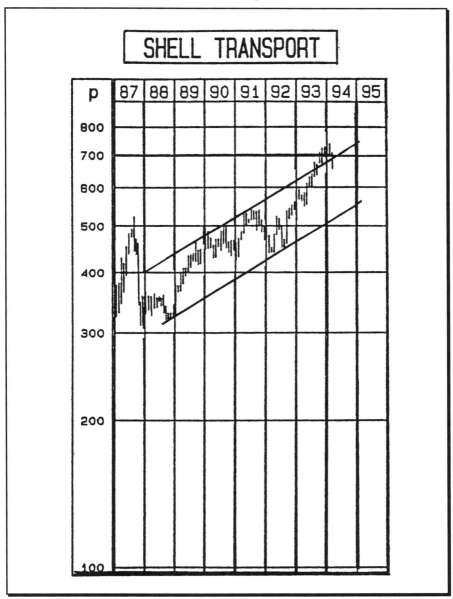

Figure 3.15   *Source:* Investment Research of Cambridge Ltd

The monthly chart of Shell shows prices moving through historic resistance from its uptrend channel.

already been stressed, I will embrace the danger of overkill and summarise them once more. The nature of the share cannot be disguised; it is either a fast trender or a sluggish performer and by the time you have compared it with others in the library you will be in no doubt as to in which category it lies; and, whatever its nature, the pace of the trend can be monitored with ease.

The history of Shell shown here identifies it as a steady-to-strong performer, without the volatility of some of the issues showing more aggression. But this is not the main point. The scaling has allowed a parallel trend channel to be drawn and, at the turn of the year 1993-94, it can be seen that prices are through the upper trendline – a signal that the move was most likely over-stretched. The most recent phase in the long-term uptrend has been sharp, with prices not quite doubling since the 1992 lows. The faster the pace of the uptrend, the more likely the subsequent reaction will be sharp too so this inclined resistance is sending a clear warning signal. Against this background a more sensitive chart needs to be analysed and this appears in Figure 3.16.

Once again the logarithmic scale is in use. This shows the rise since the 1992 low in greater detail and highlights a point not apparent on the very long-term chart – the most recent move into new high ground has fallen short of the upper parallel to the trend. This has happened before, twice in mid-1993, but then the overextension was not evident on the monthly range chart. Against an overbought background the loss of speed to the trend can be considered another danger signal – the trend could be reversed. As we can see, so far at least, the uptrend remains intact and on this logarithmic scale it comes in around 680p right now.

Earlier we looked at the shape of a fast rising price when plotted on a linear and a logarithmic grid. On the linear grid the price became almost parabolic, moving well away from any straight trend, whilst the trend on the logarithmic grid 'stayed with' the price. This is not such an exaggerated example, but the effect is the same. An uptrend line on a logarithmic scale will be broken first (whilst the first line to be broken in a downtrend will be that drawn on an arithmetic grid) giving an earlier danger signal than otherwise would have been the case. To see how real this danger is we need to look at an even more sensitive chart and this appears below, in Figure 3.17.

For the short-term picture an arithmetic grid should always be used. Over a limited timescale, the difference in where the trend lies on one grid or another is hardly noticeable. Also, the benefits of the flexibility this grid gives cannot be overrated. It has allowed the price action to be exploded so that exact points of support and resistance are entirely clear and we can examine care-fully what is happening and see how real the danger of a breakdown is. A trend channel has been drawn in and although, on an arithmetic scale over a long period of time, such lines are rarely parallel (they tend to diverge), for short-term analysis they remain a useful tool. Indeed, a familiar warning signal came through – the January peaks fell short of the upper parallel and this alarm has been followed by an actual trend breach. However, as the chart

Long-term uptrend in Shell shown in greater detail

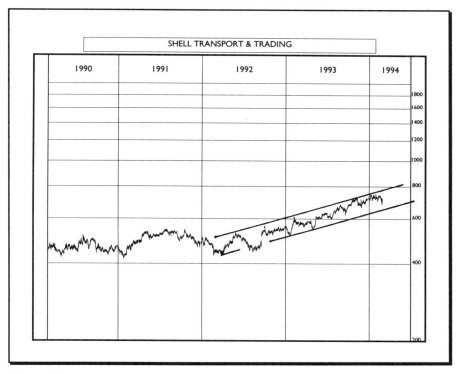

Figure 3.16   Chart by Investment Research of Cambridge Ltd: Design by NNIF

The most recent phase of the long-term uptrend in Shell is shown in greater detail here. The parallel trend channel is intact but the recent highs fell short of the upper parallel – this shows the trend to be losing speed.

shows, the actual reaction low is at 66op and, so far at least, this has not been broken. The picture is a threatening one but no definitive conclusion can be reached yet.

However, the three charts have served as a good example of how I would recommend the investor to monitor his portfolio. The very long-term chart should be used for perspective, the medium-term chart for monitoring his holdings on a regular basis and, if any danger or possible opportunity is threatened or promised, the daily, flexible chart should be brought into use to fine-tune market action.

The main aspects of trend definition by lines and channels have been addressed, as have the advantages and disadvantages of one form of scaling or another in different circumstances. The next chapter covers different, more 'automatic' ways of monitoring where the trend lies; these rely mainly on

Shell – even more sensitive chart, highlighting the critical support

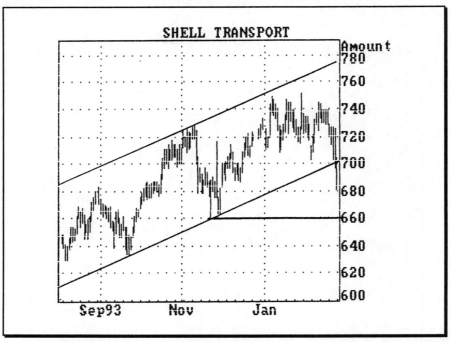

Figure 3.17   *Chart* by Reuters Technical Analysis

The sensitive daily plot has breached its trend, adding to the likelihood that a serious reaction could come through soon. The 66op support point must now be watched with care.

mathematical calculations and, to that extent, take the judgemental element out of the analysis. However, the basic rule still applies: a trend goes on until it stops, in other words, is reversed. Unless the previous reaction low or rally peak is breached, no reversal is signalled; the trend could be merely turning sideways, action that traps prices for a very large percentage of the time.

4

TREND DEFINITION BY MORE AUTOMATIC METHODS

- The moving average which forms a 'bent' trendline, trailing the price and taking on its characteristics
- The use of two or more moving averages of differing periodicities to define the short and longer term trends – and to give automatic buy and sell signals
- The different kinds of moving averages – simple, weighted and exponential; their strengths and weaknesses
- The use of filters to avoid – or attempt to avoid – false signals from moving average crossovers
- The situations in which moving average signals lead to consistent profits – or losses
- Other uses for moving averages – phasing, envelopes, Bollinger Bands
- What moving average periodicity to use
- Other calculations used for tracking trends – Parabolics, Volatility Index, Speedlines.

An increasingly popular way of defining where the trend lies is the moving average. One of the reasons for this is that, whilst the experienced analyst most probably has little difficulty in judging where to place the trendlines and channels, the moving average is a calculated value and there can be no dispute as to where it is at any time. As its name implies it is the average of past prices and it 'moves' in that it is recalculated repeatedly as each period comes to an end. The prices that are averaged are normally the closing prices for the period so that if a daily chart is being used the closes of the last, say, 20 days are added together and then they are divided by 20. The result is the 20 day simple moving average as at the last date. The following day the calculation is done again; a simple method is to take the previous day's total, add in the most recent day's close (that for day 21) and subtract the close of day 1. The resulting total is again divided by 20 and that is the 20 day moving average for day 21.

The chart of British Airways in Figure 4.1 shows how the 20 day moving average forms a gently-curving trendline as it follows the price action, offering support as prices react before their rise is regenerated. It follows the price

20 day moving average

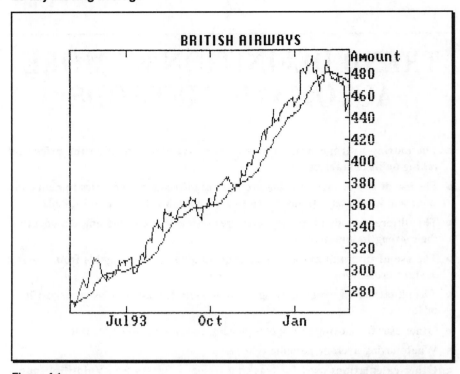

Figure 4.1

Chart by Reuters Technical Analysis

The daily closing price of British Airways is tracked by the 20 day moving average which forms a sensitive monitor of the trend.

action in a more sensitive manner than a straight trendline would and, as long as it continues to rise or move sideways and the price remains above the previous reaction low, the uptrend can be considered to remain in place.

It has become the convention to use more than one moving average at a time. The two moving averages employed will reflect different time periods; the first might well be the already illustrated 20 day moving average and the second could be another popular choice in equity market analysis, the 50 day moving average. Their relationship with each other is watched and, when this changes, signals come through.

In that the 20 day moving average is defining the short-term trend and the 50 day moving average is defining the medium-term trend, whilst the 20 day stays over the 50 day an uptrend is in place. As can be seen from Figure 4.2, British Airways enjoyed such a trend from May 1993 until the end of February 1994. At this stage two important developments occurred. First, the price fell and broke the support just over 460p – the last reaction low in the uptrend. If anyone was in any doubt that this trend was being reversed they only had to wait four trading days to see the two moving averages cross into bearish sequence. The 20 day average fell below the 50 day average for the first time in the history of the share price covered here. This crossover was strong confirmation of the signal given by the price alone. The situation had now definitely changed; whilst previously the 20 day moving average was following the price up and it was being followed by the 50 day moving average, a classic bull market sequence, the position is now reversed and bear market conditions will prevail until the relationship between the moving averages changes again.

The fact that the price gave a signal before the two moving averages is no surprise since moving averages take into account only past price data and their shape and direction is bound to lag that of the price. This is particularly true

20 and 50 day moving averages

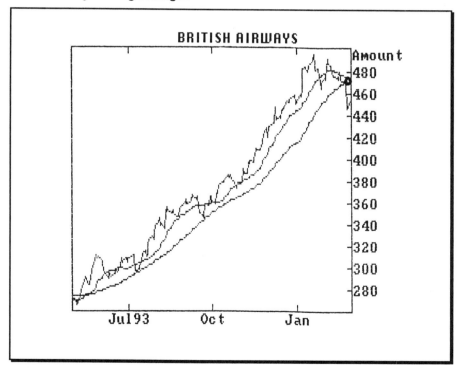

Figure 4.2

Chart by Reuters Technical Analysis

The 50 day moving average has been added to the British Airways line chart. Whilst the 20 day moving average remains above the 50 day average the uptrend can be considered intact. Once the 20 day moving average crosses down below the 50 the trend's reversal is signalled.

of the simple moving averages described here. To overcome this problem, to some extent, weighted moving averages are often employed. These are calculated differently; the most recent price is given very much more emphasis than the earlier data in the series. The most common method of calculation is to give the first price a weighting of 1, the second 2, and so on. The effect is that the average follows the shape of the price curve very much more closely and thus the moving average crossover on British Airways came through earlier and at a slightly better price (see Figure 4.3).

The other commonly used moving average is the exponential variety. It is effectively calculated by taking the previously calculated value and adding to it a chosen percentage of the difference beween it and today's price. All the prices in a particular data series are used in the calculation but, as time progresses, the earlier data points are afforded less significance (see Figure 4.4).

20 and 50 day weighted moving averages

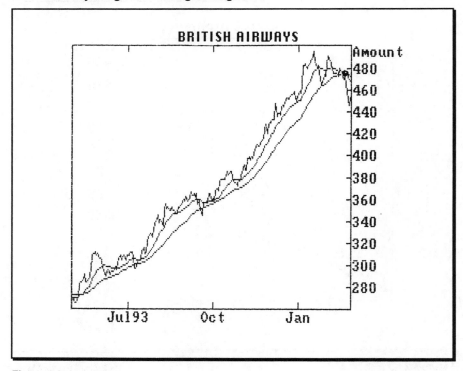

Figure 4.3   *Chart by Reuters Technical Analysis*

This chart shows the line chart of British Airways accompanied by the 20 and 50 day weighted moving averages. Such averages track the price more closely and hence the crossing occurs when prices are at a somewhat better level for sales.

Exponential moving averages

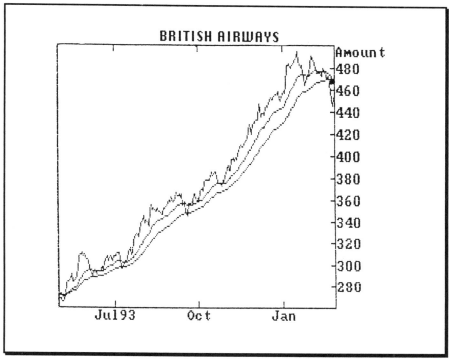

Figure 4.4   *Chart* by Reuters Technical Analysis

The daily closing price of British Airways is tracked by two exponential moving averages which use all the data in a price series, giving a heavy weighting to the most recent prices and virtually none to the first.

The advantage of the exponential variety is that a certain periodicity as such does not have to be selected. Occasionally this can be very important. If a price has had a sudden surge or fall then, once that data point is out of the calculation, the moving average can change direction dramatically even if the weighted moving average is used. In the case of the exponential moving average this effect is diminished. Figures 4.5, 4.6 and 4.7 show how the three main sorts of moving average coped with the effects of the 1987 crash. The simple moving average fell immediately and then, once the sharp fall was no longer in the calculation, rose quickly. The effect on the weighted moving average was less dramatic, but on the exponential moving average the effect was less visible by far.

The use of two or more moving averages to give automatic buy and sell signals is called 'The Crossover Approach' and is the basis of many trading systems, developed originally in the futures markets. A signal to buy is given

Simple moving average showing effects of the 1987 crash

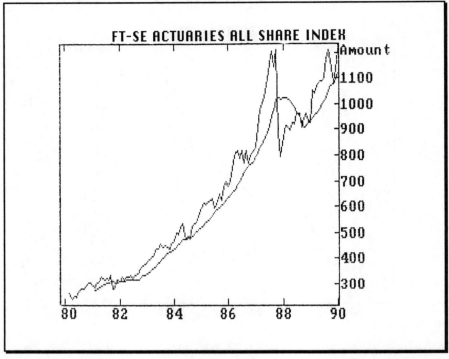

FT-SE ACTUARIES ALL SHARE INDEX

Figure 4.5   *Chart* by Reuters Technical Analysis

This monthly close chart of the FT-SE Actuaries All Share Index has a simple moving average defining the trend. This average rose sharply as soon as the October 1987 fall was no longer involved in the calculation – in late 1988.

when the short-term moving average rises above the longer-term moving average. When the reverse occurs, the trader doubles his market order; he sells his long position and also goes short, selling another contract in the hope of buying it back later at a lower price when the moving averages cross again.

Much computer research has been done to find the most profitable combinations of moving averages of different periodicities and different types. In that each market has its own characteristics it is not surprising that the optimum combination varies from market to market. But, overall, the simple moving average gives the most consistently good results in fast-trending markets. This is because it is slow to respond to any near term increases in volatility and thus does not give premature signals. So, despite the increase in computing power in recent years, these averages are still very much in use today. For the stock market investor they are a useful discipiine; sharp price

Weighted moving average showing effects of the 1987 crash

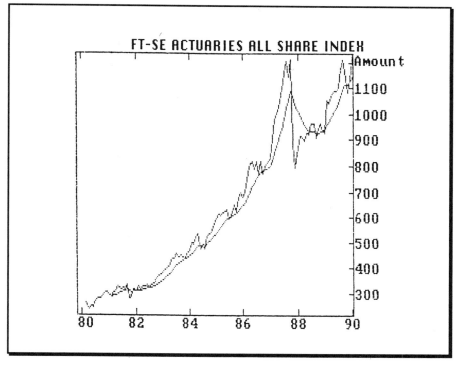

Figure 4.6

Chart by Reuters Technical Analysis

The response to the October 1987 fall leaving the calculation of the weighted moving average was more muted since the more recent prices had the dominant effect but it was quite sharp, all the same.

reactions can often be aberrations and if the averages do not cross these can be ignored, ensuring good, long-term investments are not abandoned in a panic.

Sharp reactions of this nature are by no means an uncommon feature of modern financial markets and this is particularly true if a market has been moving up at an aggressive pace. The chart of the Hang Seng Index in Figure 4.8 shows the Hong Kong stock market's explosive rise was monitored well by the 20 and 50 week weighted moving averages until April 1992 when a sharp fall came through. Not only did the price break its last reaction low, but the moving averages crossed into bearish sequence, apparently confirming the end of the uptrend. Anyone could have been forgiven for assuming the highs had been seen and abandoning their commitment to that market.

However, as Figure 4.9 shows, the price breakdown was not confirmed by the 20 and 50 week simple moving averages. Slower to respond and hence

Exponential moving average showing effects of the 1987 crash

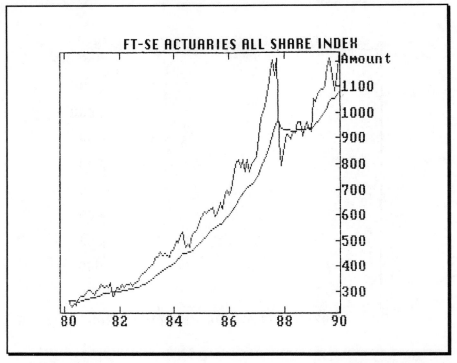

Figure 4.7   *Chart* by Reuters Technical Analysis

Since the exponential moving average never disposes of any data in the price series, it was the least dramatically influenced in 1988 by the 1987 falls; it moved broadly sideways as prices consolidated during the year and then rose sharply as the uptrend extended.

more likely to give a poorer price, as in the British Airways example earlier, they merely drew together and did not cross. The sharp rise which followed the fall was large enough to prevent a false signal coming through.

If a moving average whipsaw such as this is seen there is a great temptation to re-optimise data and come up with a solution where the false signal would not have occurred. In the case of the reaction in the Hang Seng the answer is already known – the choice of simple, rather than weighted, moving averages would have saved the day. On other occasions, however, this may not be the case.

As Figure 4.10 shows, the two years immediately prior to the strong bull market saw the subsequently successful 20 and 50 week simple moving averages give a series of poor signals. Indeed, had the 20 and 50 week weighted moving averages been used during this phase the experience would not have been so bad; less money would have been lost as the averages responded more quickly, giving better prices.

Weighted moving averages

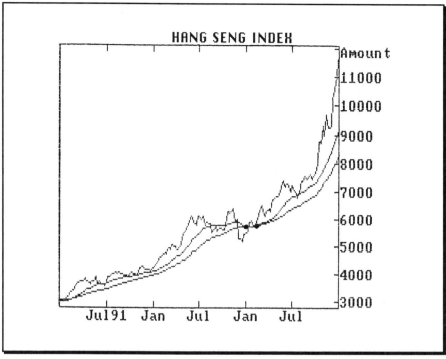

Figure 4.8   *Chart* by Reuters Technical Analysis

The chart of British Airways in Figure 4.3 showed the benefit of using weighted moving averages to get an early signal of trend reversal. However, this quickness to respond meant the sharp falls in the Hang Seng Index in 1992 caused the weighted moving averages to cross into bearish sequence, signalling a sell, only to reverse into bullish sequence when the market recovered – a classic 'whipsaw'.

In an attempt to avoid false signals from moving average crossovers confirmatory filters are introduced. Often a third, or even a fifth, moving average is employed. Long-term stock market trends are frequently defined by a 200 day moving average. If this is added to the chart of the Hang Seng and its weighted moving averages and the 'rules' are enhanced, this false signal can once again be avoided. When, on this interpretation, the 20 week moving average crosses down below the 50 week moving average a warning bell sounds. But a sell signal only comes through if the 50 week moves down below the 200 day to confirm the trend's reversal – as can be seen (see Figure 4.12), this did not occur.

Indeed, the combination of three moving averages is a popular technique for shorter-term trading (see Figure 4.13). A sell signal is given when the price, the 5 day moving average and the 10 day moving average all cross below the

Simple moving averages

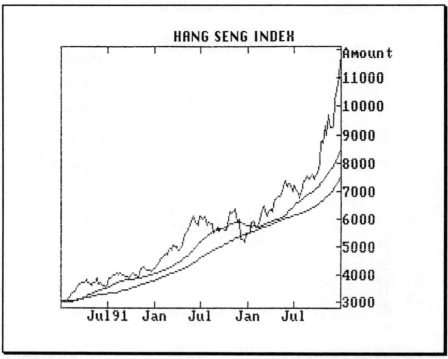

HANG SENG INDEX

Figure 4.9

Chart by Reuters Technical Analysis

The simple moving averages employed on the Hang Seng Index during 1992, being slower to respond, remained in bullish sequence whilst the price reaction was underway, leaving investors using the moving average crossover approach still in the Hong Kong stock market.

20 day average. A signal to close out the position comes through when the 5 day moving average crosses above the 10 day average.

Figure 4.13 shows how this approach would have signalled a short position in early February which would have been closed out by the 5 day moving average rising through the 10 day average in mid-March. Four days later a signal to go short again came through and this position would have been closed out in mid-April.

However, whilst this approach reduces risk it can impair profits by giving several signals and so increasing dealing charges. Also, using the three moving averages would not have improved the signals on the Hang Seng Index during 1988 and 1989 (see Figure 4.14). This is because the market conditions were different – prices were trapped in a broad trading range.

Throughout this chapter reference has been made to the use of moving averages when prices are moving in a fast up or down trend. This is no acci-

Prices trending less aggressively with simple moving averages

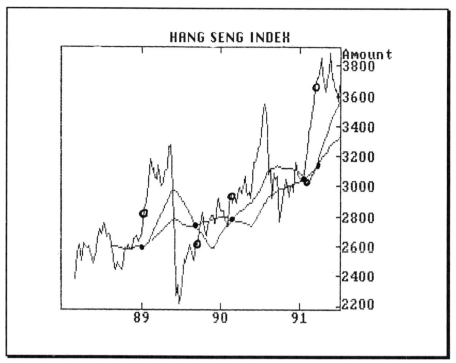

Figure 4.10   *Chart* by Reuters Technical Analysis

Moving average crossovers are only going to give reliable signals in fast-moving trends. The simple moving averages which worked so well in 1992 on the Hang Seng Index gave a series of loss-making signals over the previous two years when prices were trending less aggressively.

dent since these are the circumstances when moving averages are at their best. Indeed, some would argue it should be the only time they are used. Their strength in this role is derived from the fact that their calculation involves the smoothing of past data and they will necessarily enjoy a time lag. As such they trail the price trend and, as has been seen, ignore 'noisy' short-term swings and force the user to get maximum benefit from the trend for as long as it runs. They do this so well there is a temptation to make use of them in all circumstances – a technical tool for all seasons. But if the market is not trending up or down aggressively and is instead moving sideways, then their lagging nature will cause buy signals to come through around the upper reaches of the price range and sells will be triggered near the lows.

No amount of retesting of the moving averages, their types or their periodicities, will alter this fact. As a consequence, in almost all circumstances moving averages can be ignored when an up or down trend is not in place.

Prices trending less aggressively with weighted moving averages

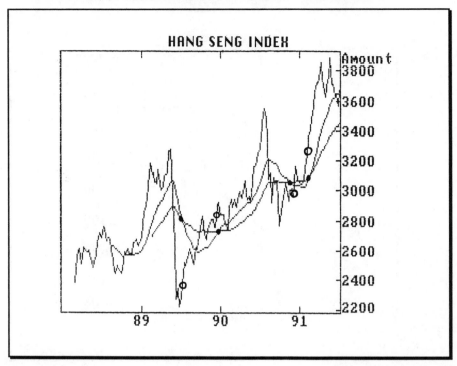

Figure 4.11

Chart by Reuters Technical Analysis

The weighted moving averages which gave the whipsaw in 1992 on the Hang Seng gave signals that were slightly more timely than those given by the simple moving averages over this earlier period. But the sell signal near the 1989 low was a particularly disastrous one.

They are lagging indicators and should be recognised as such; they have no predictive ability. However, there are some occasions when they send a strong message in a sideways trend.

The chart in Figure 4.15 appears in our chart library primarily to draw attention to the fact that, once all the moving averages have knitted together (rather like so many strands of different coloured wool in a tangle), there is a strong probability a major market move will soon come through. This config-uration is merely emphasising the fact that a major market argument has been underway long enough for all the averages to 'catch up' with the price and, on a cyclical basis, some trending action is becoming overdue. Once again the averages are not predicting the direction of the move, just emphasising the likelihood one will soon be seen.

In other situations they can give particularly useful confirmatory signals. Figure 4.16 shows the FTSE Index and the 20 and 50 day simple moving aver-

Third moving average added

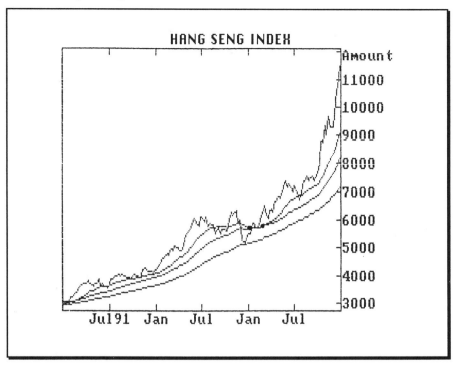

Figure 4.12   *Chart* by Reuters Technical Analysis

In an attempt to filter out whipsaws, sometimes a third moving average is introduced. Providing this is not crossed, the crossover by the two shorter-term moving averages can be used to take some profits, whilst the full position is re-entered once the upside cross comes through again.

ages from the beginning of 1993 to early 1994. A close examination of the first part of the chart will show prices moving broadly sideways and the moving averages crossing roughly in the middle of the range. Then, in early August, prices cleared their previous highs and, two days later, the 20 day moving average rose above the already rising 50 day moving average. The fact that the 50 day moving average was already rising is important; it shows the sideways trend had already gained an upward bias – the balance of the market argument was shifting in favour of the bulls. This form of crossover is called a 'golden cross' and, whilst such a crossover by no means always comes through, when it does it serves as strong confirmation that the price's upside break is a valid one. When the price breaks down through support and the shorter-term moving average crosses below an already falling longer-term average, its signficance is equally great and it is called a 'dead cross'.

Combination of three moving averages (5, 10 and 20)

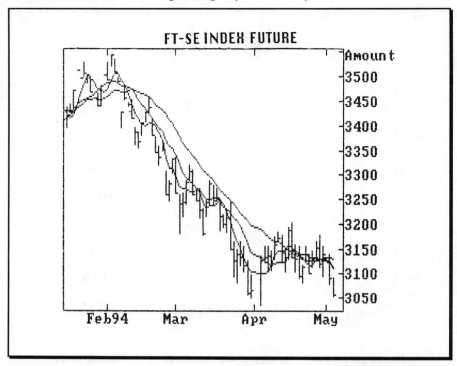

Figure 4.13   *Chart* by Reuters Technical Analysis

The combination of three moving averages is often used for short-term trading. If the FTSE future price is below the 5 day moving average and it is below the 10 when the 10 day moving average crosses below the 20 day average, a signal to go short comes through. This position is closed out when the 5 day crosses the 10 day average on the upside. In this example it would have been re-opened when all moved into bearish sequence again. This technique reduces the risk, but increases dealing costs considerably.

Whilst moving averages themselves have no predictive ability there is a situation where they are used to extrapolate a price trend. This is in cycle analysis and the technique is called 'phasing'. It can be seen from all the previous illustrations in this chapter that the moving average is plotted on the same point on the x axis as the price. This is because technical analysts use the average as an estimate of where the trend is likely to provide support or resistance on any one day. However, a statistician would plot the average half way through its timespan. In Figure 4.17 a 20 day moving average is plotted ten days back so its most recent plot is ten days before the most recent plot of the price.

The purpose of this is to cut out all the noise and show the shape of the price curve clearly. Cycle analysts use two phased moving averages to identify the short- and longer-term cycle in the price. The points where the two aver-

Third moving average added

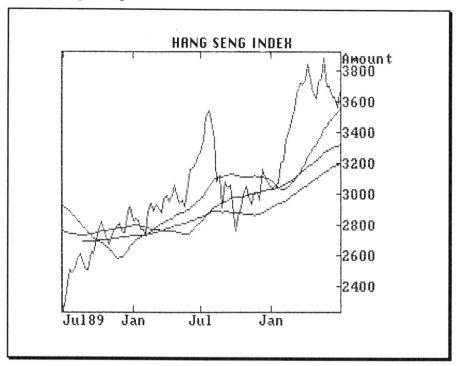

Figure 4.14   *Chart* by Reuters Technical Analysis

Going back to the Hang Seng price series, the addition of a third moving average during the early period would not have improved crossover signals. Moving averages lag prices; using the crossover discipline forces the running of profits in fast trends but causes sell signals to come through near the lows and buy signals near the highs when markets are moving broadly sideways.

ages cross each other are joined to form the core to the trend and lines parallel to it are placed where the price rallies and reactions end. Once the shorter phased moving average changes direction from an extreme a line is then drawn in, extrapolating the move across the channel to give a good estimate of the extent and timeliness of the likely price move (see Figure 4.18).

This technique is not precise (bond prices in the illustration later actually fell much further than the picture implied was likely) but, whilst trend channels give a good idea of the likely extent of a move, they lack the ability to estimate the time it might take. Using phased averages can help here.

Another use to which moving averages are put is to create an 'envelope' and this is a technique which can be used in a sideways trend. Figure 4.19 shows the FTSE Index with a 20 day moving average and its envelope. This is created by plotting two points 1 per cent above and below it.

Five moving averages

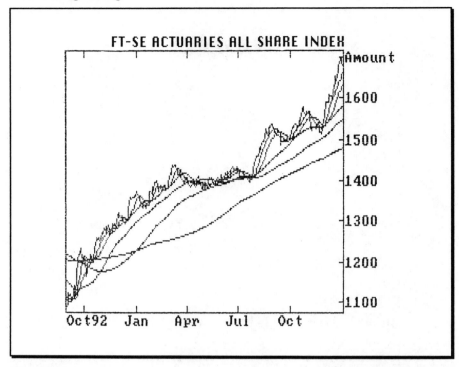

Figure 4.15   *Chart* by Reuters Technical Analysis

When prices are consolidating earlier gains and moving broadly sideways, the moving averages 'catch up' with the price and, in due course, they all bunch together. This emphasises the fact that, on a cyclical basis, a move outside the sideways trend is due. If the long-term moving average is still pointing in the direction of the original trend, and is still below the price in an uptrend or above it in a downtrend, the likelihood is the trend will extend. But the moving averages themselves have no predictive ability.

This envelope will contain price movements the vast majority of the time, much like the parallel lines employed in determining trend channels. In a sideways trend the moving average itself can be ignored and the position of the envelope lines noted as buffer zones, likely to offer support and resistance when approached. However, it is frequently found that, when a breakdown occurs, the force of the move is so great the lower limits of the envelope are cleared. During the early phase of the trend, when prices are still accelerating, the lower envelope line will offer resistance and can be used as a near term stop-loss. Once the pace of the fall slows, this line will be broken and prices should find resistance from the moving average itself. Later, when the trend has slowed significantly, the moving average could well be broken and the next

20 and 50 day moving averages

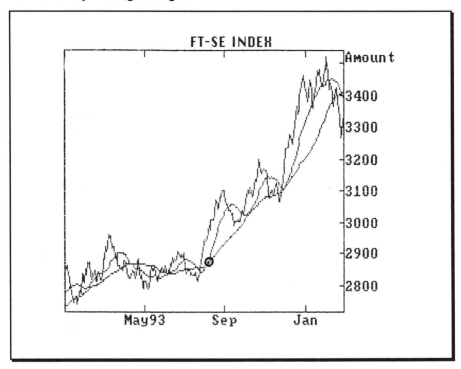

Figure 4.16   *Chart* by Reuters Technical Analysis

In a sideways trend moving averages can cross each other many times. However, if they are both rising or falling when this occurs a strong clue that a move up or down outside the range is likely to be sustained comes through.

resistance area should prove the upper envelope line. As can be seen, the moving average envelope works in the same, but opposite, way in an uptrend

A somewhat more sophisticated approach has been developed by John Bollinger (see Figure 4.20). Instead of choosing a certain percentage difference to calculate the trading band, standard deviations are used. This means that the distance of the bands from the moving average is not predetermined – it is flexible and dependent on the volatility of the underlying price. When that volatility increases, the bands widen and when prices calm down, the bands narrow. Hence the indicated support and resistance areas are calculated in direct response to trading conditions. Another useful aspect of Bollinger Bands is they highlight periods of low volatility by the distance between them narrowing; the longer they remain narrow, the greater the likelihood is a major price move will soon come through.

20 day phased average

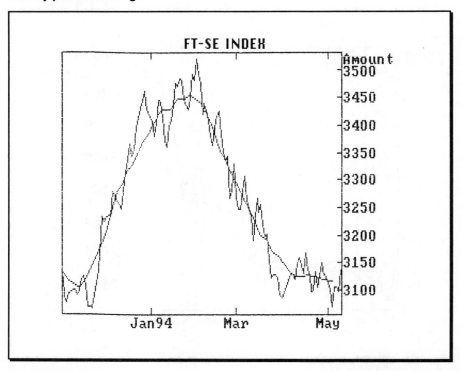

FT-SE INDEX

Figure 4.17   *Chart* by Reuters Technical Analysis

Technical analysts normally plot the moving average on the x axis at the same point as the most recent price in its calculation so it offers an estimate as to where support or resistance from the trend lies currently. Statisticians, however, place the average in the middle of its timespan: the 20 day moving average on the FTSE Index is plotted ten days 'back' so the smoothed line fits the price curve. This is called 'phasing'.

The choice of length, or periodicity, of moving averages for all these techniques vexes some whilst others are happy to accept the periodicities conventionally in use. Whilst considerable time and effort has been spent in optimising moving average periodicities for each and every market and share, this is something which I believe can be overdone. There is no doubt that the different characteristics of the various markets mean that some fine-tuning will give enhanced results. But over-concentration on optimisation following poor signals is more likely to lead to greater anxiety than greater profitability since in a truly trending market most moving averages will give reasonably timely signals.

In the United Kingdom the favoured equity market moving averages are those already mentioned: 20, 50 and 200 days. American conventions differ slightly; their longer-term moving averages are frequently 90 and 240 days.

Two phased moving averages

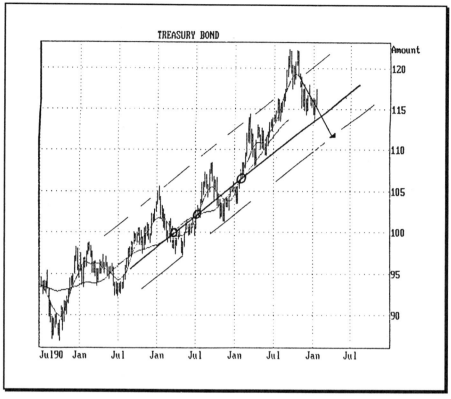

Figure 4.18

Chart by Reuters Technical Analysis

Two phased moving averages are used by cycle analysts to predict price moves. The points at which these two averages cross each other are joined by a straight line which forms the core of the trend. Lines parallel to this core are extrapolated to the region of the previous highs and lows to define the trend's boundaries. Once the shorter-term phased average turns from an extreme a line can be drawn in, extending the average to the upper or lower parallels, giving an estimate of the likely extent and timeliness of the implied move.

These periodicities were adopted many years ago, prior to the extensive analysis now undertaken. But they remain in use, suggesting that the original empirical observation has stood the test of time well.

In the shorter-term futures markets combinations of the 5, 10 and 20 day averages vie for popularity with the possibly more esoteric 4, 9 and 18 choice. Whilst the former combination reflects the 5 day trading week logicality, the latter lacks this explanation. However, it remains equally popular. Throughout the financial industry, at all time horizons, there is a fascination with Fibonacci numbers. Fibonacci's published work, 'Liber Abaci', written in

20 day moving average with its envelope

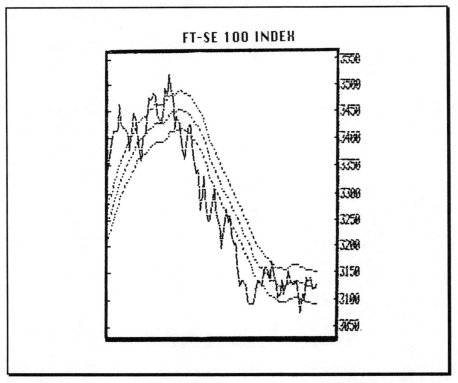

FT-SE 100 INDEX

Figure 4.19   *Chart* by Synergy Software's Technical Analyst

In the same way as trendlines have their counterparts in trend channels, moving averages have moving average envelopes. Plots are placed a certain percentage above and below the moving average. In a trending market the outer lines are often exceeded and provide resistance or support to rallies and reactions in price. Once the trend turns sideways the price bounces between the outer envelope lines.

the 13th Century, has attracted many generations of traders. He came up with a series of numbers: 1, 1, 2, 3, 5, 8, 13, 21, 34, 55, 89, 144, and so on. It can be seen that each number is the product of the two preceding it. The fascination is based on several observations. The geometry of the pyramids relied on these relationships. Each has 5 surfaces, 8 edges and a total of 13 surfaces and edges. Three edges are visible from any one side. Comparisons go on. The various ratios between the numbers were used by the Greeks in the construction of the Parthenon. The frequency with which these numbers crop up is extraordinary. Human bodies have 5 projections – 2 arms, 2 legs and a head. Arms and legs have 3 sections; hands and feet have 5 fingers and toes. There are 5 senses. A

Bollinger Bands

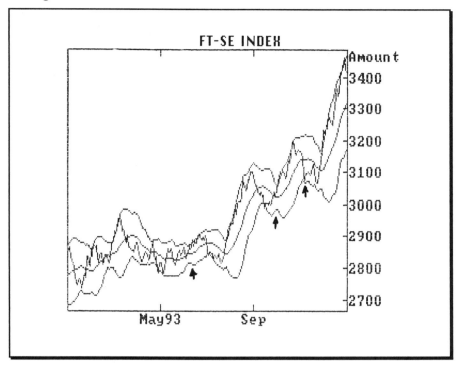

Figure 4.20   *Chart* by Reuters Technical Analysis

Bollinger Bands are a variation on the moving average envelope. The outer bands are a certain number of standard deviations above and below the average. The width of these bands varies as they move out as volatility increases and draw together when it dies down. They are expected to provide support and resistance and, additionally, when the distance between them narrows it usually suggests a move of size in the price is imminent.

musical octave is 8; there are 8 white keys and 5 black – 13 in all. And so on. These numbers are often adopted by market analysts. Figure 4.21 shows these periodicities of moving average define the movements of the FTSE well.

Many computer systems now give the user the ability to test the effectiveness of the various moving averages and the different combinations. This is useful but, bearing in mind the major caveat that if a market is trending well most combinations will give profitable signals, if such facilities are not available it is hard to beat the analytical ability of one of the best computing systems around, the human eye.

The charts in Figure 4.22 show that, whilst a 10 and 20 day moving average combination defines the short-term trends in the FTSE well, it does not suit

Fibonacci numbers for moving averages

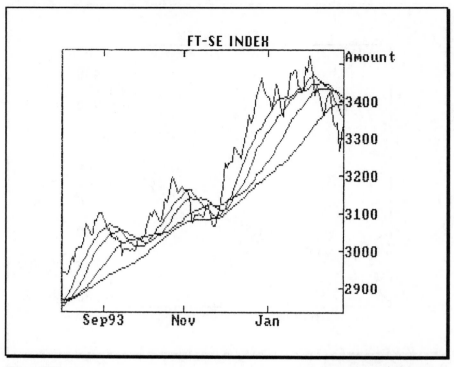

Figure 4.21

Chart by Reuters Technical Analysis

Fibonacci numbers are used in all forms of analysis, including the Elliott Wave Theory. They are often adopted for multiple moving average periodicities.

the more volatile S & P at all. It needs a longer-term approach. The best advice seems to be to adopt the conventions or do your own research by computer analysis, or experiment with what looks visually fitting.

The way moving averages define trends is important but it is not the 'Holy Grail'; false signals from moving averages will always come through from time to time – it is up to the analyst to filter all the various messages coming from the markets and reach his own balanced conclusions. This 'health warning' comes out more strongly in this section than elsewhere merely because, in my experience, I have found there is a great temptation to believe the moving average is the solution to all the problems of market analysis. Whilst it is an immensely useful tool, it is, at the end of the day, just that – a tool.

Moving averages are not the only mathematically-calculated points used to define where a trend lies. Others are often called SARs – 'Stop And Reverse' points. These are plotted as a series of dots and can often look like moving

Moving averages suitable for different markets

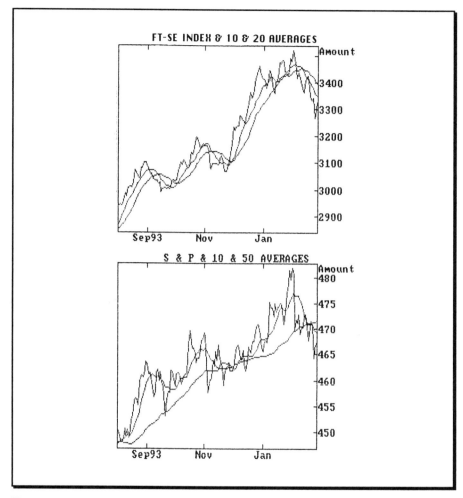

Figure 4.22

Chart by Reuters Technical Analysis

Some moving averages suit one market whilst others are more appropriate elsewhere. The FTSE Index is less volatile day-to-day than the S&P; hence the latter needs a longer-term average to encompass its moves.

averages, although their progression is less smooth. They were developed by futures traders but they have been adopted into the analysis of all financial markets. As their name implies, like the moving average crossover approach, they are designed for system trading and the basic assumption is the trader is always in the market. When an SAR is broken, the original position is reversed.

Figure 4.23 shows the FTSE Index trailed by parabolic stop and reverse points. This system was devised by J. Welles Wilder, Jnr and takes its name from the shape it adopts in a fast moving trend. In an uptrend, prices should find support above the SAR and, in a downtrend, resistance below it. When this is no longer the case the signal to reverse the position comes through. The calculation involves both price direction and time: trend acceleration factors can ensure the stop points 'hug' the price trend more closely than a moving average would. These acceleration factors do not come into effect immediately the signal comes through. There is a delay but, once the signal is given, if the price does not move in the indicated direction, the stop will eventually move towards the price and the position could be stopped out. But once the price starts to move the acceleration factors are emphasised and the trader is assured of close stop losses.

Parabolic Indicator

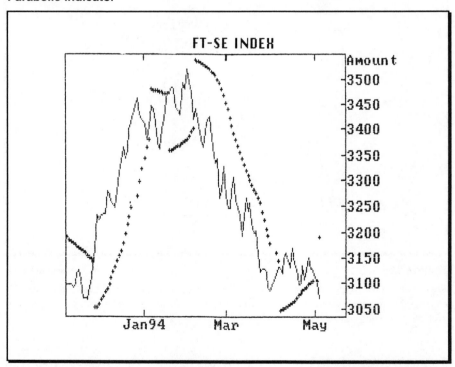

Figure 4.23

Chart by Reuters Technical Analysis

Another form of calculated trend definition is the Parabolic Indicator, so-named because in a fast-moving market it takes on the shape of a parabola. This is because the calculation involves acceleration factors which ensure the Stop and Reverse (SAR) points get nearer to the price, the faster it moves.

For users of computer software with the Parabolic SAR system on it, the sensitivity of the SAR points is determined by entering three factors: the start acceleration, the acceleration increment and the maximum acceleration. The greater the number, the more sensitive to price volatility the points become.

A similar looking system (again developed by J. Welles Wilder, Jnr) is the Volatility Index. It too employs SARs but its calculation is dependent upon the volatility of the underlying price series. If the volatility increases the stops will temporarily move away from the price so unnecessary whipsaws do not occur. Once the trend is underway again the SARs 'catch up' with the price (see Figure 4.24).

I once developed a trading system part of which was based on a similar approach; it has strong advantages during the trending phase but, should a

Volatility Index

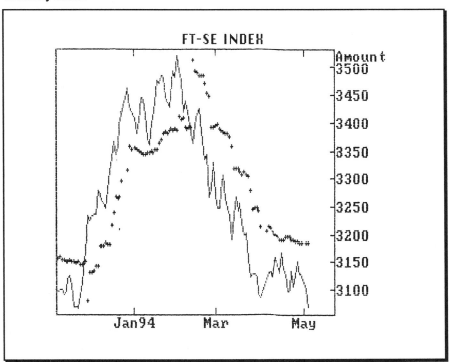

Figure 4.24   *Chart* by Reuters Technical Analysis

The Volatility Index employs SAR points which respond to increases in volatility by moving away from the price, as occurred in January when the FTSE Index saw a sharp correction. This goes a long way towards avoiding whipsaws but, if a price makes a sudden and complete reversal, the SAR stops the position out at a worse price than a moving average or the parabolic would.

Speedlines

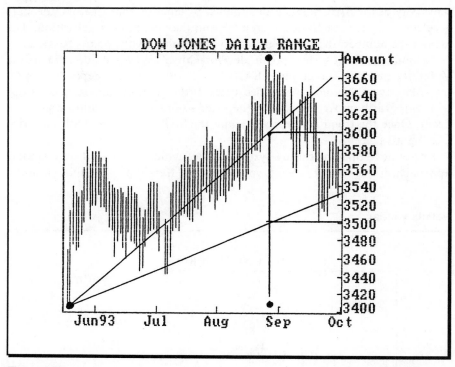

Figure 4.25

Chart by Reuters Technical Analysis

Speedlines are based on reactions in price retracing one-third or two-thirds of the previous move. The difference between a significant high and low is measured and divided into three. The one-third and two-thirds points are plotted on the x axis at the same point as the most recent price extreme (the high in this case). Two lines joining these points to the low are then drawn in. If the first line is subsequently breached by the price, the second line is the target – as happened here. They look very different from other forms of trend definition as they often pass through earlier price plots.

price top or bottom out 'on a sixpence' there is a high probability the position will be closed out at a much worse price than might have been achieved by a simpler approach such as a moving average crossover. This is because such reversals necessarily occur against a volatile background – when the SAR will have moved away from the price.

The last form of trend definition to be addressed here is the speedline. This is mathematically-based but does not need to involve the use of computers. In fact, in many ways, the pencil and ruler approach is very much easier.

Mention has already been made of the likelihood that price retracements within a trend will represent one-third to two-thirds of the previous move.

Speedlines are based on this observation but refine it to the extent they 'allow' support or resistance to come in prematurely when the market is moving fast. They are calculated by establishing the distance in terms of price between – in the case of the example of the Dow Jones Industrial Average – a significant low and the most recent high (see Figure 4.25). In a downtrend the principle of the calculation would be the same but the starting point would be the significant high and the calculations would be done (and redone) against the most recent low.

The difference between the significant low and the most recent high is taken. This is divided into three and the result is added to the low and subtracted from the high. These two points are then plotted on the price scale, at the same point on the x axis as the most recent high. A straight line from the low is drawn through each of these points and these lines are the first and

Speedlines recalculated

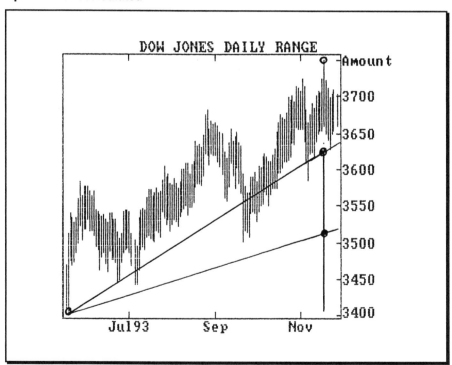

Figure 4.26   *Chart* by Reuters Technical Analysis

After the reaction in Figure 4.25 the Dow moved into new high ground. Each time this occurs the speedlines need to be recalculated. In this example the reaction from the highs is holding on the first of the new speedlines.

second speedlines. It can be seen in the above example that, somewhat unusually, the lines can go through previous prices – not something other forms of trend definition allow. But this does not affect the validity of the support the speedline should offer to prices now, immediately after the new high is formed.

The basic rule is that the first speedline should offer support to reactions in the price. If it fails to do so the fall should extend to the next speedline. In the above example the first support failed, but support from the second line and the actual two-thirds retracement point combined and halted the decline. The uptrend then extended, necessitating the recalculation of the speedlines; the difference between the low and the new high has to be recalculated and its results replotted.

Speedlines recalculated

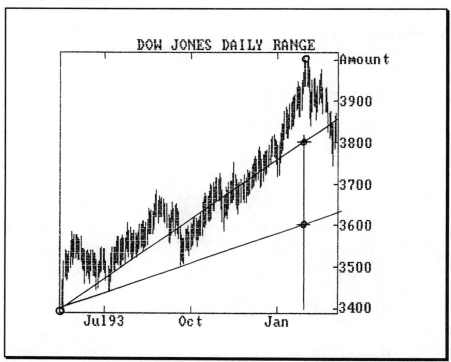

Figure 4.27   *Chart* by Reuters Technical Analysis

Once again new highs have been scored and the speedlines recalculated. The first has been breached – this targets the second which, at the current point, is standing at 3620. If, in due course, this were broken, targets would be the original low, 3420. Now that a downtrend is underway this too can be monitored with the speedline approach, measuring from the high to the most recent low.

This time the first speedline held the correction and subsequently new highs were scored (see Figure 4.26). Each time this happens new speedlines need to be plotted. In February 1994 the first speedline was broken, signalling a fall to the next speedline which, like a trendline, should offer support (see Figure 4.27). If, in due course, the second speedline were to be broken, then the prediction would be down to the original low at 3420. Meanwhile, the newly formed downtrend can be monitored in a similar manner; the 3985 point is the significant high and, for now at least, the low is 3755.

The most popular methods of monitoring rising and falling trends have now been described. As with all aspects of technical analysis the user must choose which techniques suit him, or the market conditions, best. Trend channels, moving average envelopes, Bollinger Bands and speedlines all give some form of minimum predicted move. But the major predictions come from trend reversal patterns and these we look at next.

5

TREND REVERSAL PATTERNS AND PREDICTIONS

- The rationale behind the significance of the resolution to a pattern – and the subsequent price move
- History repeats itself inexactly – hence 'classic' patterns form infrequently; thus, analysts need to interpret pattern development sensitively
- Major reversal patterns: the Head and Shoulders Top; the Reversed Head and Shoulders Bottom ('Inverse' to the American analyst); Double Tops and Bottoms: Triple – and Multiple – Tops and Bottoms; Triangles; Diamonds; Broadening Formations; Saucers; Spikes – and the volume associated with them. Sometimes their resolution can be forecast. At others, it cannot
- The 3% Rule – it is sometimes appropriate
- Patterns that do not 'work' – and the likely consequences.

One of the things technical analysis is famous for is the various patterns that form in the price plot and the predictions made from them. There are two main sorts of pattern: those that develop at market tops and bottoms and accompany trend reversal; and those that occur within an existing trend and merely mark a quiet trading period while prices 'catch their breath'. These patterns occur in charts reflecting different time periodicities: tick-by-tick data, 5 minute bars, half-hourly candles as well as the daily, weekly and monthly plots that are most in use by the stock market investor and which we will concentrate on here. Their definition and analysis is achieved in the same manner, whatever the timescale, although generally speaking the resolution to a long-term pattern will have a greater and more enduring significance than the completion of a short-term formation. The basic rules were developed with daily charts in mind; users of shorter-term data have had to adapt the signals through experience but most can be automatically applied.

Prices spend the vast majority of the time showing no statistically significant change from one day to the next and this is when patterns are building. A market 'argument' is occurring with both buyers and sellers prepared to take the going price. This argument will be resolved in due course with either the buyers or the sellers 'winning' and when this happens scrutiny of a large chart library will show that the price is likely to move by an amount which bears a relationship to the energy of the area of argument it has now left behind.

One of the reasons for this is that if, for instance, the breakout is on the upside, roughly half the trades done during the building of the pattern will now be the 'wrong' way round – in this case the sales. It may well be the sellers are happy to be out of the market and let the price get away. If, on the other hand, they feel they have misjudged the situation, they may want to get back in, buying at the higher prices and driving them higher yet. Others who had been buying as supports were approached during the period of price congestion may not have bought as much as they intended. They too could feel forced to pay more to get the balance of their holding on board. Additionally, trend followers attracted by the headlines noting the new highs could be tempted to go along for the ride.

This explains why the price might rise but it does not explain why this rise should be of a certain amount and I know of no scientific justification for the widespread acceptance of price objectives set by pattern analysis. But such predictions do have a habit of 'working' time and again and, in that all statistical estimates of future events rely on the experience of the past, it seems fair to refer to price chart patterns to give a reasonable estimate of where the price move is likely to go.

Before examining the individual patterns in detail, it is only fair to stress that the classic textbook shapes do not abound. Anyone who writes an article on pattern analysis can be forgiven for resorting to the artistic approach and not using illustrations from 'real life' as these are hard to find. This is not surprising; the analysis of charts is the analysis of prices formed by human beings operating in the market-place. Such actions are likely to be predictable but only to a certain extent; history repeats itself, but inexactly. As a consequence the chartist has to be flexible in his interpretation of what is happening, using various checks and balances to estimate the most likely outcome. Additionally, the user should not search for patterns; this can lead to interpretations being made on patterns that just are not there. The important patterns will leap out. The illustrations here are taken from real life and, where possible, they are classic examples. But additionally some less than perfect examples have been included to give the readers more of a feel for what they are most likely to come across.

Against this background it is not surprising that I take issue with those who say charts work solely because if enough people believe they do, then they will all take action simultaneously and the chart prediction will be self-fulfilling. Whilst every chart user is presented with the same information, as are economists and fundamental analysts, he will quite likely give different emphasis to different factors and can, unsurprisingly, come to conclusions which differ from those reached by others. We have already noted that different trendlines can give different breakout points; patterns may appear as one thing to one analyst, something else to another. Indeed, some years ago in answer to an article in a trade magazine that made the assumption that predictions are self-fulfilling, I quoted three different chartists' published views on gold. All held the same long-term view that it was going down but each differed on when, the breakdown points and by how much. The analysis of chart patterns is, like other forms of financial forecasting, an inexact science. Indeed, it can be argued it is an art.

The most important patterns are those that reverse major trends. At this point it is worth mentioning that one of the basic rules of pattern interpretation is that a reversal pattern is only important if there is something to reverse. Sometimes a price pattern will develop a classic reversal shape within a broad sideways trend; the pattern may be of the textbook variety but, if no major move has preceded it, then there is little likelihood of subsequent price moves being large.

Another point to bear in mind is that the longer it has taken for a pattern to form, the greater its significance. This is logical since, as has been stressed before, such patterns represent market arguments and the longer it has taken for such an argument to be resolved, the more important the conclusion is likely to be.

Lastly, as far as basic rules are concerned, basing patterns that reverse downtrends tend to take longer to form than market tops. This is primarily due to the fact that human beings, ever cautious, tend to become alarmed at the first sign of trouble and take their profits while prices are still rising, but take much longer to find the confidence to come back into the market as evidence mounts that the worst of the recession is over. Indeed, it is frequently only the poor return on bank deposits during this stage of the economic cycle that forces them to consider doing so. This effect is even more obvious in the commodity markets where supply shortages during the later phase of the economic expansion cause a rapid price acceleration and those markets often reverse their rises very suddenly indeed.

One of the most popular and reliable patterns is the head and shoulders top (see Figure 5.1). It usually follows a strong rise and its formation is evidence of an energetic argument occurring. Its main characteristics are a left shoulder forming as prices react, find support and then go into new high ground. But, not only are the new highs not maintained, prices erode the initial potential support at the top of the left shoulder and descend to test the previous reaction low. Classically, a line drawn between these two supports should be horizontal – an exact price, borne in investors' minds is likely to have the greatest psychological effect. This is the neckline; only when it is severed clearly will the top pattern form. The right shoulder forms as prices rally, usually to roughly the height of the left shoulder, and then reverse. The pattern of volume while the head and shoulders is forming is important. It should be high as the left shoulder forms, slightly less so as the head is made, and poor as the rally making the right shoulder comes through. The example in Figure 5.1 is a reasonably good one.

The breakdown needs to be made on a closing basis for confirmation. Not only does the Dow Theory recommend the use of closing prices only, there is a

Head and shoulders top

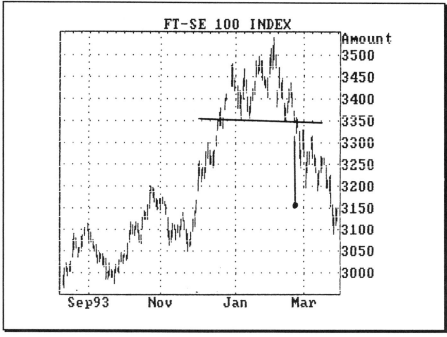

Figure 5.1   *Chart* by Reuters Technical Analysis

One of the most reliable reversal patterns is the head and shoulders top. It forms after a fast rise and its formation is evidence of a dramatic argument occurring. In a classic example volume should be highest on the left shoulder, lower at the head (which is the false break on the upside by the price) and very poor as the rally forming the right shoulder (the rally from the previous reaction low) comes through. The neckline is drawn between the previous reaction low and the support point from which the right shoulder formed; the nearer this line is to horizontal, the more reliable the downside prediction is likely to be. The prediction is made when the neckline is breached; falls are estimated by measuring the distance from the head to the neckline and extrapolating this distance down the scale from the point of breakdown. If high volume accompanies the breakdown there is a high probability the prediction will be fulfilled. (Note: This is one of the few reversal patterns where positions can be put in place, anticipating the breakout with relative impunity: as the right shoulder forms, if volume is low, the likelihood is the pattern will not abort.)

strong logic to their use in pattern resolution since closes are the most widely recognised prices across the financial community. Indeed, in the case of private investors they are often the only price they watch. Many traditional chartists will argue an important breakdown only comes through if the support is breached by at least 3 per cent and, on a long-term weekly or monthly chart where the pattern has taken time to form, it could be argued this was valid. But, with short-term trading now frequently the order of the day, this 'rule' is often ignored or adapted. In the above example such confirmation would have only come through over a week later and much of the move would have been lost.

Predictions from patterns are effectively dependent on price volatility. The likely price objective from this head and shoulders top is established by measuring the distance from the highest price in the head to the neckline and this is subtracted from the point where the neckline is breached. Falls are likely to be sharp as those previously buying around the reaction lows will be anxious to minimise their loss. But such predictions should be tempered by any barrier likely to stop such a fall being fulfilled. In the FTSE example such a stumbling block was likely to be the 3200 October rally peak which could be expected to offer support – as it did, if but temporarily.

Whilst the chart of the head and shoulders top in the FTSE had a horizontal neckline (a classic textbook example to that extent), the top formed in Medeva was accompanied by a sharply sloping neckline (see Figure 5.2). The upward angle of the neckline diminishes its bearish connotations to a certain extent as it shows buyers were still quite anxious to get into the share just before the

Head and shoulders with sloping neckline

Figure 5.2   Chart by Investment Research of Cambridge Ltd: Design by NNIF

If a neckline to a top area slopes upwards the bearish connotations are diminished somewhat as buyers have been eager enough to come in above the previous reaction low. All the same, Medeva's downside prediction was fulfilled before the large corrective rally set in.

right shoulder formed. However, this still 'counts' as a neckline since the initial support offered by the left shoulder's rally peak was severed. This is the basic rule – if the top of the left shoulder offers support then the formation is not a head and shoulders and predictions cannot be made from it in the same way. It is interesting to note in this example that, although the downside prediction was fulfilled quickly, the subsequent rally was large and the bear case was not entirely convincing at this stage. This rally stopped short of the right shoulder's high, confirming the likelihood an important top had been seen.

The chart of Body Shop International in Figure 5.3 is shown to introduce the pullback. This is the name of a rally that comes through immediately after a neckline has been broken. It 'should', as happened in this case, stop short as the back of the neckline is approached and offers resistance; a neckline, like any other previous support area, once broken, reverses its role and becomes resistance.

Pullback

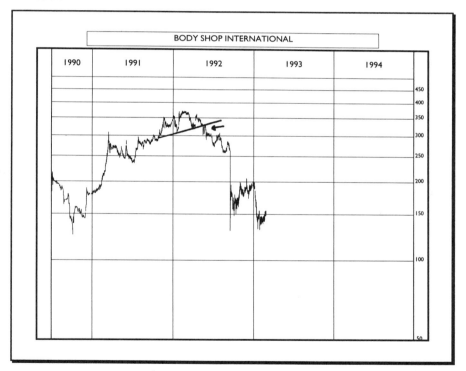

Figure 5.3   Chart by Investment Research of Cambridge Ltd: Design by NNIF

The head and shoulders top on Body Shop was followed by a pullback. This is a rally which takes prices back to the breached neckline and it offers another chance to sell. However, pullbacks to top areas by no means always come through, although they are a more likely development following a basing pattern.

Pullbacks are very useful as they offer additional chances of selling to those who failed to get out earlier. However, it can be noted that in the previous two examples no such immediate rally came through. This is not surprising. There is a saying that prices rise due to an imbalance of buyers over sellers but fall by virtue of their own weight. It is certainly true that downside objectives from top areas tend to be achieved very much more quickly than upside predictions from base areas. Once again the innate caution of investors during bull trends, and their tendency to panic when conditions change, can be noted here. The hesitancy shown by the bears in this case allowed a pullback, but it is not that common a development following the clear formation of such a top.

Head and shoulders tops usually form after prices have enjoyed a sharp rise and they have a good record of reliability. However, nothing works 100 per cent of the time and the downside potential evident on the British Airways chart was

Head and shoulders top failing

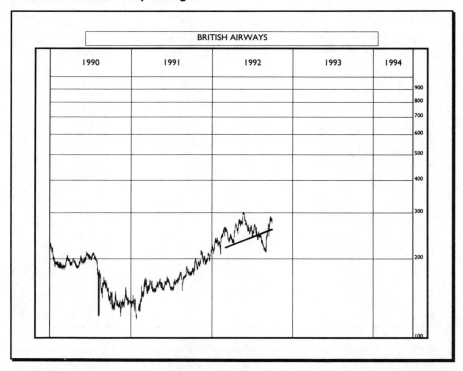

Figure 5.4   Chart by Investment Research of Cambridge Ltd: Design by NNIF

The head and shoulders top on British Airways failed. Not only did the downside prediction go unfulfilled, prices rallied back to the highs. Confirmation the pattern has failed comes through if the high of the right shoulder is cleared.

never fulfilled. It can be argued that the steep slope of the neckline invalidated the pattern but it was no more sharply inclined than that on the chart of Medeva. Indeed, following the breach of the neckline itself, prices broke the previous reaction low; good Dow Theory confirmation that the trend had been reversed. Prices were falling in a sharp enough manner to suggest the market had changed its view on British Airways radically. However, as the sharp rally shows, this bearish view came under revision. The question is, when does the pattern abort? The cautious trader would argue this occurs when the neckline is penetrated, certainly in the case of a rising line like this. But all downside predictions can be ignored if the peak of the right shoulder is overcome.

The updated version of the British Airways chart is a good example of what can happen when a pattern 'goes wrong'. If there is strong evidence that a share has gone out of favour and it starts falling sharply – as it did in this case – but then that fall is rapidly reversed, there is good reason to believe a new fundamental factor, or a reason for reappraising old ones, has emerged. What later can be seen to be a false breakdown frequently leads to a very significant move in the opposite direction; this is true of false breaks (both down and up) from all patterns, not just the head and shoulders, and it is not confined to reversal patterns either. Whereas, in this instance, the market had been dominated by sellers, suddenly there is a reversal of expectations; buying orders increase dramatically as people who had sold this blue-chip stock, recognising the new situation, scrambled to get back on board. Not only was British Airways' downside prediction not fulfilled, new highs were scored and the uptrend extended dramatically (see Figure 5.5).

The head and shoulders top has a sister pattern – the reversed head and shoulders bottom (often called an inverse head and shoulders in America). The principles for its definition and the price prediction are the same but, obviously, upside down (see Figure 5.6).

A relatively common reversal pattern is the double top. Following new highs, prices react, find support and rally to those highs but fail to close above them. At this point twin peaks are apparent but the double top only forms when the earlier reaction low (through which the horizontal neckline has been drawn) is broken by a close. The signal is a particularly strong one when volume rises on the breakdown. The price objective is obtained by extrapolating the height of the pattern from the neckline to the highs down from the breach of the neckline. In the example here (Figure 5.7), the Treasury stock's prediction was exceeded, despite potential support being in evidence in the region of the August-November trading band.

The double bottom is a reasonably common base formation. Prices rally in their downtrend and then decline, but find support at the previous low. The subsequent rise clears the previous rally high and the base is formed. In the Anglia Television example (see Figure 5.8) a useful pullback came through which allowed additional purchases as the neckline offered support. Volume

Price history subsequent to head and shoulders pattern 'going wrong'

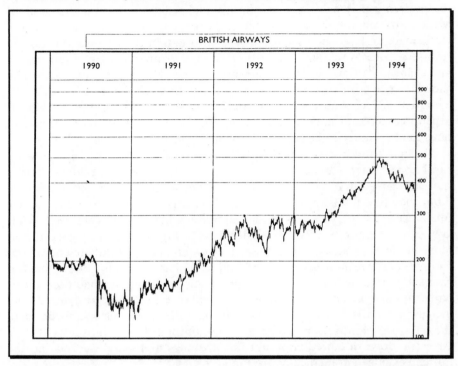

Figure 5.5   Chart by Investment Research of Cambridge Ltd: Design by NNIF

The subsequent history on British Airways highlights what can happen when patterns, not just heads and shoulders, abort. Frequently prices can go twice as far in the opposite direction as the prediction from the original pattern implied. This is due to a reversal of expectations and, in this case, the scramble to get back on board by those whose selling had caused the breakdown.

should increase upon the breakout. The prediction is achieved by measuring the depth of the pattern and extrapolating this distance up from the point of breakout. The potential resistance around 300p from the mid-1990 rally peak proved no obstacle and the prediction was exceeded with ease, prior to the company being taken over in 1994. This pattern took two years to form and it is a good example of the basic rule, the longer the base takes to develop, the greater the subsequent rise.

It was mentioned earlier that the predictions from point and figure charts were accomplished by the 'count', a method which can prove uncannily accurate. It is particularly useful if a pattern has developed in an energetic manner, but within a reasonably tight price range. In these circumstances merely measur-

Reversed head and shoulders bottom

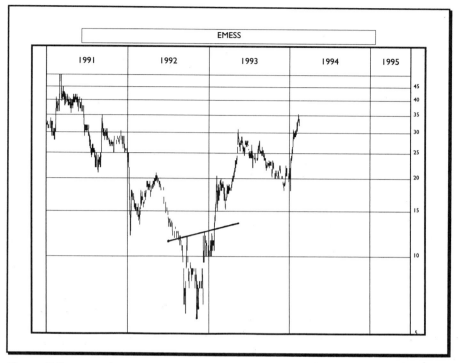

Figure 5.6   Chart by Investment Research of Cambridge Ltd: Design by NNIF

The reversed head and shoulders bottom occurs in similar, but opposite circumstances to the head and shoulders top. It comes at the end of a fast trend and the volume pattern should be the same. Once again, the distance between the neckline and head is the implied move when the pattern has completed.

ing the depth of the pattern and extrapolating it up or down in the direction of the breakout is likely to produce an underestimate of the price move, especially if the pattern has taken a long time to form and is obviously an important one.

The chart in Figure 5.9 is a three box reversal point and figure chart of London Gold, with each box given a value of $5. The base area has a similar shape to a reversed head and shoulders but it is not a classic example; it took almost exactly one year to form (between the end of 1984 and the beginning of 1986). The lowest plot is at $285 and the Summer rally peak is at $340. If the traditional bar chart method of calculating the upside objective were to be used the target would be $395 – the difference between the low and the rally peak added to the point of the upside break. However, the point and figure count gives a prediction to $500 – the high.

Double top

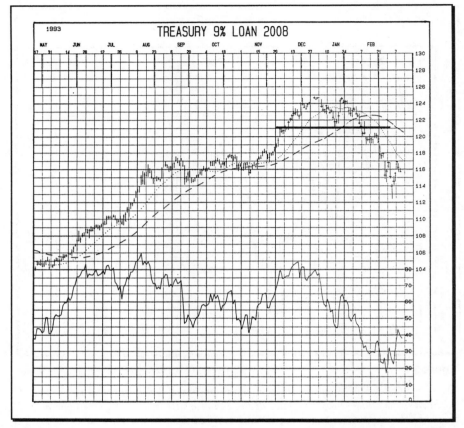

Figure 5.7   Investment Research of Cambridge Ltd

A double top is a reasonably common formation. It forms after prices rally to the recent high, fail to clear it and then break the last reaction low. Volume is usually low on the rally back to the high and should increase when the break of the support point i.e. the reaction low (the neckline) occurs. Classically, this should be the horizontal line drawn through the reaction low point. However, this is not a pattern where it is safe to jump the gun and assume, because the high has not been cleared, a top is forming. While the reaction low holds there is a considerable danger the pattern could be a rectangle; this is a continuation pattern within a trend, such as developed between August and September here.

The size of the point and figure count is not dependent upon the depth of the pattern but its width and hence the energy of the market argument. The more often price change occurs, the more frequently the plots will move over into the next column to the right, thus widening the formation. The prediction is calculated by counting across the row in which there are the greatest number of plots.

Double bottom

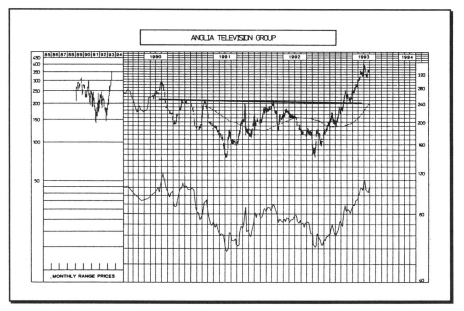

Figure 5.8   *Source:* Investment Research of Cambridge Ltd

A double bottom forms when the attempt to clear the previous rally peak fails, prices retreat, find support at the earlier low and then succeed in clearing the resistance from the top of the previous rise. This double bottom took two years to form, a factor which adds considerably to its importance. Pullbacks are slightly more common when downtrends are reversed as people are cautious and do not rush to buy in the same way as they rush to sell, and a good one came in here. The upside prediction, made by measuring the depth of the base and extrapolating that distance up the price scale from the break through the neck-line, was exceeded, before the takeover bid came through.

In the case of the chart of gold, the largest number of noughts and crosses appears in the row representing the $320 level – 12. If this were a one-box reversal chart the upside prediction would be 12 times $5 (the value of each box) added to $320 (the line across which the count is made) to give a level of $380 – not much to get excited about. However, since this is a three-box reversal chart the count needs to be expanded to overcome the effect of the compression to the market argument effected by the reversal factor. So the calculation is: 12 times 3 (or whatever the reversal factor happens to be) times the $5 box value. This gives a predicted rise of $180 and, when this is added to the $320 level, the $500 target mentioned above comes through.

This is the conventional approach. Others argue the count should occur from the lows and some would favour it being extrapolated from the point of breakout. Obviously, this gives three different targets which could be used as

Three-box reversal point and figure chart

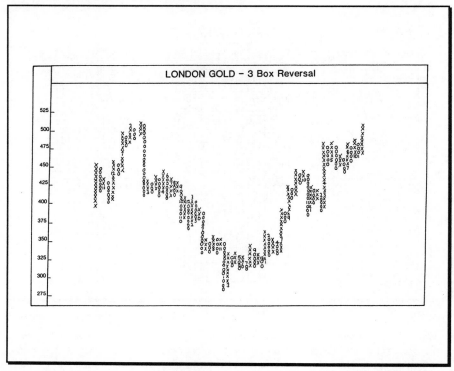

Figure 5.9

Chart by Chart Analysis Ltd

The width of the pattern which develops on a point and figure chart reflects the energy of the argument. To obtain the point and figure 'count' the number of squares filled in the widest row ($320 here) is counted and, as this is a three-box reversal chart, multiplied by 3. This, in turn, is multiplied by the box size ($5) and the result – $180 – is added to the price level of the row counted across. The predicted $500 level was achieved two years later.

first, second and third objectives if preferred. There is in addition a school of thought which argues that the horizontal count is only appropriate for the original point and figure charts which include each and every trade and not those which use, say, closing prices only.

Whilst there is considerable logic to this argument, experience does show that adapting the original count method to these 'truncated' charts does seem to work. Yet another view is to count the first column of crosses in an uptrend, multiply that by the reversal factor, and count up from the low. I have no personal experience of using this approach and, although it is said to have a good record of accuracy, I feel the logic of the width of the pattern being used for the price prediction is lost.

As with all forms of technical analysis, point and figure charting appeals to some if not to all; and the choice of method of prediction is very much up to the user. In principle, whatever method is chosen, it can be used for all patterns, whether reversal or continuation, and only the benefits of gaps and one day reversal patterns (which we will come to later) are lost. Whilst the lack of a timescale means the conventional plotting of moving averages and timing indicators is not possible, I have found the conventional point and figure count of considerable use and would not like to lose point and figure charts from my armoury simply because of this.

Close relations to the double top and bottom are the triple and, indeed, multiple tops and bottoms (see Figure 5.10). As their name implies they are variations on the same theme and the same bar or line chart principles apply. It should be noted here that, whilst the volume pattern in a head and shoulders could give early warning a reversal was underway, with these pat-

Triple multiple top

Figure 5.10

Source: Investment Research of Cambridge Ltd

A triple top forms once the price, having twice failed in its challenge of the high, breaks previous support offered by the reaction lows, across which the neckline is drawn. The prediction is measured from the high to the line drawn between these reaction lows (the neckline) and this distance is extrapolated down the scale. This is more like a multiple top – the prediction is measured in the same manner.

terns it is dangerous to jump the gun. The risk is twofold; what had appeared to be a potential double bottom could turn into a multiple bottom, lasting years, or, more dangerously, it could merely be a long-term consolidation within the prevailing trend.

Quite often a pattern such as that in De La Rue will emerge (see Figure 5.11). It is not a classic double bottom since the second low is well above that of the first. However, the fact that support came in prior to the low being tested can be taken

Rising bottom

Figure 5.11   *Source:* Investment Research of Cambridge Ltd

The rising bottom is not a 'textbook' pattern but is a fairly common phenomenon. Prices fail to clear the last rally peak but the reaction is reversed before the low is tested. Once the last rally high is cleared the pattern forms. Cautious predictions can be made by measuring from the higher low to the neckline, whilst the second prediction comes from the distance between the neckline and the absolute low itself.

as evidence of buyers' eagerness. Anyone finding other clues to a potential reversal might be tempted to jump the gun and buy with stop losses below the second low in anticipation of an upside break coming through. The measurement in this sort of case should be twofold: minimum predictions can be estimated by calculating the distance between the second low and the rally peak, with the major objective being established by measuring from the actual low itself.

The downtrend in Premier Consolidated (see Figure 5.12) was reversed by a pattern which is similar to that in De La Rue in that it exhibits rising lows, but is very much more convincing since there are two reaction lows above the actual low. It is a relatively uncommon reversal pattern called a 'triangle'. This

Triangle

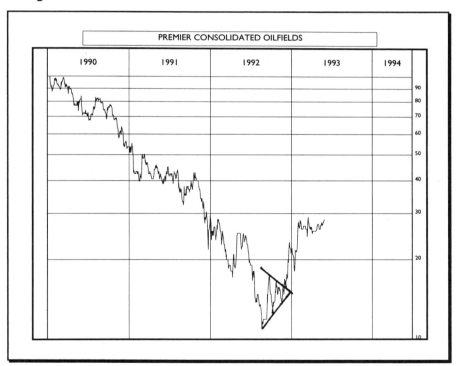

Figure 5.12   Chart by Investment Research of Cambridge Ltd: Design by NNIF

The triangle is reasonably uncommon as a reversal pattern. It is more often part of a trend and its resolution signals continuation but when it is a reversal pattern it is a powerful one. The rising lows and falling highs are evidence of a market argument tightening and, once it is resolved, the prediction – made by measuring its base – is usually fulfilled quickly. Volume will normally diminish whilst the pattern forms and increase when the breakout comes through. This should occur before prices are driven into the apex – about two-thirds of the distance across its width.

is a symmetrical triangle as the angles of the lines defining it are converging at a similar rate. A triangle forms as the argument in the market gets more intense; the range traded narrows as buyers buy at higher and higher prices whilst sellers are prepared to take less and less.

A triangle needs at least two points of contact on each side for its definition – three are preferable. Five points in total will 'do'. It can be a tricky pattern to analyse since it is not confined to a reversal formation. It can, and often does, occur within the prevailing trend; rather like the multiple tops, only when the price breaks through the support or resistance, can its role be ascertained. With the market argument tightening in this manner it is not surprising that break-outs from triangles are renowned for being sizeable. It seems as though the market is in a coil, poised to spring. Whilst a triangle is forming volume tends to diminish and then increase when the breakout comes through. Such a break-out should occur about two-thirds the way along the pattern – if prices move through the apex no prediction exists and the argument has fizzled out.

Price predictions from triangles are made by measuring the base of the tri-angle i.e. its widest part and extrapolating this distance in the direction of the breakout. In this example, following the upside break, a pullback came through. Such pullbacks are relatively frequent phenomena following the for-mation of the reasonably unusual triangle reversal and should find support from the line defining the triangle itself.

The outcome from the triangular top shown in the chart of the Italian Index (see Figure 5.13) is slightly easier to forecast. It is a descending, or flat bot-tomed triangle and the pattern is evidence of buyers remaining consistent at the same level, whilst sellers are showing signs of becoming increasingly ner-vous as they accept lower and lower prices for their shares. This formation will normally result in prices breaking down, as happened in this case.

Once again the price objective is obtained by measuring the base of the trian-gle and extrapolating this distance down from the point of breakout. This triangle has a twin sister – the ascending, or flat topped triangle. This too is likely to give a clue as to the likely direction of breakout; the sellers are remain-ing consistent and are only prepared to take a certain price, but the buyers are buying at consistently higher levels, allowing the ascending lows to form. An upside break is a strong possibility. The characteristics of triangles will be dis-cussed again in the following chapter when continuation patterns are examined.

The pattern defined on the Kwik-Fit chart looks like a triangle in reverse (see Figure 5.14). It is in fact a broadening formation and has become extremely unusual. It is a topping pattern and shows a high degree of anxiety in the market as buyers and sellers leap in and out in an inconsistent manner. It may be unusual now but apparently it proliferated on charts of Wall Street shares in 1929. Whilst this volatile price activity is occurring volume is likely to remain high.

A close look at the chart will show it is behaving very oddly. First prices break into new high ground and then fail to follow through. Not only do they

Descending/Flat bottomed triangle

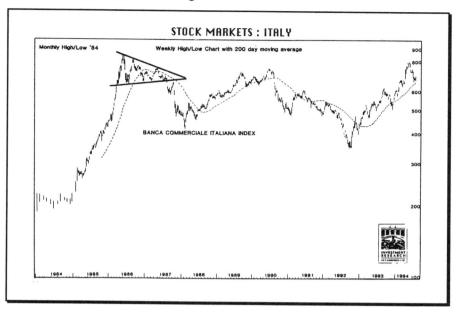

Figure 5.13   *Source:* Investment Research of Cambridge Ltd

The triangle that signalled the reversal of the Italian market's rise is of the descending or flat bottomed variety. The buyers are less anxious than the sellers, refusing to raise their bids; this normally implies a downside break is more likely. The prediction is again made by measuring the 'base' of the triangle and extrapolating this distance in the direction of the breakout when it comes through.

not make further gains, they react and breach the previous reaction low. But, instead of falling further, they rally and make new highs. A broadening formation will normally have three points of contact on the upside and at least two on the sloping line connecting the lows. It is difficult to be precise about predictions from such a frenetic argument but falls are likely to equate to the widest part of the pattern at least. They certainly did so in 1929 and in the Kwik-Fit example shown here.

Whereas heads and shoulders and multiple tops and bottoms form when prices bounce between specific support and resistance points, sometimes the shift in supply and demand is more gradual and rounding, or saucer, tops and bottoms come through. The curve drawn above the British Telecom chart in Figure 5.15 emphasises this shift as buyers gradually lose enthusiasm and sellers gain hold. A necessary adjunct to the saucer top is the mirrored saucer in volume; levels of trading diminish as prices near their highs and then increase as more sellers are attracted to the market.

Broadening formation

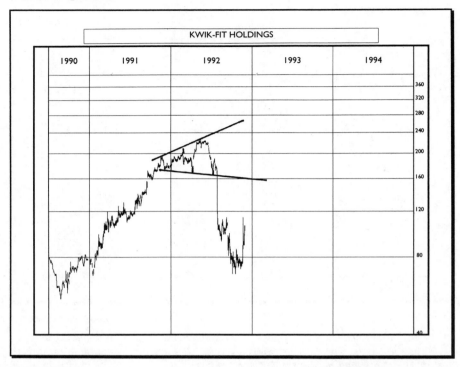

Figure 5.14   Chart by Investment Research of Cambridge Ltd: Design by NNIF

A broadening formation is relatively unusual and is most likely to form at a market top when emotion in the market-place is running high, rather than at a market bottom when activity is likely to be desultory (it is a most unusual formation as a bottom). It shows a series of false upside breaks followed by a series of false downside breaks, causing the pattern to get ever-wider. A best guess at the size of the fall is the measurement of the widest part of the pattern although the frenetic movements are such that, given the choice, it may prove wiser to stand aside. Volume usually remains high throughout the development and panic is the likely order of the day.

The saucer bottom in General Electric (see Figure 5.16) shows the gentle accumulation of long positions occurring over time; it also shows a common variation of rounding bottoms where prices rise suddenly and strongly near the mid-point of the pattern and then subside and the gentle reversal process continues. Clear breakouts from saucers are difficult to determine but in this case one did come through when the early 1991 rally peak was cleared. With a saucer bottom volume should show the same curve as the price itself. Such patterns do not succumb to the traditional measurement approach, but should be monitored by the circular uptrend applied to the example. (It should be

Saucer top

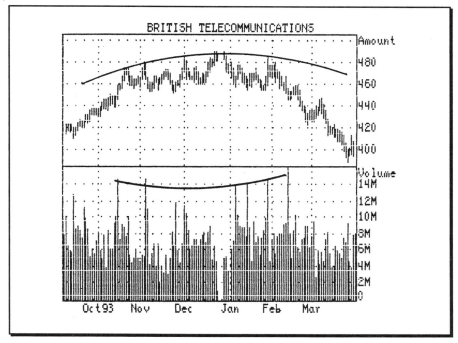

Figure 5.15   *Chart* by Reuters Technical Analysis

A saucer top shows the gradual shift in the argument as buyers slowly run out of steam and sellers gradually get more aggressive. Volume forms a mirror image of the price. Specific falls are not predictable in the normal way and prices are likely to remain trapped beneath the declining semicircular line defining the increasing selling pressure.

borne in mind this particular chart is a relatively long-term one and is plotted on a semi-logarithmic grid; were it on arithmetic paper the rise would look virtually parabolic, emphasising its energy and pace.)

The chart of Barclays in Figure 5.17 shows a diamond – an unusual top pattern which is a variation on the head and shoulders. Whilst the two shoulders form in a similar manner to those seen on the head and shoulders itself, the neckline can be drawn in as a vee, rather than a horizontal line. The measurement properties are the same; the height of the pattern is measured and extrapolated down from the point of breakout. The breakdown comes through earlier than it would on a head and shoulders, when the rising support line is breached. This is another pattern which is identified with market tops, since it usually occurs against a generally high volume level whilst the overall volume at market bottoms is normally somewhat low. Very occasionally it will also appear as a continuation pattern in a bull trend.

Saucer bottom

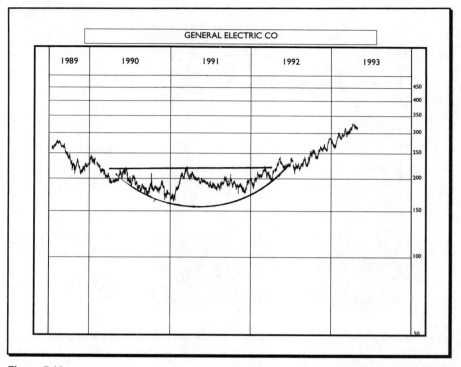

Figure 5.16   Chart by Investment Research of Cambridge Ltd: Design by NNIF

Saucer bottoms highlight waning selling pressure followed by growing confidence from the buyers. Volume usually takes on a similar curve to the price.

The last major reversal looked at here is the spike or 'V' bottom or top. As was seen in Chapter 3, sometimes a well-established trend, particularly a downtrend trend, can, at a late stage, re-accelerate. Previous experience has shown that rises or falls of this nature are unlikely to be sustained; however, with no resistance or support in the way, determining when the move is likely to stop is difficult. In these circumstances prices are likely to reverse this fast move very quickly once the turning point comes through.

In the example of Hillsdown Holdings a well-established downtrend was already in place prior to the price fall accelerating in mid-1992 (see Figure 5.18). The fall extended to such an extent the price halved. But suddenly support was found and recovery was rapid. There is no prescribed way of measuring the likely rise following such a reversal although experience will show it could well reverse one half to two-thirds of the most recent phase of the downtrend. In the case of Hillsdown the initial rally reversed one-

Diamond top

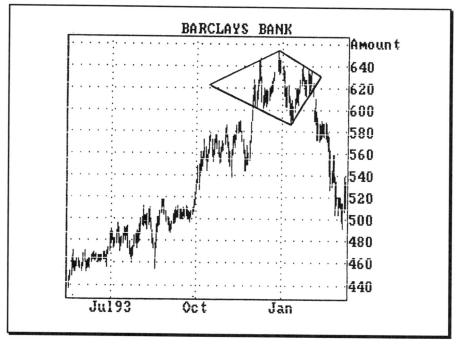

Figure 5.17

Chart by Reuters Technical Analysis

The diamond top is similar to a head and shoulders where the shoulders are shrugged. The V-shaped neckline is broken before the horizontal one would be, giving sell signals at a higher price. The predicted move is measured from the pattern's greatest depth and extrapolated down from the break point. A diamond can also form as a continuation pattern but this is more likely to occur in a bull, rather than a bear, trend. Indeed, it does not have a brother pattern as a bottom reversal – volume is reasonably high throughout.

third of the fall that had been seen since the 200p rally peak earlier in the year, and 100 per cent of the decline since the lower trend channel was breached. In retrospect it can be seen that the spike bottom formed the head of a reversed head and shoulders and, once the neckline was broken, an upside prediction to outside the trend channel could be made. As can be seen, this was fulfilled.

The patterns covered so far are reversal patterns, capable of signalling the end of a trend travelling one way and a move of some size in the opposite direction and they thus carry considerable significance. However, continuation patterns i.e. those that occur within an already existing trend, are important too. On bar and line charts they are measured in the same way as reversal patterns; their depth is extrapolated in the direction of the trend once a breakout

Spike bottom

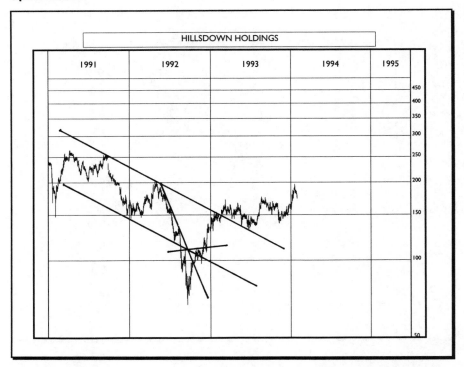

Figure 5.18   Chart by Investment Research of Cambridge Ltd: Design by NNIF

A spike bottom is normally accompanied by a selling climax, When, in the late stages of a bear trend, the price fall accelerates and panic sets in, volume tends to grow. Suddenly, after a large fall against high volume, selling is exhausted and only a small amount of buying power is needed to effect reversal. It can be seen that this bottom actually became part of a reversed head and shoulders in the longer term.

comes through. Their occurrence is far more frequent and they need constant monitoring not only to establish the size of the next likely move, but also to allow entry points to be judged if the original opportunity to get in has been missed. This is an important aspect of continuation pattern analysis since, although their development can often appear slow, when a breakout comes the subsequent move can be fast. Indeed, since these are the patterns which are forming a very large percentage of the time, their importance is considerable. The following chapter is devoted to their interpretation.

6

INTERPRETATION OF CONTINUATION PATTERNS

- The most common continuation pattern is the 'rectangle' – in other words the sideways trend – or Dow's 'line'
- It is often difficult to predetermine the direction of breakout from a rectangle since, in certain circumstances, this pattern could equally well turn out to be a multiple bottom or top. But sometimes its development offers some clues
- 'Triangles' can be reversal patterns, but they are more likely to be continuation patterns – and very reliable ones, too
- There is a family of triangular patterns and these can sometimes cause confusion. Apart from the various forms of the triangle itself, there is the 'wedge' (rising and falling), the 'pennant' and the 'flag'. They all have different connotations in measuring terms
- Sometimes warning signals from one particular trading period come through – and subsequently these can be seen to form part of a major reversal
- Gaps – occasions when prices trade completely above or below the previous sessions' range – can be very important. At other times they are not. They come in different forms – and carry different messages.

Chapter 3 already includes several examples of the most common continuation pattern, the rectangle. As its name implies, it is a pattern which develops between two price levels where support and resistance are proving effective and it is basically a sideways trend within a longer-term up or down trend. The balanced market argument will normally be resolved in the direction of the main trend but as time passes there is an increasing chance it will not be and a double, triple or multiple top could be forming instead.

The daily range chart of Boots in Figure 6.1 shows an uptrend developing in detail. Previous resistance points are subsequently providing support and there is good reason to believe the uptrend will continue.

The method of predicting the likely move once the support or resistance confining the price movements is broken is to measure the depth of the pattern and project that measurement in the direction of the breakout. As in the case of trend reversal patterns, the prediction may need to be adjusted due to the

Continuation patterns forming an uptrend

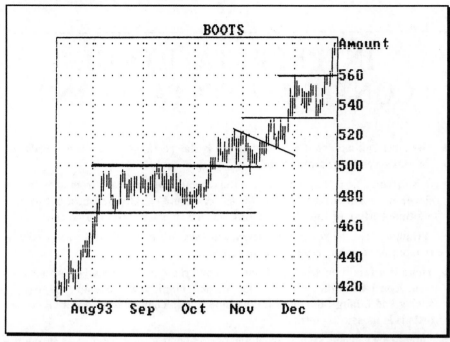

Figure 6.1

Chart by Reuters Technical Analysis

Rectangles are effectively sideways trends, or consolidation/distribution areas, which form the stepping stones to longer-term trend development. Once the rectangle's highs or lows are cleared, prices should make a move similar in extent to its depth. Subsequently the cleared highs or lows should prove effective as support or resistance as reactions set in.

proximity of previous support levels which are now likely to provide resistance, or previous resistance levels which could provide support. Additionally, if it has been possible to define a trend channel, the levels this inclined support or resistance could come in at should be noted too.

As is particularly evident on the chart of Land Securities, even though the rectangle is a somewhat unenergetic pattern in comparison to others, when its resolution comes through in an uptrend the initial move can be very fast, leaving little time to get on board (see Figure 6.2). This is because the basic rationale as to why a price should move fast when a breakout occurs still applies – not only is the area of argument attracting the buyers in the support region and the sellers around the old highs, it is disappointing others who are not trading the market but would like to do so.

Some of these are potential buyers below the current price range. As time passes they will likely abandon hope of getting the shares in more cheaply and

Breakouts followed by fast moves

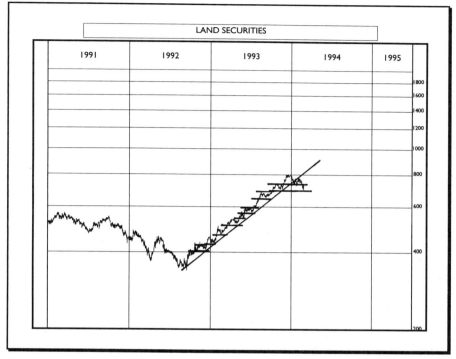

Figure 6.2   Chart by Investment Research of Cambridge Ltd: Design by NNIF

Although a rectangle appears to be a relatively unexciting pattern, the move when the breakout comes can be fast. Since such activity occurs the vast majority of the time rectangles, or consolidation/distribution areas, are more important than the charismatic reversal patterns to the professional analyst.

will either enter the market in the support region or buy another share for their portfolio instead. Whichever decision they take, the effect will be to reduce the demand in an area immediately below the current range. But, additionally, there could be would-be sellers who are looking for prices in excess of the recent highs. They may be patient and wait or, as time passes, they may accept the price that is on offer. This reduces the potential supply of shares over recent highs. Thus, when the breakout through the support or resistance comes, there is effectively a 'vacuum' immediately outside the recent price range and this is likely to be filled quickly. Not only is supply reduced, demand has also increased since the new extremes will likely attract trend followers. In addition, there is most probably a band of traders still waiting to get in at lower levels, who now have to rush to buy before the price gets even further away. (Similar but opposite, actions cause fast moves in downtrends too.)

While the strongly-angled uptrend in Land Securities remained inviolate from 1992 to the beginning of 1994, there seemed little reason to fear the rectangles which formed the building blocks to this trend would not continue to enjoy upside breaks, allowing the trend to extend. However, at the start of the new year this trendline was broken for the first time in many months and the subsequent rally was defeated by resistance from the back of it – a clear warning signal the support at 700p could give way, causing the trend to reverse.

Since the breakout from a rectangle can be explosive, it is worthwhile examining the pattern, looking for opportunities to get in before the break occurs. A close look at the chart of Next in Figure 6.3 gives strong clues that an upside break from the rectangle which completed in July 1993 could be imminent. This pattern took five months to form; during the early period prices backed

Rectangle's upside break imminent (and inverse head and shoulders)

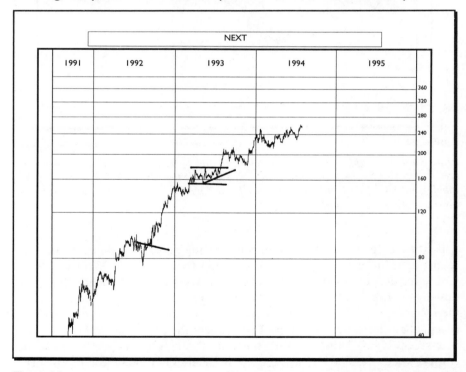

Figure 6.3   Chart by Investment Research of Cambridge Ltd: Design by NNIF

The price action within the rectangle's development can be watched for clues that a breakout could be imminent. The three higher lows in the rectangle in Next gave strong hints the buyers were becoming increasingly eager. This chart shows an additional pattern – the inverse head and shoulders, occurring as a continuation pattern in the earlier stages of the trend.

and filled between support over the previous rally peak and resistance formed by the recent highs. Then, the next three reactions held over original support as the minor downtrends reversed at higher and higher prices, allowing the overall sideways trend to gain an upside bias. This was good warning to get in then, before the price got away.

The chart of Next provides a good opportunity to introduce an unusual, but powerful, formation – the bullish inverted head and shoulders continuation pattern. Purists would argue that a head and shoulders only occurs at tops and bottoms following a large move when, as has been seen, it carries very powerful connotations. But this 'new' formation has crept into the language and it certainly gave the price considerable upward impetus here. As can be seen, it is defined by prices falling within an uptrend and then finding support around the previous rally peak; the fall is then resumed at a faster pace but this sharp decline is rapidly reversed and, in due course, the earlier rally peaks are cleared. The upside prediction is measured in the same way as it is in the case of a reversed head and shoulders reversal pattern. In theory it has a sister, the bearish head and shoulders continuation pattern but, in that rallies in bear trends are rarely sharp enough to form such a head, this pattern can usually be treated as a rectangle for measuring purposes.

Part of the Dow Theory mentions a formation called a 'Line'. This is a variation on the rectangle. The rule states that if, following a move in the direction of the main trend, prices move sideways and consolidate within a range no greater than 5 per cent of the price, then this action substitutes for a reaction and the trend will eventually resume – as it did in this case (see Figure 6.4).

We now come back to triangles, this time in their somewhat more common role as continuation patterns. Again, the triangle forms rather like the rectangle does but the market argument is somewhat more intense. Thus, as the pattern develops, the area of the argument narrows and while this is happening volume tends to diminish. On daily charts a triangle, whatever its shape, tends to take between one and three months to form (although this one took longer) and the presumption is the breakout will favour the prevailing trend unless there is evidence to the contrary.

In the example of the Australia and New Zealand Banking Group in Figure 6.5 an upside break was almost a foregone conclusion since the downtrend had only just been reversed when it formed and there was little, if anything, of a rise worth reversing. It is a symmetrical triangle and it enjoyed an upside break some time before prices would have been driven into its apex. Again, as a general rule, a breakout should occur, roughly speaking, after two-thirds of the area covered by the triangle has been traversed and, as confirmation of its validity, volume should increase. The pullback to the triangle found support over the formation itself – a fairly classic pattern. The measurement is obtained by calculating the triangle's base and extrapolating this distance upwards.

Dow theory 'Line'

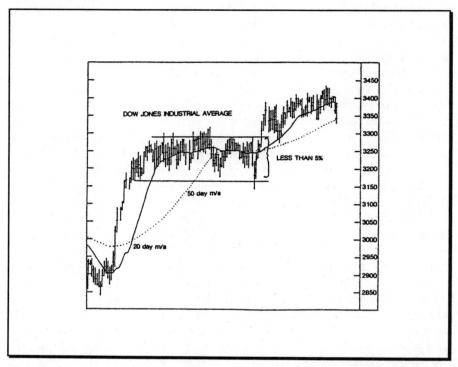

Figure 6.4

Source: Investment Research of Cambridge Ltd

Dow recognised the rectangle (he called it a 'Line') specifying that, were prices to consolidate within a 5 per cent price range, then a sizeable correction to the trend was unlikely to come through. Would-be buyers (or sellers in a downtrend) would have to get in in the current region before the main trend extended.

Some markets 'adopt' triangles and they appear again and again, in others they form not at all. Among the commodity markets silver is famous for continuously allowing triangles to form.

Bank of Scotland, during 1993, was in a fast moving uptrend and formed two triangles in quick succession. The first was of the symmetrical or equilateral variety and the prediction following its upside break was rapidly fulfilled. The second was marginally unusual in that it was descending, or flat bottomed, but was resolved on the upside. A flat bottomed triangle is a more frequent occurrence in a downtrend where sellers show a tendency to be evermore anxious to sell. However, the resolution was a positive one and, once again, the upward prediction was quickly fulfilled (see Figure 6.6 below).

The triangle which formed in Campari International during 1993 is a particularly interesting one (see Figure 6.7). Not so much for its shape as it was,

Symmetrical triangle

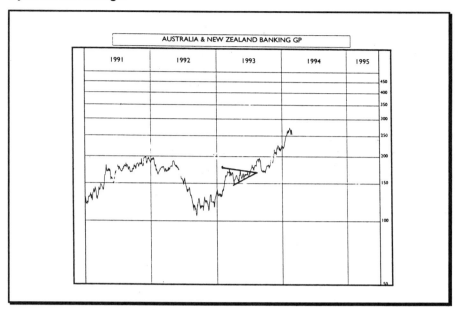

AUSTRALIA & NEW ZEALAND BANKING GP

| 1991 | 1992 | 1993 | 1994 | 1995 |

Figure 6.5
Chart by Investment Research of Cambridge Ltd: Design by NNIF

The triangle is normally a continuation pattern within an existing trend. This example is a symmetrical triangle – the lines defining the rising lows and falling highs are tilted at the same angle. Usually a triangle (on a daily chart) takes between three weeks and three months to form; this is an imperfect example as it took four months. However, it fulfilled the crucial criteria that the price should not travel through the apex (which signals the argument has fizzled out and no prediction can be made), and made its breakout about two-thirds of the way along its length. Volume characteristics and measurement principles are the same as when the triangle comes through as a reversal pattern.

once again, of the symmetrical or equilateral variety, but because the downside break saw a large 'gap' in the prices traded. Gaps will be addressed later but suffice it to say, if a breakout from a pattern occurs in such an aggressive manner that prices do not trade in the range established over the previous period at all, then the move is a very significant one and the chances of the prediction being exceeded are considerable. Indeed, in this instance, the prediction was fulfilled almost immediately.

The triangle has a near neighbour called a wedge which looks very similar in some ways but this can lead to confusion. Whereas an ascending triangle, where the top is horizontal and the lower support line is rising, is a potentially bullish pattern, the ascending wedge is bearish. Also, whilst the descending triangle – where support is proving effective at a particular level, but rallies are running out of steam at consistently lower prices – is bearish, the descending

Two triangles formed in quick succession

Figure 6.6   Chart by Investment Research of Cambridge Ltd: Design by NNIF

Triangles appear time and again in some price series, never in others. The predictions from the depth of the base are usually fulfilled quickly, as happened on both occasions here. The first is an equilateral, or symmetrical, triangle and the second is a descending triangle – which is slightly unusual in an uptrend. But the breakout was on the upside and the prediction was exceeded.

wedge has bullish connotations. Wedges come through, generally speaking, as counter-trend moves but, instead of adopting roughly parallel boundaries, defining a consistently paced rise or fall, the lines defining the wedge converge.

In the Johnson Matthey example in Figure 6.8 prices are rallying across their downtrend; the boundaries to the rally can be drawn in and, in that they draw together, they take on an appearance similar to that of a triangle. However, this merely implies that, although the rally is consistently gaining support at higher and higher levels, its minor upthrusts are running out of steam. This is a warning that the rise might soon reverse and, when the lower line defining the wedge is broken, falls back to its start at least are signalled.

Much in the same way as a rising wedge is bearish, a falling wedge is normally bullish – particularly if it occurs in an uptrend (see Figure 6.9). The pattern is formed by the same converging trendlines and, once the declining line defining the lower peaks is broken, the rise can be expected to extend back to the point where the wedge began to form, at least. Whilst a breakdown

Downside break with 'gap' in prices traded

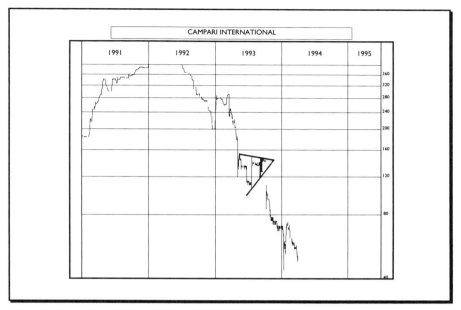

Figure 6.7   Chart by Investment Research of Cambridge Ltd: Design by NNIF

The large triangle that formed in Campari was resolved on the downside by prices break-
ing down, leaving a gap between the last trading period in the triangle and prices traded
the following day as the breakdown occurred. Such a gap adds to the significance of the
breakdown and the prediction is often exceeded, as it was here.

from a rising wedge is likely to be fast, it is a frequent occurrence that, once a
falling wedge is breached, prices consolidate before moving ahead. However,
in this instance the buying power was adequate to allow an immediate advance
– into new high ground. In both situations volume should expand once the
breakout from the wedge has come through.

Wedges normally form as counter-trend moves, as has already been stated.
When they come through in different circumstances alarm bells ring. The chart
of ASDA in Figure 6.10 shows a rising wedge when there was already a strong
possibility the uptrend was being reversed. Whilst prices had already breached
the last reaction low, the reaction had held over the previous one and the trend
channel was intact. Against this background, the rally is enjoying consistently
higher lows, yet the minor peaks were failing to complement the momentum –
they were losing speed. This action often comes through near market tops and,
as can be seen from this example, it did so here. Indeed, once the rally (the
wedge) failed, prices broke the more important support and an almost classic
head and shoulders top formed.

Ascending wedge – bearish pattern

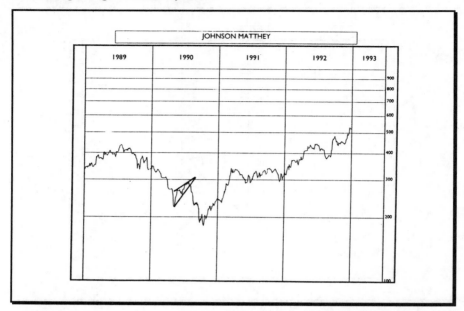

Figure 6.8   Chart by Investment Research of Cambridge Ltd: Design by NNIF

The triangular shape is common to several patterns but they must be distinguished care-fully as they carry different connotations. The ascending wedge in Johnson Matthey is a bearish pattern, unlike the ascending triangle which usually occurs in an uptrend and breaks out on the upside. This illustration shows a rally in a downtrend but, instead of the rise occurring within a roughly parallel trend channel, the minor waves peter out before the would-be upper parallel is neared. Thus the lines defining the highs and lows converge, forming an ascending wedge, highlighting the point buying power is failing to follow through. A breakdown signals a reversal to the lows of the wedge at least.

The triangle seems to cause a lot of confusion to the unversed technical ana-lyst. It is a word that is bandied about without too much thought as to what it means. This is unfortunate since predictions from triangles differ from predic-tions from wedges and, again, from predictions from pennants – the formation shown in the chart of Allied Domecq in Figure 6.11.

Whilst the wedge is a rather different formation from the triangle, the pen-nant is not and so confusion can be forgiven. However, the implied measured move is very different indeed, so it is advisable to get it right. Whereas the tri-angle represents an urgent argument within a continuing trend, it does still take some time to form – between one and three months on daily charts. When the breakout comes the measurement is taken from the base of the triangle itself. But the pennant is a very different creature. It takes on the same shape

Falling wedge – bullish pattern

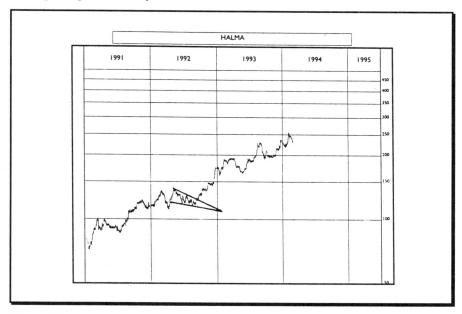

Figure 6.9   Chart by Investment Research of Cambridge Ltd: Design by NNIF

The descending wedge, unlike the descending triangle, is a bullish pattern. The price is falling in a longer-term uptrend and the lines defining the reaction converge, highlighting the fact the selling pressure is failing to carry through consistently. An upside break implies a move back to the highs of the wedge at least. Often, when a falling wedge comes in, prices, having broken out of the upside, then come back to test the back of the breached wedge for support before rising strongly. This did not happen here but it frequently does.

as a triangle (hence the confusion) but only forms in a very fast trend and its formation usually lasts less than three weeks. It is normally accompanied by very low volume and indicates an area where short-term profit-taking is coming through. It effectively acts as a 'halfway hesitation'; in other words, once the price has cleared the line defining its triangular shape, the rise or fall can be expected to extend by the same amount as the rise or fall seen immediately prior to its formation. In the case of Allied Domecq this would mean a rise equivalent to the one that preceded the pennant's formation – a move far greater than the one implied if the pennant were treated as a triangle – merely the depth of its base.

The pennant is so named as it takes on the appearance of the small flag flown on boats and the analogy is drawn between the rise (or fall) in price and the subsequent measurement being similar to a flag at half-mast. The 'flag' formation itself has similar connotations, but it is a different shape (see Figure 6.12).

Bearish rising wedge as part of a head and shoulders top

Figure 6.10   Chart by Investment Research of Cambridge Ltd: Design by NNIF

Mid-1993 saw a large, rather ugly head and shoulders top develop in ASDA and the right shoulder was, in fact, a bearish rising wedge. Once the breakdown from the wedge occurred, the breach of the head and shoulders' neckline was almost a foregone conclusion.

A flag forms against a similar background to the pennant; after a fast move in price some profit-taking occurs and causes a minor reaction against the trend. The rally in the case of British Telecommunications can be confined within parallel channels and this is typical of the flag. Once the breakout from the flag comes through, the move can be expected to extend by the same amount already seen. Volume should increase once the breakout comes through and the move is measured by establishing the distance between the point at which the price broke down from its top formation (in this instance) to the low prior to the flag forming. This distance is then subtracted from the flag's high or, if feeling less cautious, from the point at which prices broke down from the flag itself.

The chart of the Treasury stock in Figure 6.13 has already been seen since it was used to illustrate the double top (Figure 5.7). The breakdown from that double top was a fast one and, around 120, a reasonably common pattern formed. It is not a textbook example of a flag since the short-term price consolidation highlighed on the chart does not show rising lows – they are horizontal, rather like a short-term rectangle. But it took only days to form and I find that, as a mark of a halfway hesitation in a fast up or down move, once it breaks

Pennant formation

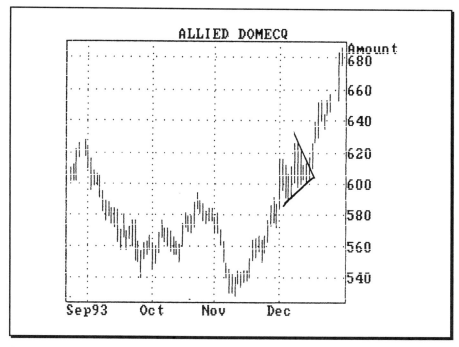

ALLIED DOMECQ

Figure 6.11   *Chart* by Reuters Technical Analysis

The baby sister to the equilateral, or symmetrical triangle is the pennant. It forms the same shape but, in daily bar charting, takes only three days to three weeks to do so. It occurs in a fast trend and, most importantly, the method of prediction is different. Once the break comes the price is indicated to extend the current fast trend by the same distance already travelled; it is a 'halfway hesitation'.

support it is a very reliable indication that the fall should extend down the scale by the same amount already covered.

The chart of HSBC in Figure 6.14 is an apt end to the coverage of triangles and similar formations since it emphasises the different interpretations placed on the different patterns. The descending wedge that formed at the beginning of the year is a classic example; it formed in an uptrend and is a bullish continuation pattern. The subsequent rise was greater than the extent of the wedge itself and the prediction was exceeded. At the end of February a head and shoulders top with a sloping neckline formed and prices fell quickly. The first week in March saw a sharp bounce which was reversed quickly; thereafter a pattern very like a descending triangle emerged but it took less than the minimum three weeks and, in this fast moving market, should be interpreted as a pennant despite its flat bottom. In other words, it is a halfway hesitation and signals further considerable falls, far greater than just the measurement of its base.

Flag formation

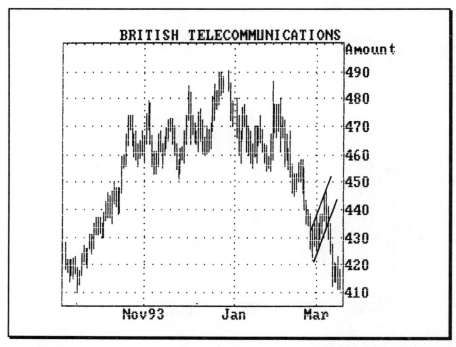

Figure 6.12

Another 'halfway hesitation' is the flag. This is a short-term formation in a fast trend which, over three days to three weeks, reacts against the trend within parallel lines. Once the break comes, prices should extend the trend by the same distance already covered. It, like the pennant, is a pattern which denotes short-term profit-taking.

All the patterns seen so far have taken some time to form but there are, additionally, such things as reversal days. In themselves they do not give predictions but warning signals that the sharp move in the market is probably over. Later, they can often be seen to form part of the pattern actually responsible for reversing the trend. Typically they occur after very significant gains or falls have been seen and are accompanied by very high volume – probably the highest enjoyed during that trend. In a falling market they are called selling climaxes and can be expected to herald a sharp rally at least.

The chart of Argyll Group in Figure 6.15 shows a selling climax on 7 June; relatively heavy volume was traded as prices fell rapidly but by the end of the day both the close and the high were higher than the high of the previous day. This constitutes an 'outside day', usually a strong signal that the worst of the decline has been seen for now. Such action often signals that the actual lows have been seen.

Halfway hesitation

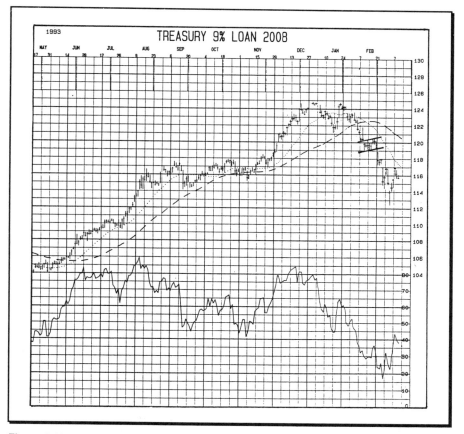

Figure 6.13

Investment Research of Cambridge Ltd

The pattern illustrated in the daily range chart of the Treasury stock is a small rectangle, with prices moving within horizontal lines following the earlier sharp fall. It evidenced some profit-taking on shorts which was not enough to cause prices to rally within a flag. However, it only took eight trading days to form and, as it was within a fast trend, the breakdown carried the same connotations as the pennant and flag – it was a halfway hesitation.

Sometimes, as in the case of the peak in British Airways (shown in Figure 6.16), the reversal takes two days to form. On the Wednesday, backed by high volume, the price rose into new high ground; but on the Thursday, having opened firm, it fell back and closed near its low – below Wednesday's low. This, following new highs, signalled a considerable degree of uncertainty; what had started as a good day turned into one where profit-taking was taking place. In retrospect it can be seen that an important high had been hit, confirmed when the trend was reversed by the formation of the double top in

Falling wedge and descending triangle contrasted

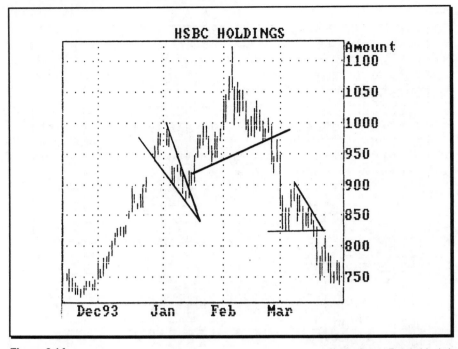

Figure 6.14   *Chart* by Reuters Technical Analysis

This chart highlights the difference between a falling wedge and a descending triangle. The falling wedge occurred in an uptrend and its bullish predictions were exceeded. But, once the trend was reversed, a pattern much akin to the descending triangle emerged. Its connotations were, however, more bearish since it took less than three weeks to form. Hence it can be treated as a pennant and the fall should extend far further than the mere measurement of the base would imply.

double top in February. This classifies it as a 'key reversal'. This is an impressive sounding phrase often bandied around, however it requires hindsight to give it this name. Until further evidence comes through that the trend has reversed it is merely a reversal day and the trend could, in due course, resume.

Other near term developments which are not patterns as such but which give strong clues something interesting is occurring are gaps. These are spaces which appear on high/low charts (but, as with reversal days, not on line or point and figure) reflecting a gap in the trading between one period and the next. In other words, prices open above the previous period's high and remain above it for the rest of the period, or open below the previous period's low and stay below it for the rest of the period. Such gaps occur very frequently on the very short-term

Reversal day

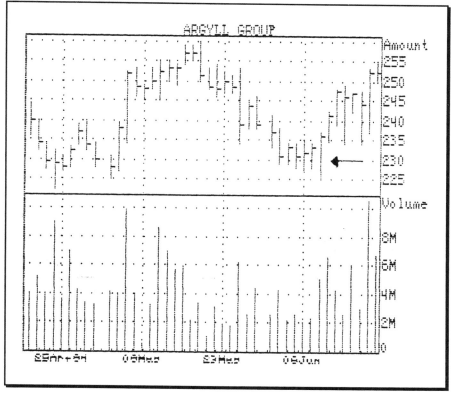

Figure 6.15

Chart by Reuters Technical Analysis

Towards the end of a trend the price action over one particular period can give the alert that the end is nigh. Prices start the period by moving into new high or low ground and then reverse, with the other extreme and the close exceeding the low or high of the previous period. This is referred to as a key reversal – although whether or not it is 'key' can only be known for sure in retrospect. The likelihood of the action signalling the end is much enhanced if volume on the occasion is high.

charts such as 5 minute bars, reasonably often on daily charts and sometimes on weekly charts. They are an infrequent occurrence on monthly charts.

Gaps can carry great significance but to use them properly it is necessary to understand when they are unlikely to do so. This is when they are classified as 'common gaps' which normally form in a chart of a narrowly traded issue or in the middle of a trading range. The gaps in 600 Group (see Figure 6.17) are only useful as a warning to a would-be investor that the market is a thin one and he might have difficulty in getting out at a decent price – they carry no specific technical significance.

Key reversal

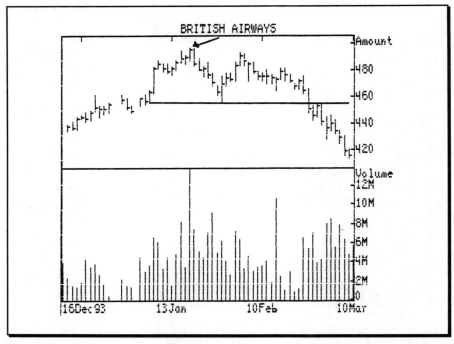

Figure 6.16   *Chart* by Reuters Technical Analysis

The action in British Airways shows a two day reversal. Prices moved into new high ground and closed firm on the first day. The following day, however, prices reacted, exceeding the previous day's low, and closing below it. Volume was high on the first day, but only reasonably so on the second. However, the action can be seen to have been 'key' – the trading of those two days proved to be the highs.

However as Figure 6.18 shows, the gap in British Aerospace does carry import. The chart shows prices trading sideways between August 1993 and January 1994; the formation is a rectangle, with a slightly sloping line defining the upper boundary.

Prices frequently leave a gap when they make a break from a consolidation pattern, particularly if this pattern has held prices for any length of time. As discussed previously, this is because every time the price rallies to the resistance area it meets selling and the longer this continues the greater amount of selling it absorbs. In due course the immediate supply of shares will be used up, creating an effective vacuum overhead. Breakouts are often rapid but, when accompanied by a gap, the signal carries even greater import. This gap is called a breakaway gap and when it occurs against high volume there is a very strong likelihood the upside prediction will be fulfilled quickly. The same is true if the break is on the downside but the volume is unlikely to be quite so large.

Common gaps

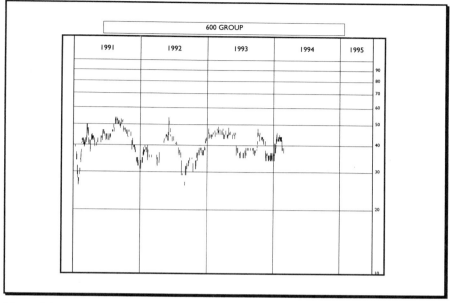

Figure 6.17   Chart by Investment Research of Cambridge Ltd: Design by NNIF

Gaps between prices traded during one period and the next can be very important indicators. However, at other times they are not; this is when they are 'common gaps' occurring within a sideways range and/or in a narrowly traded issue. Both circumstances existed here.

The FTSE chart in Figure 6.19 shows several important gaps. The first is a breakaway gap. The second gap followed the formation of a flag. It is a 'measuring' or 'runaway' gap and the energy it emphasises makes it highly likely the flag will prove to be a halfway hesitation – as it was. However, once a breakaway gap and a measuring gap have been seen, it is likely any further gaps are highlighting the very frothy state of the market and they could prove to be signalling the exhaustion of the trend. But no real danger is signalled until they are 'filled'. Once an 'exhaustion' gap is filled – by prices, in this case, retreating to fill the area on the scale left by the gap – there is a high probability the trend is tiring and will soon reverse and after the fifth gap on the FTSE this is just what happened.

It is often said that 'the gap will be filled', suggesting that the investor can look forward to the price retracing and giving him another opportunity to get into the market or sell at a better price. This, however, is very misleading and shows a lack of understanding of why the gaps form. A breakaway gap will rarely be filled; it is rather like assuming a pullback will always come through and, as has already been discussed, this is by no means a certainty. Indeed, there is a high probability that the gap made on a breakaway will only be filled

Breakaway gap

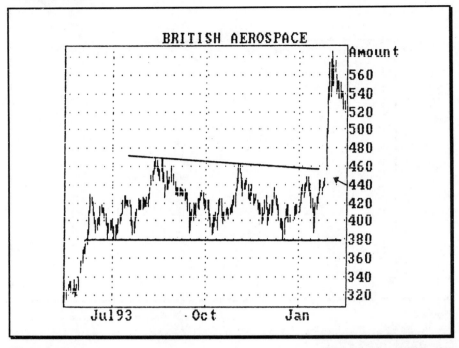

Figure 6.18   *Chart* by Reuters Technical Analysis

One of the most important signals a gap can give comes through if a price abandons a trading range against high volume, leaving a gap behind. This is called a 'breakaway gap' and it adds to the probability the prediction from the pattern will be fulfilled. The area in which the gap occurs should offer support or, if the break is downwards, resistance.

once the trend has been reversed. Additionally, if a runaway gap is filled it is not the wished for opportunity to get into the market again, it is a warning that the implied measurement on that upside break is now questionable – the pace of the rise is faltering and it may not be sustained. As we have seen, once an exhaustion gap is filled, the alarm bells ring loud.

The daily chart of Campari has already appeared as an example of a triangle as a continuation pattern. It is shown here in Figure 6.20 because, as the breakdown occurred at the beginning of the month, the monthly range chart shows a gap, a rare phenomenon. It shows a large double top formed over seven years. Some would argue patterns which build over such a long period of time cannot carry the same predictive ability since the immediate psychological build-up is not there but this top's downside prediction was certainly achieved.

Sometimes more than one runaway gap comes through but individual

Breakaway gap, running gap and potential exhaustion gaps

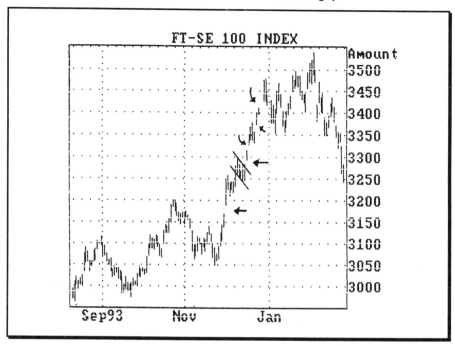

Figure 6.19

Chart by Reuters Technical Analysis

Several gaps are shown here. The first is a breakaway gap. This is a strong signal and the gap left behind should not be 'filled' as the gap denotes the enthusiasm of the market and, while this level of emotion is sustained it will not be. The next gap, following the flag, is almost equally as positive. It is called a runaway or measuring gap. Its occurrence suggests strongly that the implied upside measurement from the flag – in itself a halfway hesitation – will be fulfilled. But, in any energetic market move, once both a breakaway gap and a runaway gap have come through, other subsequent gaps could well be signalling overheating. The next three gaps are potential exhaustion gaps; once they start coming in they highlight frothy conditions and, once filled by subsequent price reactions, the market's move has likely neared its end. In this case, once the end-year gap was filled, the best of the move had been seen.

trends rarely see more than two. Any further gaps, particularly in a fast trend, are likely to be exhaustion gaps and, once they are filled, the danger of the trend reversing is considerable. Such reversal may not happen immediately but it will likely come through in due course.

The chart of Alfred McAlpine in Figure 6.21 shows a runaway gap in April 1993 and then, after a six-month consolidation, a breakaway gap came through in December. By February 1994 both the upside prediction from the original base area (a multiple bottom) and the rectangle formed in 1993 had

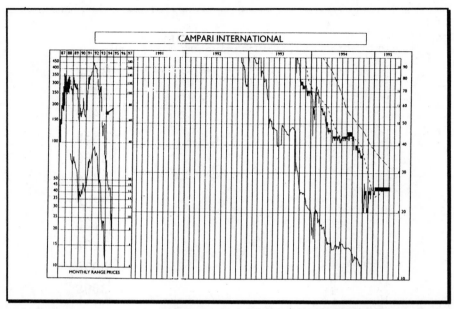

Figure 6.20

Chart by Investment Research of Cambridge Ltd: Design by NNIF

The daily chart has already been seen in Figure 6.7. Unusually, a gap also shows on the monthly range chart. Since such gaps have to appear over the turn of the month, and are probably a coincidence, they are rare and do not carry any particular import.

been fulfilled and the next gap seen as prices broke up from the flag was most likely to be an exhaustion gap. Indeed, it was; the upside prediction from the flag had to be abandoned when this gap was filled.

Whilst in a fast moving market exhaustion gaps may well be preceded by runaway gaps, there is no hard and fast rule that states they have to be. As with all technical analysis, personal judgement has to come into play when categorising the signal the gap is giving. The chart of Pentos in Figure 6.22 shows a steady decline which suddenly accelerated at the end of 1993 as the temporary support at 40p was breached. Then a large gap formed at what was very obviously a late stage in the trend. This has subsequently been filled, giving a strong suggestion the worst of the fall is over, for now at least.

One of the most powerful warning signals that can come through is a combination of the exhaustion gap and a one day reversal. It is called an island reversal and, as the chart of the Swiss Franc future shows, it is just that (see Figure 6.23). In fact this chart shows a double island reversal. First, prices gap into new high ground and consolidate briefly before doing so again. The following day, however, prices open well below the previous day's low, back in

Runaway gap followed by breakaway and exhaustion gaps

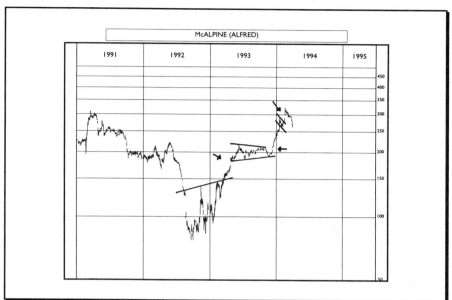

Figure 6.21   Chart by Investment Research of Cambridge Ltd: Design by NNIF

Previous descriptions might imply there was a particular order in which the various types of gaps came through. This is true if they appear within the same phase of a trend; first the breakaway, then the runaway followed by the exhaustion gaps. However, as in the two-year chart of McAlpine, where the trend developed in two distinct stages, the runaway gap appears first. The breakaway gap comes through after the share has had a respite and formed a six-month consolidation. The next gap signalled exhaustion.

the range of the short bout of consolidation seen two days earlier. The next day prices gap down again, leaving two small islands of trading at the top of the market. This is not an infrequent occurrence in a fast trend in the futures markets, but it is seen less often in shares.

However, in equity markets it is not abnormal to find island reversals forming over several trading periods. In the case of Norcros, shown in Figure 6.24, prices moved sharply into new high ground, consolidated (and formed a tiny head and shoulders reversal) and then gapped down, leaving the trading block stranded as a peninsula, rather than an island. The gap was in fact filled by a subsequent rally which failed to clear the highs. Later a more substantial head and shoulders formed and prices fell to fulfill its downside prediction.

All the basic patterns which form on bar charts and the method of predicting the likely extent of the subsequent move have now been discussed. With the exception of the gaps and one period reversals, these rules apply to line charts too. The point and figure count has also been addressed. There is one

Exhaustion gap

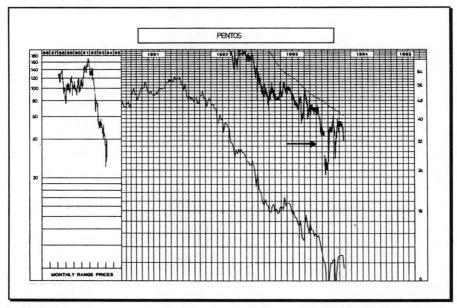

Figure 6.22   *Source:* Investment Research of Cambridge Ltd

As with all patterns, gaps should be viewed in context. Whilst during the early fall in Pentos no gaps appeared, the one that did so in late 1993 occurred against a re-accelerating downtrend. The pace of the fall could not be sustained; the probability was this, although it was the first gap, was all the same signalling exhaustion.

form of pattern analysis which is still to be discussed and that is the Japanese candlestick approach. Although there are some similarities between the interpretation of candlesticks and bar charts, there are some considerable differences too; for this reason the next chapter serves as an introduction to this Eastern methodology.

Island reversals

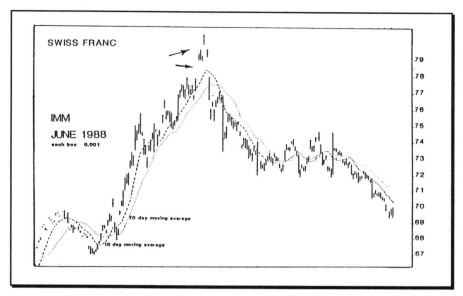

Figure 6.23 *Source:* Investment Research of Cambridge Ltd

Exhaustion gaps herald the end of a fast move. If, as prices rise during the late stages of the uptrend, such a gap comes through and the price, instead of reacting and filling it, then gaps down, leaving the price range 'stranded', this is an island reversal and is a very important signal the highs have been seen. This example shows two such islands, making the warning even more significant. The opposite occurs in a late accelerating downtrend.

Island reversals forming over several trading periods

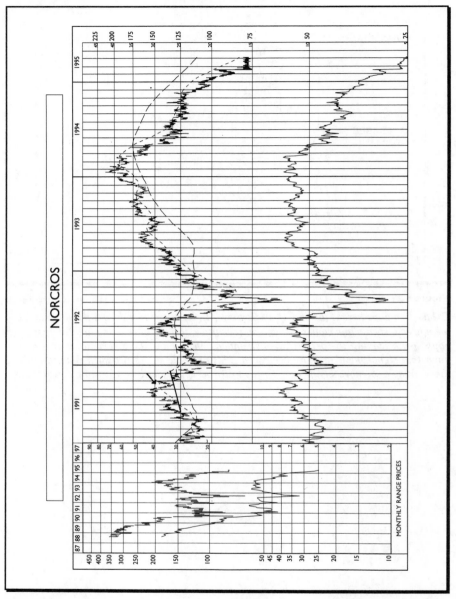

Figure 6.24   Chart by Investment Research of Cambridge Ltd: Design by NNIF

In daily share prices islands are relatively unusual. However, the mid-1991 gap down in Norcros left a pattern similar to an island. As with many of these short-term formations, this subsequently proved to be a significant part of a major reversal pattern – the top of the head in a head and shoulders reversal.

7

JAPANESE CANDLESTICK CHARTS

- The Western 'gap' becomes the more important 'window' in Japanese Candles. A window is not 'filled' it is 'closed'
- Potential short term reversal patterns abound – including: Engulfing Pattern; Dark Cloud Cover; Hammer and Hanging Man; Stars and Dojis; Morning Star; Evening Star; Harami
- There are continuation patterns too: Rising/Falling Three Methods; Three Soldiers; Tasuki Gap.

Throughout the book so far it has been emphasised that the techniques used to interpret charts are basically the same, whatever timescale or form of plot is used. Broadly speaking this is true. However, having already looked at various short-term formations and reversal days in bar chart terms, we now need to look at the somewhat different approach taken by Japanese candlestick chartists.

When it comes to major reversal formations the differences are not large. The Japanese names for these patterns are generally more emotive than their Western equivalents, emphasising the recognition that technical analysis is based largely on market psychology. Where they are not emotive they are nicely poetic. The Head and Shoulders is the Three Buddha Top and the Reversed Head and Shoulders is the Inverted Three Buddha Bottom. The Triple Top is the Three Mountain Top and the Triple Bottom is the Three River Bottom. The Saucer Tops and Bottoms are Dumpling Tops and Fry Pan Bottoms. The list goes on but the analysis is very similar. There are, however, two main points of difference: the respect paid by candle chartists to 'windows' (gaps in Western terminology); and the stress laid on the significance of very short-term formations.

As we have seen, Western bar charting techniques recognise gaps as important but consider them as an added bonus. The basic rules of candlestick interpretation tend to regard them as a prerequisite. A gap, or window, is the empty space left on the chart when a price moves up or down, failing to trade within the previous period's range, emphasising the sudden eagerness of the buyers or the sellers to get on board. Once a gap or window has formed it should, in the same manner as broken highs or lows, provide support or resistance to subsequent reactions. They should not be 'closed' or 'filled' as those in the West would say.

Whilst this is a fairly big difference between the two regimes, I do not believe it is the major one. This is the fact that candlestick charting is famed for short-term formations – signals whose bar chart equivalents are considered as warnings rather than de facto reversals. This implies all important candlestick formations are reversals rather than continuation patterns. This is not true; some classic continuation signals exist but the most famous suggest trend reversal.

This chapter will build on the warning signals already mentioned at the end of Chapter 6 and the reader should gain some insights into the importance placed by candlestick users on the sensitivity of signs that can come through when a trend has gone too far. This is not to suggest that the coverage of candle formations is comprehensive as it is not – whole books have been devoted to this subject. However, the following examples should serve to give a flavour of the sort of signals that come through which suggest the trend will reverse for now or, sometimes, continue. It is a fine-tuned approach which can warn seriously of dangers to come.

One of the most reliable and hence, popular patterns is the engulfing pattern. It can be bullish or bearish and offers strong, clear signs that the low or high has been seen – for now at least. The price must be in a definable up or down trend and, providing that is the case, these trading patterns form over just two trading periods. In a downtrend a bullish engulfing pattern appears when a small black candlestick's real body is followed by a candle with a white real body which engulfs the black one. If prices are in an uptrend a bearish engulfing pattern will come through if a relatively small white real body is exceeded in range by a black real body during the following period.

Figure 7.1 shows a good signal from a bullish engulfing pattern that ended an eight week downtrend (although the purist would argue the black candlestick was a little on the large side) and another that signalled the reversal of the secondary correction. The bearish engulfing pattern that followed was not a textbook example as the white real body was rather larger than it 'should' have been, but it signalled a temporary high anyway.

The dark cloud cover and piercing pattern are similar to the bullish and bearish engulfing patterns but they offer slightly weaker signals. A dark cloud cover comprises two candlesticks in an uptrend; the first is a large white candle and it is followed by a black candle which opens above the previous candle's high but closes within the white candle's real body. The lower the close within the white real body, the stronger the signal: a good sign the highs have been seen is a close half-way down the white real body.

Figure 7.2 shows the dark cloud cover which signalled the February 1994 highs. Additionally, in early January, it shows a piercing pattern – the opposite of the dark cloud cover. This formation highlights the likelihood that, in a

Engulfing patterns

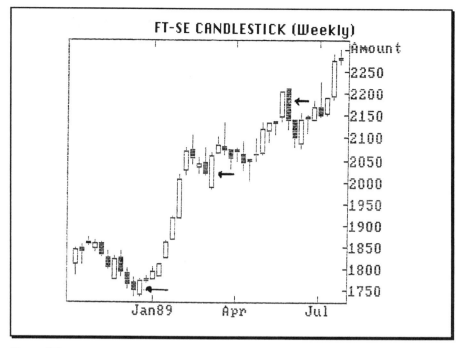

Figure 7.1   *Chart* by Reuters Technical Analysis

The arrows highlight engulfing patterns. The first is a bullish engulfing pattern. A large white candlestick in a downtrend opens in new low ground but closes above the open of the previous black candle. Thus the white candlestick's real body completely engulfs the previous smaller black candlestick's real body, signalling a likely reversal. The same pattern came through and ended the secondary correction ten weeks later. Also the highs were temporarily signalled when, in June, a pattern similar to a bearish engulfing pattern occurred. It is not a perfect example as the black candlestick was only marginally larger than the preceding white one. In these circumstances confirmation of the implied direction from the next candle that a bear signal has come through is essential. This happened and it was effective for the short term, at least.

downtrend, the lows have been seen; the first candlestick is black and the second, which opens in new low ground for the move, is white. The close should be well within the black real body, preferably half-way through it.

A popular reversal pattern is the hammer. It occurs over one trading period in a downtrend. It has a long lower shadow, little or no upper shadow and a small real body (it can be black or white) near the top of the period's trading range. It is probably signalling the end of that trend, as happened after its formation in Figure 7.3 on the FTSE towards the end of 1992, although a

Dark cloud cover and piercing pattern

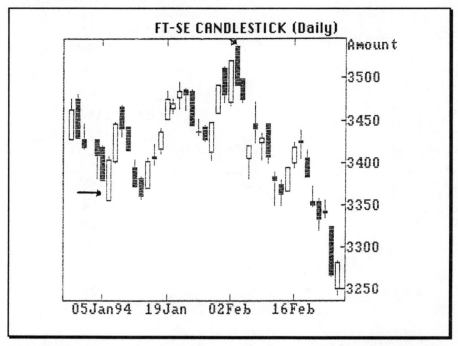

Figure 7.2   *Chart* by Reuters Technical Analysis

The dark cloud cover and piercing pattern give similar, but weaker, signals to the bearish and bullish engulfing patterns. The first arrow highlights a piercing pattern where, in a downtrend, the first candle is black and the second, opening in new low ground, is white. With the close coming through over half-way up the preceding candle's black real body, the pattern is a good indication the lows have likely been seen. The candle for the next period should, for confirmation, move in the direction of the implied reversal – as it did here. The second arrow accompanies this pattern's counterpart i.e. the dark cloud cover. Here, in an uptrend, a black candlestick opens in new high ground, but closes at least half-way down the real body of the white candlestick. Both signals worked well.

hammer can be seen during early July – one that did not work. Ideally the lower shadow should be at least twice the length of the real body, as it was in this case, and the signal should be confirmed by prices moving in the implied direction during the following session.

Stars have small real bodies which gap away from a previous long real body and they are often part of other patterns. A shooting star warns of an impending top and it was certainly successful in that role in late 1993 on the stock market as Figure 7.4 shows.

It occurs in an uptrend; prices open near their lows and then rally strongly. However, the rally is not maintained and prices close relatively weak, leaving a

A hammer

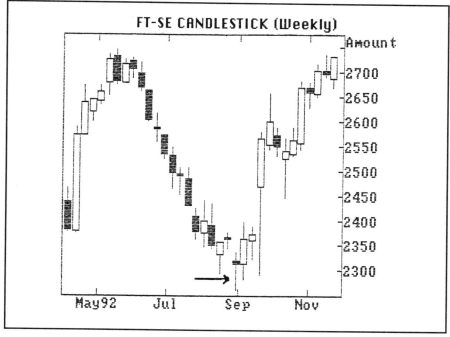

Figure 7.3

Chart by Reuters Technical Analysis

Hammers are indicative a downtrend 'has gone too far'. A hammer has a long lower shadow, preferably twice the length of the small (black or white) real body, and the real body should be very near the top of the range. For confirmation, the price should move up during the next session.

long upper shadow and a small real body near the low. Little or no lower shadow should be present. In this example a small black body can be seen but its colour is not important. Prices need to move lower during the next trading period but in this case they did not. However, it was a good warning. Five weeks later a similar pattern (lacking the preceding window) was seen. The poor performance the following week went a long way towards confirming a significant high had been seen. This formation can come in at the end of a downtrend, in which case it is called an inverted hammer and a strong close during the following period is needed to confirm the likelihood the downtrend is liable to reversal.

The morning star is an important bullish reversal pattern which comes in at the end of a decline; it is formed by three candles. The first has a relatively long black body, denoting the domination of selling pressure. The second candle has a small real body, showing the diminution of bearish influences; ideally it will

Shooting stars

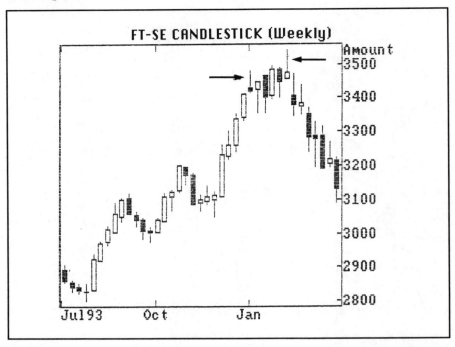

Figure 7.4   *Chart* by Reuters Technical Analysis

The shooting star is the counterpart to the hammer. It warns of an end to the uptrend; it is probably signalling the high. The pattern has a long upper shadow, a small real body and little or no lower shadow. Prices need to move lower during the next trading period to confirm its significance. The arrows appears by two shooting stars: the first did not 'work' but the second, although not preceded by a window, did.

be preceded by a window. The following candle will be white and, again, the signal will be strengthened if the price gaps up and closes well into the first candle's real body. The example in Figure 7.5 is a strong one; not only are the three basic requirements for a morning star all present, the long lower shadow on the second candle makes it a hammer – a double signal the downtrend was ending had come in – and the third candle closed over the high of the first.

The evening star is the bearish counterpart to the morning star and it occurs when prices are in an uptrend. A long white real body is followed by a star – a small real body – which gaps away from the previous candle. This in turn is followed by a black real body that goes into the white real body of the first candlestick in this formation. The example in Figure 7.6 would demonstrate a clearer signal if the dark real body had gapped down from the star and penetrated the white real body to a greater degree but it was a good signal, all the same.

Morning star

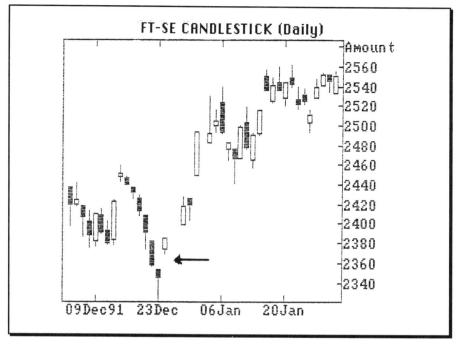

Figure 7.5

Chart by Reuters Technical Analysis

*A more reliable pattern is the morning star as it forms over three periods and, as a conse-
quence, should not 'need' confirmation. This example is a good one – classic textbook
material. The first candle, within a decline, has a relatively long black body. The second
gaps down, leaving a window; it has a small real body. The third candle is white. It should
gap up and penetrate the black candle's real body, as it did here, to give a strong signal.
There is a strong probability the low has likely been seen.*

A doji can be an important candle formation in its own right; if the market
is a liquid one the formation is rare and usually carries considerable import. It
also adds to the importance of others when it forms as part of them. It looks
like a normal high/low/close bar chart because the open and the close are at
the same, or virtually the same, level (see Figure 7.7).

If a doji comes through in an uptrend after a large white candle is followed
by a window it is a danger signal that carries particular portent. If, following
the doji, a black candle forms that penetrates the white candle's real body,
then an evening doji star has formed and it carries a high probability the highs
have been seen. The opposite formation is the morning doji star; here the doji
represents the low in a downtrend. An even stronger signal is given when the
doji is isolated by windows; at the top the doji gaps up from the long white

Evening star

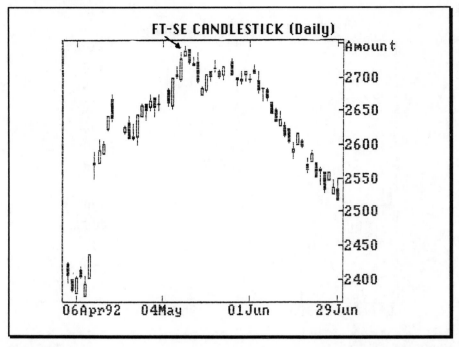

Figure 7.6

Chart by Reuters Technical Analysis

The counterpart to the morning star is the evening star which signals the end of an uptrend. Again, it is formed by the combination of three candles. A long white real body is followed by a small real body which, preferably, gaps up, leaving a window. The next candle has a black real body that penetrates the first candle's white real body. This is not a perfect example but it worked.

candle and is followed by a long black candle which gaps down. This is called an abandoned baby and it carries the same name when it is at the end of a downtrend; the doji stranded below two windows. The first window is left after a black candle and then the doji forms. Prices for the following period gap up and form a strong white candle. Both are reasonably rare.

We have already looked at the hammer, which is not entirely dissimilar to the star patterns, and now the time has come to examine the hanging man – the hammer's 'brother' pattern. It occurs at market tops and warns of retreats. There is a small real body and a long lower shadow which is at least twice the length of the real body. The two hanging men in Figure 7.8 gave good warning the rallies were over, but were not classic signals since prices did not immediately head in the opposite direction.

A doji

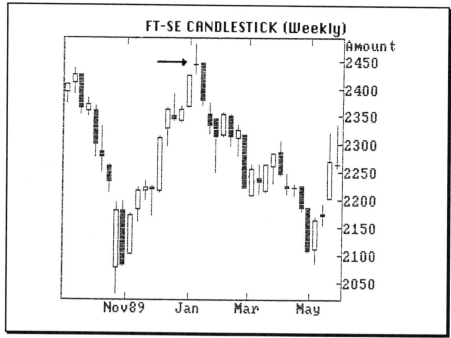

Figure 7.7

Chart by Reuters Technical Analysis

A doji represents a high/low/close chart as the open and the close are identical, or nearly so. In well-traded markets at certain junctures it carries considerable import. If the second candle in an evening star formation is a doji the signal is much stronger and is called an evening doji star.

The Harami (as shown in Figure 7.9) is what Western analysts would call an 'inside day'; you will note this is not a pattern that was mentioned in the previous chapter. This is because, in my experience, it rarely has significance. However, it is viewed with slightly greater reverence by candle chartists when it turns up in the form of the Harami. The Harami is a warning the trend might be liable to change – it is hesitating, rethinking the fundamentals. The range of the day is well within that of its predecessor. There is a slightly stronger signal if a Harami cross forms. This means the small candle comes through in the form of a doji. As far as both patterns are concerned, in an uptrend the first candle will have a white real body and in a downtrend it will be black. The colour of the subsequent small real body can be either black or white.

The candlestick formations dealt with so far have all warned, to a greater or lesser extent, of the imminence of a trend reversal and this is what candle

The hanging man

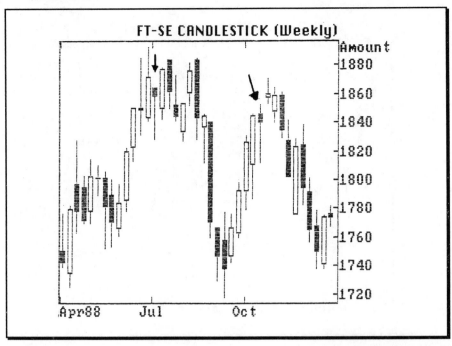

Figure 7.8

Chart by Reuters Technical Analysis

The hanging man has the same configuration as a hammer, but it occurs in an uptrend. It very definitely needs confirmation from prices moving in the direction implied by its formation during the next session. In neither of the examples shown here did this occur but the signals were reasonably timely all the same.

patterns are primarily renowned for. However, there are some continuation patterns and the three methods is one of them. It is a short-term continuation pattern within an uptrend or a downtrend. In an uptrend it is called the rising three methods: a tall white candlestick is succeeded by three small (usually black) real bodies that are within the white candlestick's range. The fifth candlestick must be white and close at a new high. The formation in Figure 7.10 is a particularly bullish one, since only one of the three small candles is black and the fifth gapped up before closing at the new high. The falling three methods formation is just the opposite: the first candlestick is black, the three small candles usually have small white real bodies within the range of the long black one, and the fifth candlestick has a long black real body and closes at a new low.

Another continuation pattern is the three white soldiers formation. These come through after a period of consolidation and start from near the lows.

The Harami

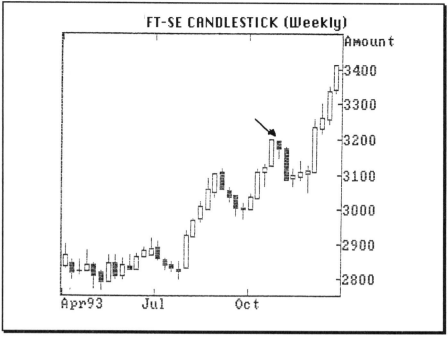

Figure 7.9   *Chart* by Reuters Technical Analysis

The Harami involves a candlestick which, in an uptrend, has a small real body that follows one with a large white real body. The signal is not a particularly strong one but it is strengthened if the second, small, candlestick is a doji.

Figure 7.11 shows the three white candles advancing firmly from a test of the support around 2800. Each has a higher close, as should be the case, and they imply further strength is likely. In that this is a weekly chart, it could be argued that the move at the end of the year was also accompanied by three white soldiers although the consolidation preceding them only lasted a shortish while.

A rather rare continuation pattern within a moving trend is chosen to end this section on candlestick signals – it is called a Tasuki gap. There are downside and upside Tasuki gaps and they occur when a fast moving trend is well underway. The upside Tasuki gap is formed when a white real body gaps higher. This is followed by a black real body of similar size which opens within the white real body and closes below the white candle's real body. The example in Figure 7.12 is imperfect in that the black real body is considerably smaller than the preceding white one but the message was clear and it 'worked'. With a downside Tasuki gap the opposite occurs.

Rising three methods

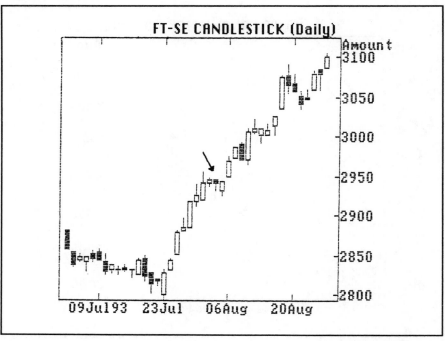

FT-SE CANDLESTICK (Daily)

Figure 7.10

Chart by Reuters Technical Analysis

The rising three methods is a continuation pattern within an uptrend. A tall white candle is followed by three small real bodies which are within the white candle's range. The fifth candle is white and closes at a new high. The falling three methods is the opposite.

Some might argue that a disproportionate amount of space has been allotted to candlestick patterns since no pretence has been made to cover the subject fully. However, I would argue that although candlestick charts are relatively new to Western investors, their popularity is continuing to increase and there is a very significant interest in them. One of the reasons for this, I suspect, is their very clear visual impact. An advancing line of white candles very obviously identifies the fact that buyers are in control. Equally, regardless of how oversold a market may appear, a downtrend containing almost all black candlesticks will impress even the novice that selling pressure is dominating still and there is a real danger prices could be pushed lower yet.

This section serves as an initial guide to the few continuation patterns that may appear within such trends and to some of the signals that alert technicians these trends could be liable to change direction. All can be used in conjunction with other signals, such as moving averages and overbought/oversold indicators (which we come to later), and can add a further dimension to the overall analysis.

Three white soldiers

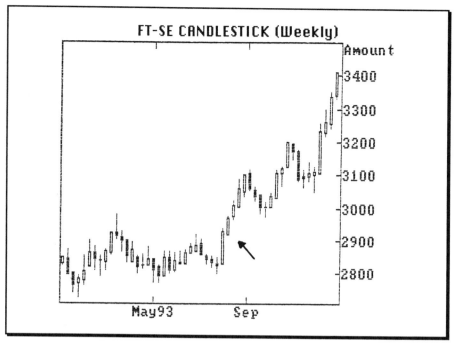

FT-SE CANDLESTICK (Weekly)

Amount

3400

3300

3200

3100

3000

2900

2800

May93   Sep

Figure 7.11

Chart by Reuters Technical Analysis

The three white soldiers is another continuation pattern which comes through following a consolidation. The advance of the three white candles starts from near the lows and implies further gains are likely.

Upside Tasuki gap

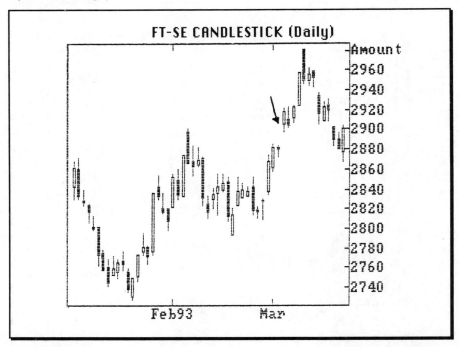

Figure 7.12
Chart by Reuters Technical Analysis

The Tasuki gap is a relatively rare continuation pattern. There is the upside Tasuki gap, as shown here, and its downside equivalent which forms in a downtrend. The upside Tasuki gap forms when a white real body leaves a window in an uptrend. This is followed by a black real body (of similar size) which opens within the white real body, but closes below it. This, as can be seen, is not a perfect example, but it worked.

8

THE ANALYSIS OF THE STOCK MARKET AS A WHOLE

- Advance/Decline Line – a measurement of the 'breadth' of a move
- Other indices – their varying constructions can give very different results
- New highs and lows – an indication of how overextended a market move may be
- Yield Gap Ratio – how expensive are equities versus government bonds?
- The interrelationships between the trends in Government stocks and equities
- Other influences include: the cyclic influences on stock markets and economies; the effect of currency factors; the sometimes contra-cyclical behaviour of commodities such as gold and industrial metals
- The analysis of share price behaviour, bearing in mind the above factors and how the share is behaving against the market as a whole – 'relative strength'.

Whilst most of this book is concerned with the analysis of an individual price series, this chapter addresses how to attempt to ascertain not only what 'the market' itself is likely to do, but also see what is happening among the issues that make up the market-place as a whole. Indices can be examined on their own but interrelationships need to be examined too.

There are two main indices used to establish what the UK Equity Market is doing. The first and, by now, the best-known is the Financial Times-Stock Exchange 100 Index. This contains the 100 largest shares quoted in London on the International Stock Exchange and is calculated throughout the day: the Stock Market futures are traded against it. It started in 1983 when it took the place of the Financial Times Ordinary Index as an intraday monitor of what the market was doing.

The FT Ordinary was calculated on an hourly basis and is still published. It has its uses in that its history (including the old Financial News Index) extends back to the 1930s but, for normal purposes, it is considered flawed. In the first place it contains only 30 stocks and, secondly, it is calculated as an unweighted geometric mean, a method which gives it a downward bias over time. This problem was compounded in the 1970s when those responsible for its constituents failed to replace some earlier industrial giants – such as Rolls Royce and British Leyland – which were suffering such serious problems they were no longer representative of British industry as a whole, and their dire price falls caused the downward bias of the Index to be even further exacerbated. Thus the FTSE 100 has taken over the role of market monitor for the near term and it is the one that is quoted on the radio and in the press.

The other popular index is called the FT-SE Actuaries All Share and dates back to 1962 when the whole group of FT Actuaries Indices were started. It contains all the major issues quoted (over 900) and is used primarily as a comparison for portfolio performance. It is calculated at the close of business only. Both it and the FT-SE 100 are weighted arithmetic means; the calculation involves the measurement of the percentage change of the price of each of its constituents, adjusted to reflect its market capitalisation. Thus, in that the top 100 companies are very much larger than the vast majority of the rest, both indices put up a very similar performance.

On a simple level these two indices can be used as normal price series and their plots interpreted on a straightforward technical basis as Dow originally advocated. Indeed, throughout the earlier part of this book charts of these two indices have been used frequently to illustrate the various points made. However, as 'the market' consists of more than one share, this means what is happening within the market can be examined too. One of the ways of doing this is to use the Advance-Decline Line as a measure of confirmation that the indices are showing a true picture of what is happening to shares in general.

The A-D Line is a simple device, designed to measure what all the shares in the market are doing, ignoring any undue influence from the blue chips with high market capitalisation. A large starting number is taken, 100,000 for example, and each day the number of shares that rise is added to it and the number that fall is taken off. The resultant line should take on the shape of the indices themselves. If it does not do so it suggests the indices are not representative of the market as a whole and warning signals could come through. This goes back to the basic Dow Theory tenet of the need for confirmation of a particular move by the Dow Industrial Average.

The comparison between the performance of the All Share Index and the Advance-Decline Line in Figure 8.1 shows some useful signals. In the summer of 1989 the Advance-Decline Line made a triple top and began falling in what turned out to be a serious downtrend. This warned that shares in general were not enjoying the stability that the All Share Index's broadly sideways trend implied. Indeed, it was good warning since the All Share itself eventually followed the Advance-Decline Line down when the short bear market of 1990 was born. The Advance-Decline Line gave further good warning when, in May 1992, the All Share Index hit new highs; it failed to breach its earlier peaks and, in due course, the rise in the All Share Index was reversed. Since then the two lines have formed similar shapes.

This sort of performance from the A-D Line made it a very useful indicator in the past. Figure 8.2 shows the A-D Line's downtrend from 1964 was not

Comparison between the performance of the All Share Index and the Advance/Decline Line

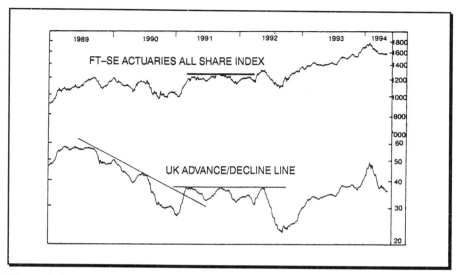

Figure 8.1

Source: Investment Research of Cambridge Ltd

The Advance/Decline Line is a running total of rises and falls and gives a simplistic picture of what the market as a whole is doing. When its shape differs from that of the major indices alarm bells ring. It forewarned weakness when it topped out in 1989 and failed to confirm new highs in 1992. Thereafter it confirmed the All Share's movements.

broken when the All Share Index made an apparently important upside break in the summer of 1966. This move was suddenly reversed and a sharp, but shallow, bear market set in. Both the All Share Index and the A-D Line recovered simultaneously but the A-D Line broke down at the end of 1968 – giving five months' warning of the All Share's eventual reversal.

However, although the Advance-Decline Line has given some useful signals in the past, it fell heavily into disrepute during the long bull market of the 1980s. As Figure 8.3 shows, it was very reluctant to confirm the energy of the market's rise and then compounded the error by moving strongly higher during 1987, just before the market crash.

Views differ as to why this previously reliable indicator should suddenly become so misleading. It is most likely that its simplistic calculation had not allowed for the considerable change which the London market underwent during that period; the All Share Index currently has over 900 constituents, whereas they numbered less than 600 when the comparison in Figure 8.2 was done. There is a suggestion that an indicator based on the ratio of the net rises or declines to the number of issues tracked as a whole would put up a more

A/D Line as useful indicator in the past, 1964–1969

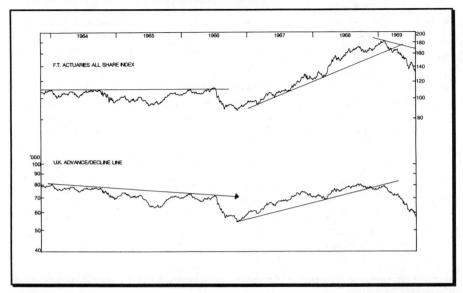

Figure 8.2   *Source:* Investment Research of Cambridge Ltd

The Advance/Decline Line enjoyed a good history of reliability prior to the long bull market of the 1980s. The illustrated period (1964-1969) shows some excellent signals. The false upside break in 1966 by the All Share Index went unconfirmed by the down-trending A/D Line, and the latter broke its uptrend in early November 1968 – several weeks before that in the All Share Index went too.

robust performance. Certainly, in that such a calculation would allow for the constant change in the number of issues quoted this is logical. Unfortunately, the rises and falls are not figures which are stored in this manner on readily accessible databases and at the moment it is not possible to judge how such a line would have performed.

The US Advance/Decline Line, however, retained its reputation for reliability during the 1980s and thus, when it failed to confirm the S&P Industrials' move into new high ground in 1990, the warning was heeded (see Figure 8.4). The S&P is calculated in much the same manner as the FT-SE Actuaries All Share Index and hence was highlighting the strength of the major issues. However, the A/D Line remained firmly in a downtrend and, in due course, the S&P's rise reversed. Subsequently, both recovered simultaneously and a new leg to the long-term bull market started.

We have used the Dow Jones Industrial Average on several occasions to illustrate a point, although professional investors might argue that its actions are irrelevant. This is because it still only comprises 30 shares (like our old FT

A/D Line failing as indicator during the 1980s

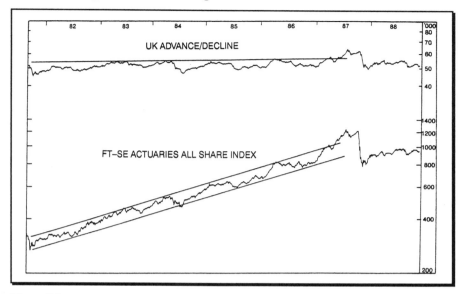

Figure 8.3

Source: Investment Research of Cambridge Ltd

The Advance/Decline Line let analysts down badly during the 1980s. It consistently failed to confirm the aggressive uptrend in the indices and then, to compound the error, burst into new high ground as the late, and unsustainable, re-acceleration to the uptrend came through in 1987.

Ordinary – although the Dow is an unweighted arithmetic, rather than geometric, mean) and cannot usefully be used for portfolio performance comparisons. However, despite its deficiencies, the rises and falls of the Dow are those that are quoted still as a measure of what Wall Street is doing and, as a consequence, its numbers have the greatest psychological impact on the investment community as a whole. Thus it should be monitored still.

The Advance/Decline Line is not the only indicator that warned rises into new high ground by the US market were not to be trusted. Figure 8.5 shows the Dow Jones Industrial Average two years later enjoying a similar fate to that of the more sophisticated S&P and achieving new highs which were later to prove unsustainable. But the S&P futures contract did not confirm the move.

Futures prices have a reputation for being more volatile than the underlying cash price series. This is undeserved and indeed, untrue. Futures prices move in line with cash prices and the volatility actually refers to the fact that they are traded on margin; in other words, people only have to put up a certain percentage of the value of the bargain. Thus, for each percentage point the price moves, the trader's gain or loss is very much greater. From time to

US Advance/Decline Line

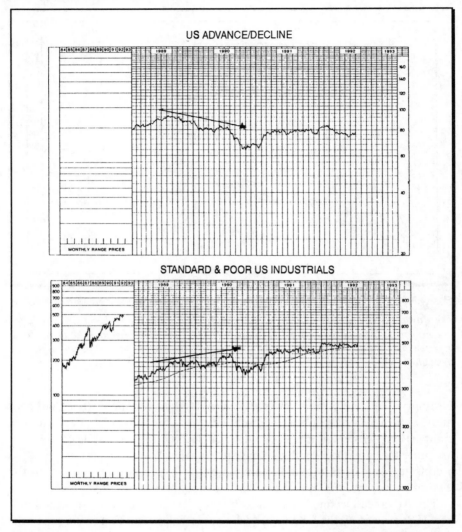

Figure 8.4

Source: Investment Research of Cambridge Ltd

The US Advance/Decline Line has, however, retained its reputation for consistency. Here it gave a clear warning that the move into new high ground by the S&P Industrials in 1990 was unlikely to be sustained.

time the price movements of the futures may differ as sharp moves get underway. However, in that this offers a potentially profitable arbitrage opportunity to market traders (buying the cash if it is underpriced and selling the futures, and vice versa), such pricing differences will be closed quickly.

New highs on Dow unconfirmed by other market indices

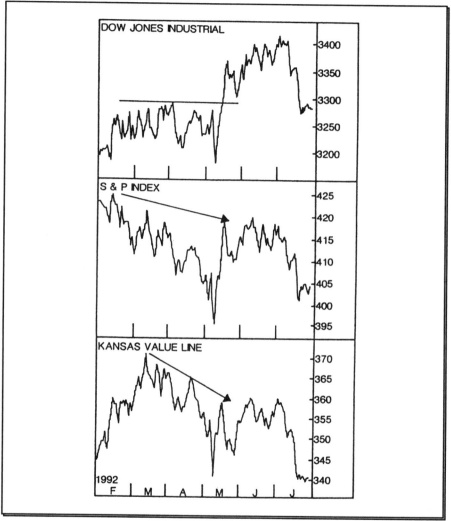

Figure 8.5

Chart by Reuters Technical Analysis

If one important market index moves into new high ground others should confirm this move. In 1992 the Dow Jones Industrial Average cleared its highs but the S&P and Value Line Futures failed to do so. Constructed differently, they were signalling that the Dow's move was unlikely to be sustained.

This means that the futures contracts – after taking into account the valuation of future dividends, etc. – can be used as confirmatory indicators of what the cash price has done.

Not only did the S&P future not confirm the new highs, but the Kansas Value Line future did not do so either. The KVL is an unweighted index, rather like an Advance/Decline Line, and I find it often lends a strong clue as to whether or not a move implied by the major American indices is going to carry through. On this occasion it remained firmly in its downtrend and it was no surprise to anyone watching it when the aberrant move by the Dow Industrials into new high ground was reversed.

This brings us to the point where, perhaps, we should have come in. It was Dow's observation that when his Industrials Average moved into new high ground this action was likely signalling further dramatic gains. We have already seen the extent of the rises which came through in the 1920s and 1980s after the earlier highs around 100 and 1000 were cleared. Wishing to ensure that the signal was a true one, he came up with the Railroads Average and built in the rule that its action should confirm that of the Industrials before the import of the new highs was acted upon.

At the end of the last century Railroad stocks were the largest sector in the American market but, in the intervening 100 years, with methods of transportation changing radically, their importance has diminished significantly. However, the original Railroads Average has long-since changed into the Transportation Average published today. This is dominated by airline stocks and, although the goods originally shipped by the railroads do not necessarily use the airlines, this Average serves the same purpose in confirming the moves made by the Dow. After all, it is acknowledged that during recessions the business of the airlines is hit hard whilst during times of affluence they do notoriously well. As a consequence, the basic Dow tenet 'The Averages Must Confirm' is alive and well today.

Indeed, as Figure 8.6 shows, Dow's principle has served us well in the recent past. In the early 1980s when the Dow Jones Industrials made new highs, the Transportation Average confirmed this action within a matter of days. Subsequently, however, when the Industrials moved into new high ground (again, in 1990) the Transportation Average fell short of its earlier highs. I remember a conversation with a Wall Street bull during that period when he said the comparison was no longer valid. He argued, justifiably, that the 1989 highs on the Transportation Average were due to unusual circumstances; various of its constituents were takeover targets during the junk bond era. He went on to say that now this was no longer the case the stock market was healthier for it. Long term that remark is true but it is typical of a really energetic bull market that unrealistic valuations prevail at the top.

Indeed, in the search for better value, funds are often switched into smaller shares that have not yet performed. As an aside during the last stage of the rise in UK equities over the turn of the year 1993-94 the FT-SE Actuaries All

'The Averages Must Confirm'

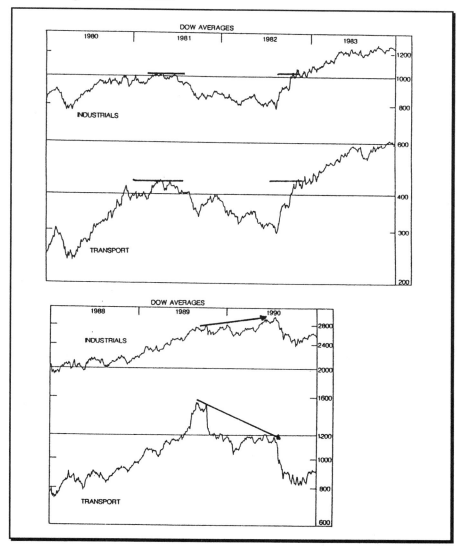

Figure 8.6
Source: Investment Research of Cambridge Ltd

A core tenet of the Dow Theory – 'The Averages Must Confirm' – still works today. The start of the major bull run in 1982-83 was confirmed by both the Industrials and Transports making new highs. However, the Industrials' move into new high ground was not confirmed by similar action in the Transports in 1990 and the move by the Industrials subsequently reversed.

Share rose 9 per cent whilst the FTSE Mid 250 Index (containing the next 250 largest stock issues, after the 100 in the FTSE 100 Index itself) rose over 22 per cent. It can be considered a good clue that the market is becoming vulnerable when the sudden, but late, rise in smaller stocks comes through. Optimists argue this is 'orientation of interest' but it usually represents a desperate hunt for anything that has not become overvalued. Once things get cheaper the upward impetus has gone. Indeed, one of the wisest sayings of the founder of my company was 'cheap is nasty'. On that basis alone he would not have been a Wall Street bull in 1990. As the chart in Figure 8.6 shows, he would have been right.

Another way of looking at an overvalued, or undervalued, market is by historic comparison of the number of new highs (or lows) scored over the past 12 months. At some stage these will come in in such numbers that they will suggest the market is very vulnerable to reversal. Unfortunately, the *Financial Times* to this day adopts the same principle as it did in the pre-easy-computing age. On the London Share Service pages it publishes the highs and lows of each share for the year; when the turn of the year comes about it expands its time horizons and looks back to the previous January – until March, when it looks back to the start of the current year. This is obviously a statistical nonsense and, bearing in mind the huge computing capabilities in the current era, it is more than a shame since it is misleading.

However, some 20 years ago, when the FT adopted the identical approach, I instigated a manual observation of the new highs and lows on the IRC chart library on a rolling 12-monthly basis and the total each week was plotted. In that the number of shares covered in our library is not constant, I cannot suggest our approach is entirely scientific either. However, it is better by far than the FT's alternative and, as can be seen in Figure 8.7, recent experience has shown that new highs or lows in excess of 100 suggest some danger and when they are in excess of 150 they sound serious alarm bells. The Investment Research Library of individual UK equities has, over time, tended to average around 500 so we are talking about long-term overextension coming through when between 20 and 25 per cent of the market is in new high or new low ground for 12 months.

'Value' is a somewhat difficult concept in that it is always changing. This is because it does not exist in its own right – it is relative to alternative investment media. The primary comparison is made with the virtually risk-free return on money on deposit which, in itself, is ever changing. It used to be the case that government securities, which offered a known yield and were almost entirely risk-free, would yield less than ordinary shares where the greater dividend yield compensated for the equity risk. However, the Reverse Yield Gap came about at the end of the 1950s and has now become the norm; shares traditionally yield less than government paper. This, it could be argued, lacks logic, unless a certain amount of capital growth can be guaranteed. Such guar-

IRC new high/low indicator

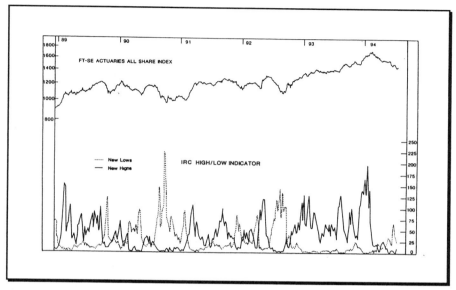

Figure 8.7

Source: Investment Research of Cambridge Ltd

The IRC new high/low indicator each week charts the number of shares in the library in new high or new low ground for a 12-month period. Levels over 100 suggest the market is overextended; over 150 it is particularly prone to reversal.

antees obviously do not exist. However, there is a built-in assumption that the economies of the developed world will continue to grow and successful companies will enjoy consistent dividend payments and capital appreciation. This can be called the 'confidence factor' and the chart of the ratio of the yield on Consols to the yield on the All Share Index in Figure 8.8 shows that, in recent years, a ratio of around 2.4 is relatively high and the stock market is vulnerable to reversal, whilst 1.8 is relatively low and shares are 'cheap'.

Consols 2½% is used as a representation of what government stocks are doing. There are two reasons for this; firstly, the Consols stock in question is effectively irredeemable and thus the price does not discount any maturity date. Secondly, the dividend is paid quarterly, so the price trend is not disturbed to a significant degree when the payouts come through.

There is a more straightforward way of comparing the interrelationship between bonds and stock markets – a direct comparison of the price curves themselves. Whilst discussion of the 'confidence factor' is logical, it is, after all, a ratio and the trouble with ratio analysis is that it can sometimes become confused – a turnaround in the line in question can be due to one price falling or the other rising. A strict comparison of the two lines can be clearer, and the

Yield Gap Ratio

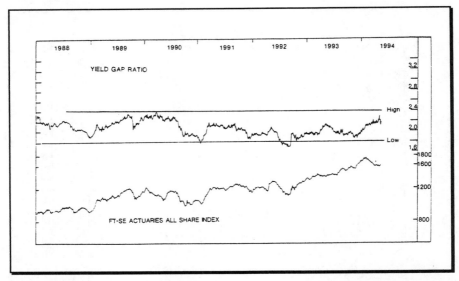

Figure 8.8   *Source:* Investment Research of Cambridge Ltd

The Yield Gap Ratio expresses how 'cheap' or 'dear' equities are in relation to the guaranteed yield on gilt-edged stocks. Recent experience suggests levels around 1.8 show equities to be relatively low and 2.4 shows them to be high, although this ratio went to 3.3 in 1987!

logic is better too. Simplistically, the stock market cycle relies on the comparison of the two factors already mentioned: the desire to achieve a reasonable return on monies invested, with a risk profile reduced as far as possible.

During phases of economic expansion demand for money causes interest rates to rise. This will have a negative effect on bond prices and they will begin to fall. Meanwhile, prices for money on deposit will become competitive and stock market investors will query whether or not the potential for capital growth is so great that they can ignore the high risk-free returns offered by the banks. If the answer is no, then profit-taking will begin. This is likely to cause the pace of the stock market's rise to falter and this, in turn, will force others to examine the risk profile of their portfolios. Should they decide the best of the capital growth has been seen for now, then further profit-taking will set in and, in due course, the stock market indices will top out.

Providing the judgements about future profitability are correct, news will come through that the best of the economic recovery is over and share prices will fall further. Eventually, confirmation of the economy's reverse will come through and shares will fall further still. Meanwhile, against the poor economic background, demand for money will begin to decrease and, in due course, interest rates will begin to fall. Shares will fall further and bonds will rise. However, there will come a stage when the low interest rates offered by the banks will no longer look attractive to investors and a hunt for undervalued shares with safe yields will begin. Once found, some buying will come through and, in due course, it will likely prove adequate to stem the decline. Additionally, the low interest rates should attract borrowing for industrial investment and the economic decline should slow. Eventually, these factors should prove capable of reversing the stock market's decline. This is the simplistic economic cycle noted by Dow when, ignoring the relationship with interest rates per se, he formulated his reasoning on why the US stock market led the economy. It may be simplistic, but there is clear evidence it has been working right through to the present day.

Figure 8.9 shows the relationship between the US stock market and Treasury Bond. It can be seen that highs in the Bond have frequently preceded those in the stock market by many months; economists would argue this is the phase when the economy's recovery has gained enough speed that predicted capital growth is enough to ignore any income comparisons. However, technical analysts have long argued that a reversal in Bonds is a good leading signal

Relationship between the US stock market and Treasury Bond

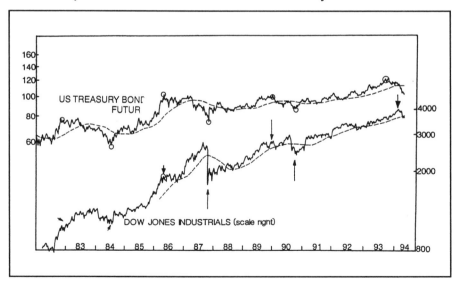

Figure 8.9   *Source:* Investment Research of Cambridge Ltd

There is a strong relationship between long-term interest rates and equity prices. US bonds normally reach their peaks some time before shares do – the lead used to be a long one. There is a growing tendency for the lows to be scored simultaneously.

that the rise in the stock market does not have much further to go. The Bond's reversal in 1982, 1986, 1989 and 1993 gave good warning the rise in the stock market was not likely to be sustained for long.

However, the experience of the period covered by Figure 8.9 shows that the lows in bonds and the stock market were virtually simultaneous. As the description of the simplistic economic cycle implies, this should not be the case. Indeed, it used not to be. But it is beginning to look very much as though investors, having recognised this relationship, have embraced the opportunity to move from low-interest-paying cash to undervalued equities as soon as bonds have been seen to turn. Indeed, although the chart shows long leads from bonds on the equity market reversal at tops, there is an increasing likelihood that this useful relationship is no longer in the domain of technical analysts alone and has, rather like the fact stock markets discount future events, become accepted wisdom across the markets as a whole. I suggest this as a scenario because as I write, European bond markets and shares, having taken fright from falls in the US Treasury Bond and a rise in short-term interest rates, are falling fast. This is despite the published views of economists that the economic recovery in Continental Europe, lagging that in the States, has much further to go and can support further falls in interest rates yet. Time will tell.

The relationship between bonds and stock markets is not confined to the United States; it has also been long-established between the UK stock market and gilts. As Figure 8.10 shows, Consols consistently gives good leads to equity tops although, here too, the lows were scored simultaneously, with the exception of 1990, where a five-month lead from Consols came through.

So far mention has been made of the Dow Jones Industrials and Transportation Averages only. In fact Dow went on to develop two other indices – the Home Bonds Average and the Utilities. The former puts up a very similar performance to the Treasury Bond but the latter can sometimes prove even more far-sighted.

Utilities stocks are extremely interest rate sensitive and any fear of an increase in interest rates, or hope of a fall, can cause considerable leaps in price (see Figure 8.11). Hence, this Average also provides good warning that the stock market might be about to reverse. The new FT-SE Actuaries series now has a Utilities sector too.

So far it is too young to have established a record; but it could prove useful for comparison purposes and, for now at least, it is far enough from the media's eye that the record of a good lead-lag relationship may not become accepted wisdom yet. This may sound an oversensitive remark but there is a very real danger that some of the more convincing (and logical) concepts of technical analysis are, after a century of use, becoming self-fulfilling. A 'disguised' relationship can be very useful to the inner circle.

One aspect of analysis common to all disciplines which has not been touched on yet is cycle analysis. It has been proven that many things move in cycles; some

Relationship between UK gilts and equities

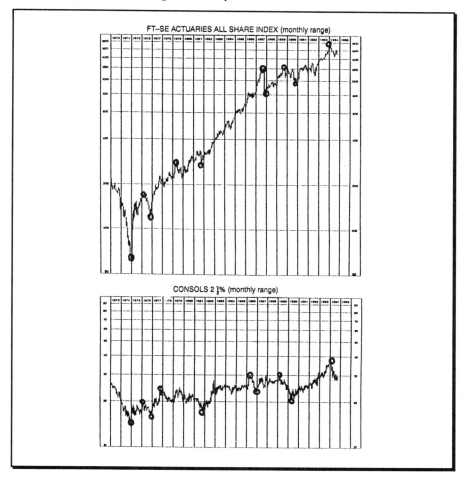

Figure 8.10
Source: Investment Research of Cambridge Ltd

The relationship between gilts and equities is much the same as that experienced in the US markets. Consols' highs tend to come in before those of the All Share Index and the lows are either simultaneous or, as in 1990, the gilt takes a slight lead.

are very obvious such as night and day, seasons and tides. In Biblical times Joseph noted that seven years of plenty led to seven years of famine. Each day newspapers publish lighting up time – and so on. These calculations are all based on cycles and they exist in all walks of life: earthquakes, disease, animal abundance and economic matters. The four-year cycle on Wall Street is laid largely at the door of the four-year Presidential term. Whether or not this is the main cause, there is very clear evidence that this cycle does exist. The chart in Figure

Dow Jones Utilities Average

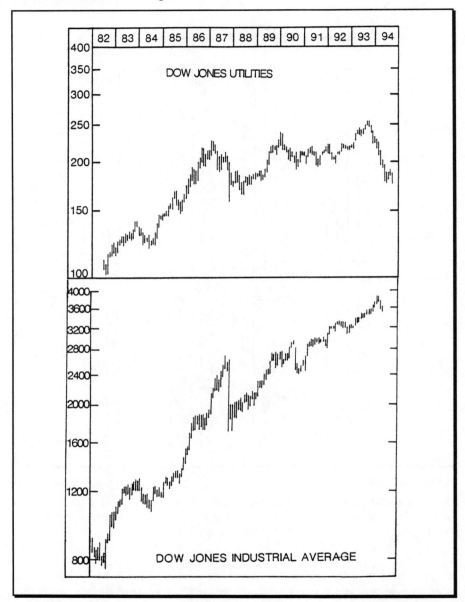

Figure 8.11

Source: Investment Research of Cambridge Ltd

The Dow Jones Utilities Average is particularly sensitive to interest rate movements. The chart shows its turning points giving good leads to the Industrials.

8.12 is a very long-term one (it covers 44 years) and cyclic lows in the Dow Jones Industrial Average come through in a convincing manner every four years.

Cycles are measured from low to low and a glance at this chart will show why. When the indices are in very long-term uptrends, as from 1950 to 1965 and 1982 to now, the bull markets within this cycle last a lot longer than the bear markets. This means the peaks of the rises are roughly three years from the lows, automatically implying the bear markets will be short and shallow. This is called 'right translation' and means that measuring from peak to peak would not give a good idea as to where the underlying cycle lay. However, from 1966 to 1982 Wall Street was caught in a wide trading band, in which far more regular (two years up, two years down) cycles came through. Extrapolating the predictability of the cyclic effect through to now, the strong suggestion is that a cyclic low was due in 1994; prices on Wall Street are already falling but the major uptrend drawn in on the chart, although slowing, had not been severed. On this basis alone, the bear market should be a short one.

Wall Street's four-year cycle

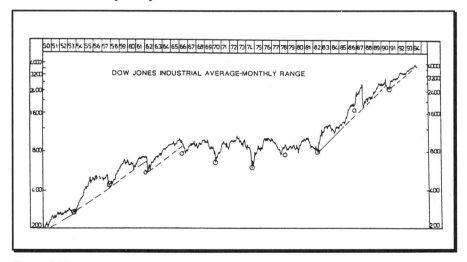

Figure 8.12

Source: Investment Research of Cambridge Ltd

Economic cycles exist and they influence market prices to a very great extent, particularly on Wall Street where it is said the four-year Presidential term has a considerable effect. The chart shows the Dow's history since 1950 and the four-year cycle over that 44 year period. Cycles are measured from low to low: this is because, when a market is trending over time, prices spend more of the cycle moving in the direction of the trend than against it. As a result 'slippage' occurs and the recent cyclic highs on Wall Street occur almost three-quarters of the way through the cycle.

Unfortunately, cyclic analysis of the UK market is not handed to us on such a plate. Whilst stock market behaviour during the early part of the period of comparison was very similar to that of Wall Street, since the lows of 1974–75 the UK stock market has been in a secular uptrend – and remains so. This tends to disguise cyclic influences and it may be some time before they become easily identifiable again. But, in that this major uptrend is slowing, there is a high likelihood that in the UK too 1994 has hit a cyclic low (see Figure 8.13).

This book is a basic introduction to technical analysis and there is no room to go into cycle analysis in great detail. However, this is no reason not to clarify a common misunderstanding – cyclic lows are based on time, not on price. This can mean confusion as to 'where the cycle lies'. It is tempting to assume a major low in price, such as that seen in Western stock markets in October 1987, was a major cyclic low but it was not. For cycle analysts it was either an aberration, or a low (due in 1986) which suffered considerable 'slippage'. The recognition of when a cyclic low is due is of great importance; but it is part of the argument not its entirety. The dates should be borne in mind but they should not be acted on alone.

It is possible to argue, as the financial press does, that, in the modern world of interconnected markets and rapid communications, individual stock mar-

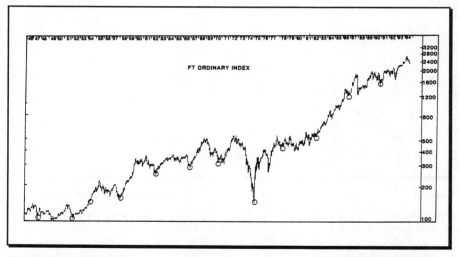

Figure 8.13

Source: Investment Research of Cambridge Ltd

Prior to the 1970s cycles in the UK stock market were similar to those on Wall Street and reasonably easy to identify. But since the 1970s a secular uptrend has been in existence and cyclic observations have been largely disguised. It is, however, possible they are returning now.

kets cannot be expected to put up separate performances – all will be influenced by the news coming from the major economies. The logic of this argument is good, and is enhanced by the experience of the 1980s when all markets rose to a greater or lesser extent but, in my view, it is not proven.

As the last two charts have shown, there are undoubtedly long periods when economic influences combine and stock markets enjoy secular uptrends. During such phases the probabilities favour all developed economies enjoying the same experience, to a greater or lesser extent. However, the intervening periods tend to be dominated by problems, or benefits, particular to individual economies and the chart in Figure 8.14 (showing the history of a random selection of markets over the past 10 years) suggests this is likely to remain the case. The charts are all on an automatically comparable semi-logarithmic scale and it can be seen that, overall, the experiences have been very different. This is included so that interested investors are persuaded to watch these lead-lag relationships and, should things on the home front not look encouraging, they can direct their investments to another area. There is no reason to suppose the worldwide bull markets of the 1980s will automatically lead to worldwide bear markets (enjoyed simultaneously) during the 1990s.

Prior to the 1980s it was, for very many years, the accepted wisdom that since commodities in general were contra-cyclical to stock markets, once domestic equities looked vulnerable, a considerable proportion of a portfolio should be switched to gold shares – always a haven when economic problems prevailed. Gold shares, rather than gold itself, were favoured since it was also assumed that, with their profit gearing, they would outperform the metal itself; indeed, it became a 'rule' that, once the shares recovered, they would lead the metal higher. These series of assumptions oversimplified the situation to a substantial degree.

The charts in Figures 8.15 and 8.16 are provided by Ian McAvity, an analyst for whom I have considerable respect, and are chosen because my own chart library offers the price of gold in US dollars but the F T Gold Mines Index is quoted in sterling – a point which makes immediate comparison impossible. But both of Ian's charts are based in dollars and expose this theory as a myth. The bottom line is that gold shares can, and do, enjoy periods of increased profitability due to factors, such as currency movements, which are not directly connected with the movements of gold itself. This does not mean that a commitment to gold shares should not be considered when industrial equities look likely to undergo a period of underperformance, but it does mean they should not be viewed as an automatic alternative.

In that technical analysis is based on the analysis of price, the question sometimes arises as to what price should be used. This is particularly the case where an international commodity such as gold is concerned. As is almost always the norm nowadays, the official quotation is in US dollars. But, the argument goes, there are several areas in the world where there is considerable

World stock markets

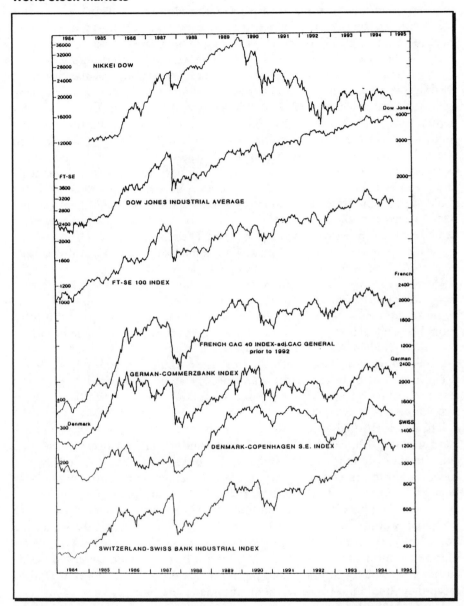

Figure 8.14

Source: Investment Research of Cambridge Ltd

Anyone reading the financial press or listening to financial broadcasts could be forgiven for believing the stock markets of the world move in unison. During the 1980s they did. But from time to time they do not. This chart highlights their very different shapes – long-term experience is likely to vary from economy to economy.

interest in gold, but only when priced in the local currency. The Japanese, for instance, buy it in considerable quantity; the Australians and South Africans mine and sell it; the Swiss buy it as an anti-inflationary investment. Obviously this applies not only to gold; the Indians have a considerable interest in silver and the Japanese in base metals in general and aluminium in particular.

For the technical analyst the answer has to be US dollars. This is is the price everyone recognises, even though some may value their commitments differently, and this should form the basis for the core analysis. However, this does not mean a watch should not be kept on the numbers in other currencies. A glance at Figure 8.17 will show why; whilst gold's base which formed at the beginning of 1986 supported a rise in excess of its minimum upside prediction in dollar terms, the downtrend in gold prices valued in Swiss francs was never breached. Indeed, it continued for some years to come. This meant that the apparent appreciation in gold was due to dollar weakness – something anyone interested in the gold market at that time would need to bear in mind.

This is an appropriate point to comment on the relationship between stock market and commodity market cycles in general. The received wisdom is that, during the early stages of economic recovery, industry uses up the above-ground stocks of commodities and, as the expansion continues, demand for those commodities increases. Thus, the pressure of this demand causes com-

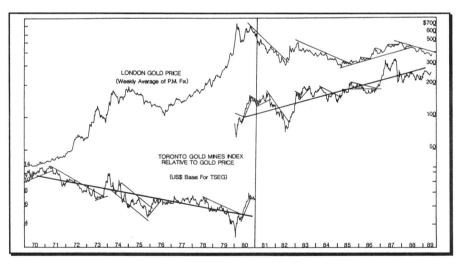

Figure 8.15   *Chart* by Ian McAvity's Deliberations

These charts are published by the kind permission of Ian McAvity, editor of 'Deliberations'. They go a long way towards scotching the myth that gold shares always outperform gold. The decline in the second line – the ratio of the shares to the gold price itself – shows how, during the major 1976-80 bull move in gold, this was not the case. However, sometimes it is. The ratio should be watched at all times.

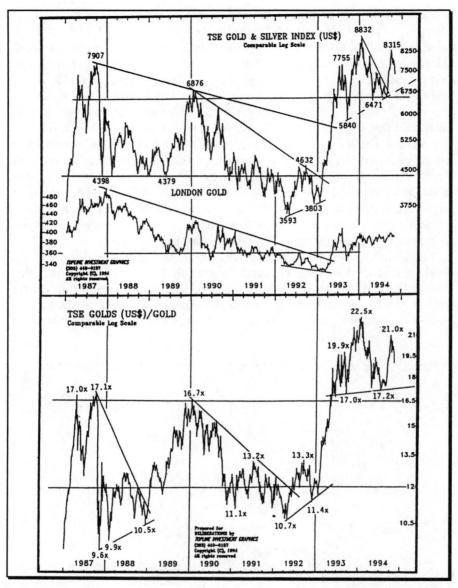

Figure 8.16

These charts are published by the kind permission of Ian McAvity, editor of 'Deliberations'. They go a long way towards scotching the myth that gold shares always outperform gold. The decline in the second line – the ratio of the shares to the gold price itself – shows how, during the major 1976-80 bull move in gold, this was not the case. However, sometimes it is. The ratio should be watched at all times.

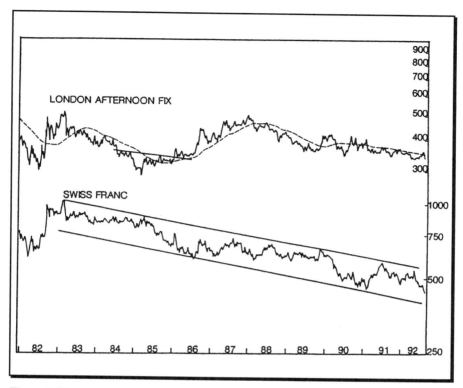

Figure 8.17

Source: Investment Research of Cambridge Ltd

Technical analysis is based on the fact that people react to certain price levels being traded. Thus, the chart upon which trading decisions are taken should be priced in the currency in which the international commodity is quoted. However, its performance in other currencies is worth watching, particularly if the commodity in question is likely to be included in a valuation in terms of the local currency. Anyone long of gold during 1985-87 should have been aware that the rise was due to dollar weakness, rather than inherent strength in gold itself.

modity prices to rise but only in the late stages of the economic cycle. Hence, rising commodity prices can be the signal that the stock market rise is due to end. Indeed, it can at times be an extremely useful sign. However, life is not as simple as that. The problem lies with the fact that the cycles in commodity prices are far longer than they are in shares, even in the base metals where there is a direct connection between industrial revival and metal demand. Whilst the equity market cycle in most developed economies is roughly-speaking four years, in commodity markets the cycles average out at between five and six years. This suggests that, give or take several months, every 12 to 20 years or so, bull markets in both stocks and commodities can, and do, start simultaneously (see Figure 8.18). When this occurs the rise in commodities is not giving an immediate bear signal.

It is interesting to note that, as I write in the second quarter of 1994, the US bond and stock market looks to have topped out, after finding a cyclic low in 1990, and commodity prices in general are rising, having probed an important low (a coincident 40 month cycle low and a 5.25 year cycle low) over the turn of the year 1992–93. In that the 40 month cycle low for commodities is not due until the beginning of 1996 at the earliest, these prices could have considerably further to go yet. This implies fears of commodity price-led inflation will increase, and the stock markets of the world could suffer further falls.

Whilst it is arguable how much influence commodity price rises have on overall inflation – there is considerable evidence the worst inflationary input comes from domestic wages – rising commodity prices bring up the question of how the stock market investor can benefit from them. At this point is it worth mentioning that whilst the CRB Index is generally considered a good measure of commodity price trends, it should be recognised it is compiled from the major US commodity futures contracts prices. This means that, among the base metals, only copper is included. The other base metal futures i.e. aluminium, aluminium alloy, tin, lead, zinc and nickel all trade on the London Metal Exchange and hence are not part of this US-based index. Other indices have been developed but the CRB remains the most closely watched for now. However, having made this major proviso, it is not unusual to find all major commodities enjoying significant price gains simultaneously. Indeed, this looks to be happening, or about to happen, now.

One of the largest producers of metals is Rio Tinto Zinc and a glance at Figure 8.19 will show that it can often enjoy strength when commodity prices rise. But, rather like the gold/gold mines analogy, it does not automatically respond to commodity price trends alone. Indeed, it enjoyed an important low coincident with the UK stock market in 1990 – long before metals prices even began to think of reversing their declines. But, despite having achieved considerable rises since (over 100 per cent), in early 1994 it has just moved into new high ground and looks set to enjoy further gains – as could other mining stocks.

The implication that further gains will be made in RTZ does not come from the fact new highs have been achieved alone. Not only is the price rising above the rising 200 day moving average, the relative strength line has made an upside break and is rising too (see Figure 8.20). In stock market terms relative strength is the expression of the ratio of the stock's performance to the market as a whole. In this case the relative line is the result of dividing the price of RTZ by the price of the FT-SE Actuaries All Share Index and, as it is rising, it shows that this share is outperforming the market in general. Apart from the basic logic that anyone would rather have an overperforming share in their portfolio, monitoring the relative strength line as though it were a price itself fits nicely with Dow's Theory of Confirmation and is an established part of equity analysis today.

Bull markets in stocks and commodities starting and rising in tandem – 1977–1980

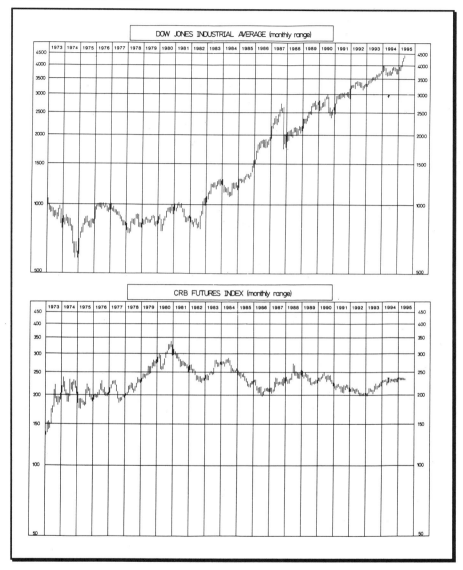

Figure 8.18   *Source:* Investment Research of Cambridge Ltd

The basic economic cycle infers a rapid run-up in commodity prices as the economy gets overheated and thus commodity price strength often comes through just as the rise in equities is nearing its end. However, this is not always the case: as commodities in general enjoy a cycle lasting on average between five and six years and the equity cycle is four years, every so often (between 12 to 20 years) their cyclic lows will coincide and the two bull markets can start and rise in tandem – as from 1977 to 1980.

Rio Tinto Zinc – able to ignore bearish stock market influences

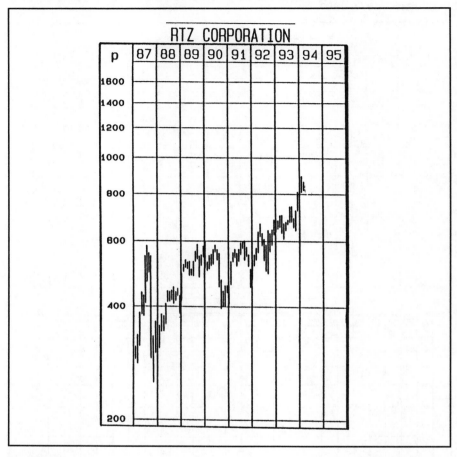

Figure 8.19
Source: Investment Research of Cambridge Ltd

Rio Tinto Zinc, one of the world's largest mining companies, responds to the basic stock market cycle in general but, additionally, it can ignore bearish stock market influences when metal prices are strong – as in early 1994.

The chart of Powerscreen in Figure 8.21 shows the price outperforming the market from the January 1991 low until the uptrend in the relative strength line was broken in May 1993. This was a strong warning signal to holders since, although the reaction in the price held on the rising 200 day moving average in June, the subsequent rally failed to clear the earlier highs. Then, in November, the relative line formed a top and it was only a matter of weeks before the price did so too. Downtrends in both the relative and the price have persisted since.

Relative strength line

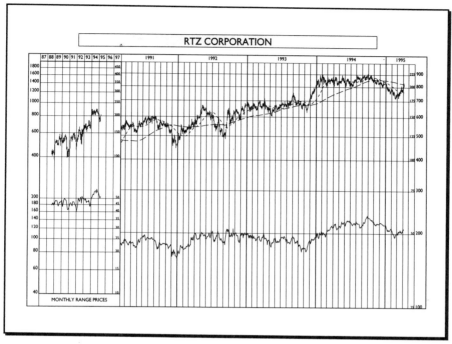

Figure 8.20

Chart by Investment Research of Cambridge Ltd: Design by NNIF

The line below the share price of RTZ is a relative strength line, showing how RTZ is performing compared to the market as a whole – it is a ratio of the price to the All Share Index. When the line is rising it highlights the fact RTZ is outperforming.

The relative strength line on Pilkington did not take a lead on the price but it confirmed its action (see Figure 8.22). Both formed a base in December 1992 and then the relative broke its downtrend in April 1993. Here it was leading and the price's trend did not enjoy a break until some weeks later.

Rather like very long-term trends in price, those in relative strength can persist for a considerable time and when, in due course, they are reversed, the effect can be significant. British Steel and Courtaulds reversed their roles at the end of 1992; the serious underperformance of the former became dramatic outperformance whilst Courtaulds suffered the opposite fate. Meanwhile, RTZ's relative had been moving broadly sideways but when, in December 1993, the price made new highs, the relative confirmed the move. (See Figure 8.23.)

As the relative strength line is a ratio it needs to be examined carefully to determine the message it is giving. Sometimes it will merely move sideways highlighting the fact the share is moving in line with the market itself. As can

Relative strength analysed

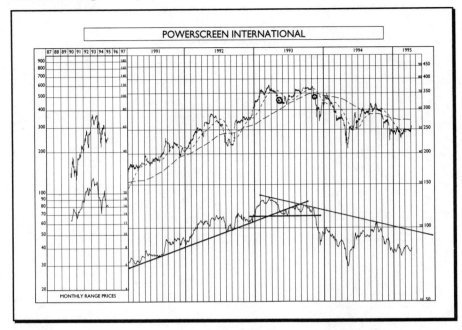

Figure 8.21   Chart by Investment Research of Cambridge Ltd: Design by NNIF

Relative strength can be analysed as though it were a price. A break in its trend can often warn that the trend in the price might soon be vulnerable too, as was the case here. The subsequent top formation in the relative line also formed before that in the price.

be seen on the monthly range chart of Courtaulds, although the relative fell heavily from the end of 1992, the share merely adopted a broadly sideways trend. The fall in the ratio was due to the fact the market at that time was rising and Courtaulds was not.

The same, but opposite, effect is coming through in mid-1994 in the FT-SE Actuaries Extractive Industries sub-group Index (see Figure 8.24). Prices, as can be seen, are moving sideways but, since the FT-SE Actuaries Index itself is falling, the relative to it is rising. This will also happen when a price is falling more slowly than the market itself. It does not mean the price is about to rise – it is not a lead indicator to that extent. Indeed, some would argue it is not a point of interest on the basis they do not wish to lose money, albeit at a slower rate than everyone else. However, for those who need to retain a commitment to equities on a consistent basis, rising relative strength during a bear market will help their funds outperform.

Relative strength confirms the base in the price

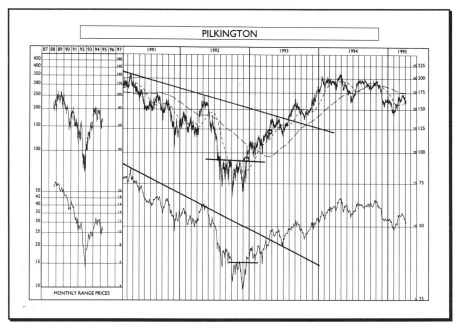

Figure 8.22   Chart by Investment Research of Cambridge Ltd: Design by NNIF

In this example the reversal pattern in the relative line came through simultaneously with that of the price but the downtrend in the relative was broken some weeks before that in the price.

I have left to last one of the major indicators of the strength (or lack of it) behind a market move – volume. Dow noted its importance and part of his Theory states 'Volume Goes With Trend'. Throughout this text when dealing with trend reversal and pattern analysis in particular, volume has been mentioned. Basically, an important move needs good volume to confirm it. In a bull market volume rises on strong days and falls back as prices react. In a bear market volume will likely increase on weak days and peter out as prices rally. (See Figure 8.25.)

Whilst Figure 8.25 shows good increases in volume as the uptrend in the Dow is resumed, the individual plots of volume do not show a clearly rising trend. Several indicators have been devised to incorporate volume's role more easily and one of the best known is On Balance Volume (see Figure 8.26). This line is constructed by amalgamating the price and volume; if the price closes up on the previous day volume is given a plus value and vice

Long-term trends in relative strength reversed

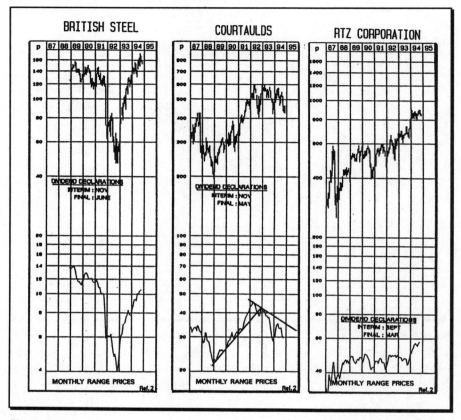

Figure 8.23

Source: Investment Research of Cambridge Ltd

Trends in relative strength can last for a long time and, when they are reversed, the effect can be considerable – as in the case of British Steel. The break in the relative strength line of Courtaulds did not signal an immediate downtrend in price, but it was a useful signal all the same and the share underperformed drastically thereafter. The RTZ relative has confirmed the break into new high ground by the price.

versa if the price closes down. The OBV Line is a running cumulative total and it should confirm the price trend. If it does not do so loud warning bells sound. The same approach is taken by a similar indicator called Volume/Price Trend.

A considerable amount of space has been given to background indicators and some market interrelationships and their leads and lags together with the danger signals they can give; but their primary role is confirmation of what the market indices are doing themselves. It has been consistently stressed that the

Rising relative strength does not imply new highs in price

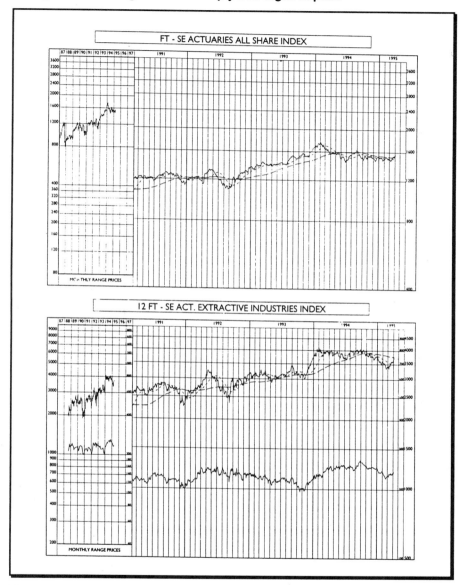

Figure 8.24

Chart by Investment Research of Cambridge Ltd: Design by NNIF

A break into new high ground by a relative strength line on its own does not necessarily imply new highs in the price will follow. As it is a ratio, the fact it is rising in early 1994 on the chart of the FTSE Actuaries Extractive Industries Index does not mean the sub-group's price is rising; rather it is highlighting the fact it is moving sideways during a period when the market as a whole is falling. Hence, this sector was holding up 'relatively well'.

'Volume Goes With Trend'

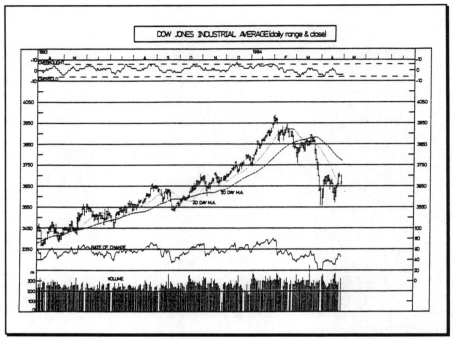

Figure 8.25
Source: Investment Research of Cambridge Ltd

Part of the Dow Theory states 'Volume Goes With Trend'. In a bull market volume should rise on days when prices are strong and diminish as prices react. The opposite is generally the case in a bear market.

Principle of Confirmation and its opposite, Divergence, is at the core of technical analysis and it certainly does not apply to the market indices alone. The most popular application of this rule is in the analysis of oscillators and these are used on all price series and in all time frames. Their main purpose in life is to monitor trends and highlight overextended conditions that leave prices vulnerable to reversal; these are addressed in the next chapter.

On Balance Volume and Volume/Price Trend

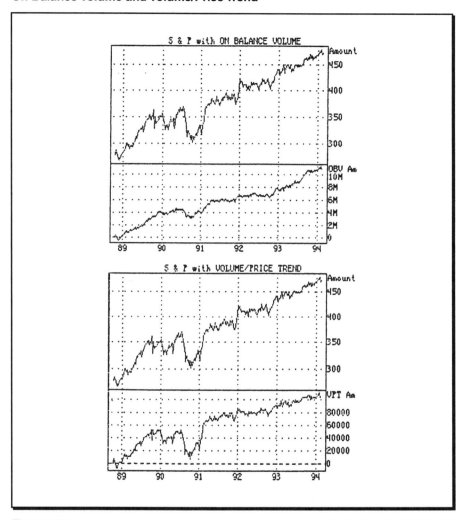

Figure 8.26

Chart by Reuters Technical Analysis

In recognition of the importance of the role played by volume, both these indicators – On Balance Volume and Volume/Price Trend – amalgamate volume and price and the result should ape the price trend itself. When they fail to do so warning bells ring.

9

THE ANALYSIS OF
INDICATORS & OSCILLATORS

- Momentum – a generic term for speed measurement – is also the name of a specific indicator in its own right. It forms trends – as do others – oscillating around zero and reaches high and low levels from which prices have reversed before. Thus it operates as a monitor of the speed of the trend and its over extension. An indicator which is very similar – and is interpreted in the same way – is called Rate of Change.

- 'Modern' indicators are normally presented in the form of oscillators, confined within the 0–100 parameters. This allows the identification of predetermined overbought and oversold levels (conventionally over 70 and below 30) on all indicators in all markets. These readings can be refined. The coverage includes: Welles Wilders' RSI; George Lane's Stochastics; Larry Williams' % R; George Appel's Moving Average Convergence/Divergence; Coppock's Momentum, Meisels' Overbought/Oversold; Donald Lambert's Commodity Channel Index; Accumulation/Distribution; Rise & Fall; Granville's On Balance Volume; Volume/Price Trend; Welles Wilder's Directional Movement Index.

The analysis of oscillators is one of the most popular aspects of technical analysis today. These indicators give leading signals that the trend in price could soon reverse before any signs from the moving averages (etc.) come through that this could be the case. They are effectively measures of the speed of the trend (velocity) and, as the pace of price increase or decrease often slows before the trend is reversed, they give early warning. Additionally, these lines rise and fall to upper or lower areas on the scale from which they have reversed previously; these extremes show the market's overextension, highlighting the fact the move in price has likely gone far enough for now and profit-taking could set in.

The chart of the FTSE 100 in Figure 9.1 shows the parallel uptrend channel. As we have seen previously, the channel lines provide inclined support and resistance as they are approached and, in due course, this forces prices to reverse. Adding an oscillator to the picture gives better clues as to when such reversal is likely to occur.

Changing role of trend channel

Figure 9.1

Chart by Reuters Technical Analysis

The trend channel containing FTSE values for the first six months' history of this chart provided inclined support and resistance on several occasions. Subsequently, when prices cleared the upper parallel, it changed its role and the previous inclined resistance became inclined support.

A generic term for the study of the speed at which price change occurs is 'momentum' and there is a specific technical indicator with this name; it appears below the FTSE plot in Figure 9.2. Momentum is the simple arithmetic differential between the current price and one a constant 'n' periods ago – in this case, 22 days. The resultant line oscillates around a horizontal zero line. When prices are higher than they were 22 days ago the plot will be above zero – and below it if prices have fallen over the working month.

A glance at the oscillations of this line will show that during the first six months 'overbought' readings come through when the momentum figure is over 200, and oversold conditions are registered when levels are around –100. These readings remain pertinent while the uptrend in the FTSE stays in place and they alert watchers to overextension. Had the trend in the FTSE instead been sideways, it is probable the plus and minus values would have been similar – plus or minus, say, 150. Now the stock market is in a downtrend, the

Momentum

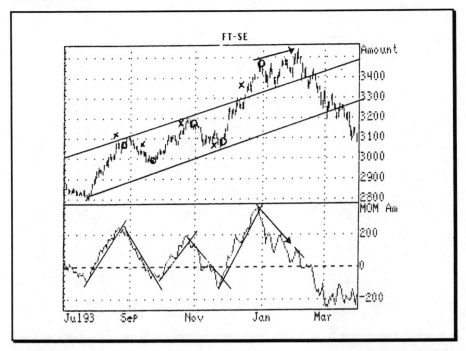

Figure 9.2   *Chart* by Reuters Technical Analysis

Momentum is a generic term for indicators which measure the speed of price change i.e. velocity. This particular indicator has the name 'Momentum' and it highlights periods when the market is overbought or oversold and thus prone to reversal. The points where the indicator has reversed from previously overextended territory are marked with crosses on the price chart. The circles highlight the points at which the trends in momentum were broken, pinpointing prices very near the absolute extremes in most cases. These indicators take on the shape of the price. When they do not do so, for example, when the moves into new high ground in early 1994 by the price were not confirmed by momentum, alarm bells ring. This signals that the new highs in price are unlikely to be sustained.

previous observations have been reversed – minus 200 is oversold and over-bought readings would likely register around plus 100 if rallies came through.

When adopting a periodicity for momentum it is normal to choose a number of periods representing roughly half the cycle in force so the comparison is likely to prove to be between the high and the low etc. In this case the three low points evident on the chart are two months (44 working days) apart, hence the choice of one month. The crosses on the price represent the points at which the overextended readings came through and they were reasonably timely. Whilst, as can be seen, they did not necessarily catch the absolute high or low, they served their purpose well in warning that trend reversal could be imminent.

The end-1993 reading was, however, extremely early; the reversal came through six weeks later and at a considerably higher price. Readers may recall that in Chapter 3 it was stated several times that a move through the upper parallel line to an uptrend which occurs after that trend has been in place for some time highlights danger. Late re-acceleration can carry prices considerably higher but it is unlikely the move will prove sustained. So here we already had good warning that the move in the UK stock market was suspect; then momentum gave us another. It can be seen that the peak on momentum that came through in January 1994 was lower than that seen in December, despite the level of the FT-SE being over 50 points higher. This is classic non-confirmation, or divergence, and is one of the signals for which these indicators are justly famed. The market in question is not only overbought, the lower high in momentum reflects the fact it is losing speed. This is a background against which trend reversal, or a long consolidation, is almost automatic.

In the previous chapter we looked at several comparisons and adopted the 'rule' that when one line failed to do the same as the other, then divergence had occurred and alarm bells rang. One of the factors we were monitoring was the trend in the lines which were being compared to the price. If the same approach is adopted with the momentum line some very interesting signals come through. A close look at the chart will show that, had the investor noted the points of overextension, but awaited the subsequent breaks in the trend in momentum (marked by circles on the price), his market timing would have been very near spot-on.

Three main points have been gleaned from an examination of Figure 9.2: firstly, overbought and oversold readings highlight danger when the momentum number gets to an extreme from which it has previously reversed; secondly, when a price moves into new high (or new low) ground and the momentum line does not do so the trend is losing speed and is vulnerable to reversal, particularly if the numbers are in overextended territory; and thirdly, the trend in momentum itself is important. These are the basic rules for the use of indicators which measure the speed of price change, and they can give very good leads.

The simplistic momentum line has its disadvantages, however. The main one is that, over long periods of time, considerable price change can occur and this means that the arithmetic differentials which originally represented overextension can become outdated quickly. An approach which partly overcomes this is a calculation called 'Rate of Change'. Instead of expressing the change between the two prices in question as an arithmetic difference, it shows them as a ratio. The resultant line looks similar to momentum, but the highs and lows respond better for the purposes of historic comparison.

Figure 9.3 shows how the break in the downtrend in the rate of change indicator on Tarmac alerted the investor to the likelihood that the falls in price were nearing their end, and subsequently the break in the rate of change's

Rate of Change

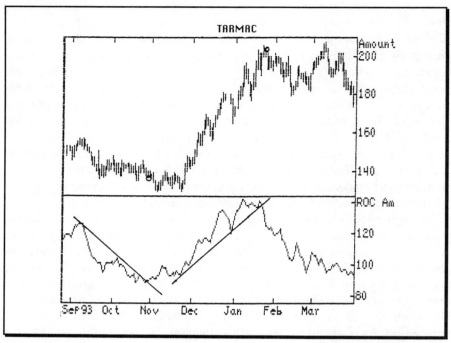

Figure 9.3

Chart by Reuters Technical Analysis

Whereas the Momentum line in Figure 9.2 is the arithmetic difference between the price now and that a set number of periods ago, Rate of Change is the ratio between the two. It is interpreted in the same manner.

uptrend almost caught the top in the price itself. However, it additionally shows the danger of using such signals in a slavish manner. Whilst the downtrend in the rate of change continued unabated for the balance of this chart, the price rallied significantly. The use of such signals to close long positions is sensible but, were this technique applied to reverse positions in the futures markets, the results could be costly.

The chart in Figure 9.4 shows the Dow Jones Industrial Average and an indicator called the MACD (Moving Average Convergence–Divergence) which we will look at in detail later. Its buy and sell signals come through when the two lines cross – one is the moving average of the other. It can be seen that the signal to sell in September 1989 was very similar to the signal from the rate of change indicator on Tarmac; it came in very near the high but, although the indicator continued to decline, the price did not. Indeed, in the case of the Dow it consolidated and then rose into new high ground.

Moving Average Convergence – Divergence (MACD) as a measure of acceleration of a trend

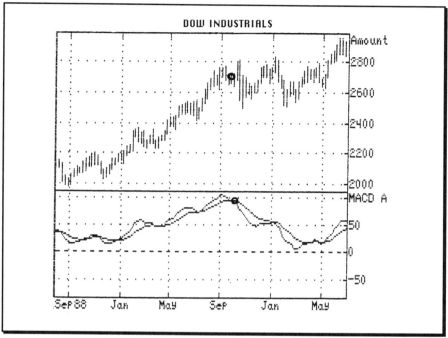

Figure 9.4

Chart by Reuters Technical Analysis

Indicators which measure the speed of a trend should not be used automatically to reverse positions. This is because an apparent sell signal can come through, as occurred in September here when the two lines in the lower window saw a downside cross, when the speed at which prices were increasing merely slowed. The price trend may not have reversed, but just stalled.

To explain the way these indicators work I use an analogy with driving a car. Let us say that during the early stages of this chart the MACD lines are representing the increasing speed of a car as it first pulls out from the kerb, then gets into the traffic and, around 'summer', enters the motorway. As it gets to its peaks it is moving into the fast lane. However, the driver then notices that ahead is a wall of red lights. He takes his foot off the pedal; the car continues to go ahead but the speed is declining. Once the red lights clear, he re-accelerates – in May 1990 for the purpose of this analogy. In other words, when a trend in price loses speed it is vulnerable to reversal but such reversal will not necessarily come through. Confirmation the trend had reversed would only come through on this indicator if the numbers went through the zero line. While they are above it prices are advancing over the period in question, albeit at a slower pace. To draw on the analogy for an ultimate conclusion, going short automatically upon the indicator's reversal can be as risky as going into reverse gear in the fast lane and buying prematurely because the trend has slowed can have similarly disastrous consequences.

This is is a 'health warning' which is meant to caution the user of these indicators, rather than dampen his enthusiasm. Their use hinges on the type of market background in force when the signals come through. There are no areas of analysis where automatically risk-free trades can be generated and momentum indicators are no exception. But, if the market background against which the signals occur is correctly analysed, the aid they can give to market timing can be excellent – making them virtually indispensable. The basic rules, as described above, work extremely well when markets are in either a broadly sideways trend, or a gentle up or down trend. When a market is moving fast in one direction or another – in other words when moving averages and other such lagging trend-defining systems are at their best – the buy/sell signals cannot be obeyed automatically. This is equally true of the popular oscillators such as the RSI and Stochastics which we shall come to shortly.

Another simplistic method of measuring the speed of the trend is an indicator called, simply, 'Oscillator'. A glance at the price chart of the ASDA in Figure 9.5 will show the 1991–92 downtrend monitored by two moving averages which, as the decline nears its end, can be seen to draw nearer together. In the window below the price is the oscillator, a straightforward arithmetic difference between the levels of the two moving averages. A classic divergence comes through as, in August, prices fall into new low ground, but the oscillator is rising strongly.

One of the things all three of the simple indicators already mentioned have in common is that the levels at which overbought and oversold conditions in the price are registered can vary considerably over time. It can be seen in Figure 9.6 that the oscillator was signalling overbought on at least two different levels – at 100 and twice at 65, and oversold readings came through at –130, –15, –20 and –40. This is due to the fact the oscillator and momentum both rely on arithmetic differentials and there had been considerable price change over the period in question. Even though the Rate of Change indicator employs ratios, this problem is not surmounted.

A breakthrough came during the 1970s when different sorts of formulae were developed. J. Welles Wilder, Jnr published a series of indicators which did not suffer from this problem. Immediately below the oscillator in the illustration is Welles Wilder's RSI (Relative Strength Index) which moves on a scale confined within the 0–100 parameters. Two lines have been emboldened: the line which shows registrations of 70 or above and the one showing 30 or below. These highlight overbought conditions (70 and above) or oversold situations (30 and below). It can be seen that the signals on the RSI are very clear

Parks Bookshops

Serving the
Business, Financial & Legal Professions

Principal Bookshops

243/244 High Holborn
London WC1V 7DZ
Tel: 0171 831 9501
Fax: 0171 405 9412

■

119-122 London Road
London SE1 6LF
Tel: 0171 928 5378
Fax: 0171 261 9536

■

11 Copthall Avenue
London EC2R 7DJ
Tel: 0171 638 1991
Tel: 0171 920 8537
Fax: 0171 638 1594

■

19 Brown Street
Manchester M2 1DA
Tel: 0161 834 4019
Fax: 0161 832 9240

■

83 St Vincent Street
Glasgow G2 5TF
Tel: 0141 221 1369
Fax: 0141 221 1440

■

3 Windsor Arcade
Birmingham B2 5LJ
Tel: 0121 233 4969
Fax: 0121 236 3652

■

Also at

Holborn Law College
South Bank University
Sandwell Management Centre
Birmingham College of Food,
Tourism & Creative Studies
Manchester Metropolitan University

Central Administration Office
36 St Paul's Square
Birmingham B3 1QX
Tel: 0121 236 0646
Fax: 0121 236 6621

Internet:
htt://www.bookshop.co.uk/parks

Oscillator

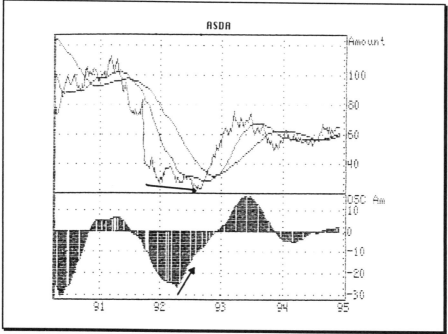

Figure 9.5

Chart by Reuters Technical Analysis

The Oscillator measures the arithmetic difference between the levels of the two moving averages used to define the trend. When the speed of the trend slows, the averages draw together and signals that the trend is prone to reversal come through when new lows in price (or new highs in an uptrend) are not confirmed by the oscillator.

warnings, whilst the actual points on the oscillator, over the same periodicity, varied so widely as to be little less than confusing.

Before looking at the ways J. Welles Wilder, Jnr recommends for interpreting the RSI, it is worth stressing that the rules regarding the analysis of momentum indicators in general remain the same – Welles Wilder's version just makes them more specific. The shape of the plot adopted by the indicator should be the same as that traced out by the price and, when it is not, the warning signals come through. As far as Figure 9.7 is concerned, this was the case until the Index hit new highs over 2250 towards the end of December 1993. The RSI did not enjoy the same fate, its high was equivalent to the one seen in the early part of the month. This was the first hint that the two lines might be diverging. Confirmation of this came through when, over the turn of the year, the Index moved clearly into new high ground and the rise in the RSI fell short of its previous peaks. As can be seen from the chart, the Index's rise

Oscillator and RSI

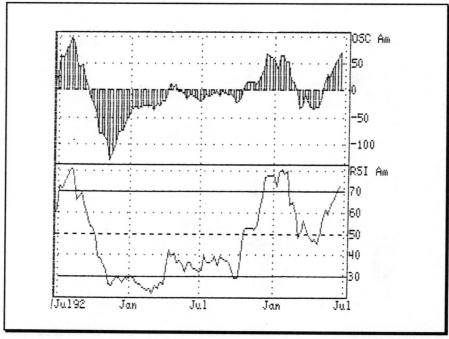

Figure 9.6

Chart by Reuters Technical Analysis

Momentum, Rate of Change and Oscillator all have a common fault – the levels at which they signal overextension can vary from one peak or trough to another. The RSI, confined to oscillate between 0 and 100, gives warnings that the market is overbought around 70 and oversold around 30 (predetermined numbers).

reversed and the two lines moved in harmony, both enjoying a downtrend which continued until early March. Here the Index clearly hit new lows but the RSI did not – divergence again. Subsequent to that signal, the decline in price has reversed and the RSI is confirming every move.

The initials RSI stand for 'Relative Strength Index'. This name is not to be confused with the relative strength lines we have already looked at and which are used in stock market analysis to evaluate an individual share's performance against the market as a whole.

As far as Welles Wilder's calculation is concerned, the relative strength being referred to is that of the current price in the series to its performance 'n' periods ago. He does this by summing the amount by which the price has risen close-to-close over a certain period and, additionally, summing the total of the close-to-close falls over the same period in question. They are then averaged; if

Over extension and diverging signals from the RSI

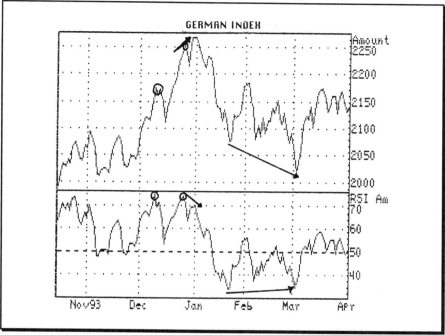

Figure 9.7

Chart by Reuters Technical Analysis

During December the RSI highlighted the overbought condition by going over 70 on two separate occasions. Each time the price reacted and then recovered. However, the new highs scored at the year-end were not confirmed by new highs in the RSI. When this happens while the RSI is in overbought territory it is called a failure swing and warns of impending reversal. The same, but opposite, signal came through in March when new lows were scored by the price but the oversold RSI did not go below January's lows. Subsequently the price reversed.

the period is 14 days, which is the default with Welles Wilder's indicators, the totals are divided by 14 (although most computer programs will allow any period to be entered). The final calculation involves the ratio of one average to the other and then, to confine the result into the 0–100 levels which allow the use of absolute overbought and oversold parameters, this ratio is added to 1 and divided into 100. The RSI is the result of 100 minus this figure. It should be noted that Welles Wilder developed this, and his other indicators, on a programmable calculator with little storage space. Consequently, the calculation uses exponential moving averages of the two series summed. Should 'raw' data be used instead, the line is more volatile and overextension registers at much higher, or lower, levels.

RSI forming reversal patterns

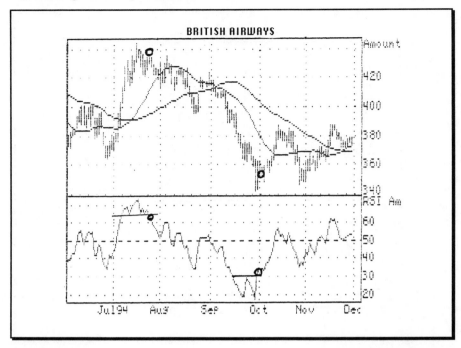

Figure 9.8

Chart by Reuters Technical Analysis

The RSI will normally form a reversal pattern before the price itself does so. On both these examples the timing was good.

The method for calculating the RSI was published by Welles Wilder at the end of the 1970s and nearly produced a revolution in technical analysis. This was due to the fact that the overextended observations could be predetermined at certain levels and this appeared to take out much of the judgemental element of the analysis. It was greeted with acclaim and the rules for its interpretation recommended by Welles Wilder have been adopted in principle for all oscillator analysis today.

These rules are basically the same as those mentioned several times already i.e. watch for divergence between price and the indicator, particularly at extremes. But they are more specific: tops and bottoms in price are indicated when the RSI goes above 70 or below 30. Additionally, the RSI will normally form a reversal pattern before the price does itself. If this pattern comes through in the overextended regions, it is a very serious warning signal that the price trend is about to end. Another important signal comes from the 'failure swing'; if a price in a downtrend goes into new low ground and the RSI is below 30 (oversold) but does not itself find a new low, this is a failure swing. A failure swing will come through if a price in an uptrend goes into new high ground and the RSI is above 70 (overbought) but it does not hit a new high. Failure swings are a strong indication of imminent trend reversal or correction in price.

The strongest signals from the RSI come through when it is registering overextension. However, there are others. Welles Wilder points out that the RSI frequently forms patterns ahead of the price chart; it shows up support and resistance levels that are not as clear on the price chart alone and it can fail to confirm price moves, suggesting they are an aberration. This latter is similar to a failure swing but the results are less likely to be so significant as the market is not showing serious overextension. The official title of this signal is 'divergence'.

The daily range chart of British Airways in Figure 9.8 shows two good examples of the RSI forming reversal patterns below 30 and above 70 before the price did itself. It can be noted that, during this period, British Airways was in a wide, but gentle, downtrend – a background against which signals from all these indicators are likely to be most successful.

The chart in Figure 9.9 shows prices moving in a sideways trend; each time the RSI registers 70 or 30 near term rally peaks or reaction lows are seen.

Overbought and oversold readings in a sideways trend

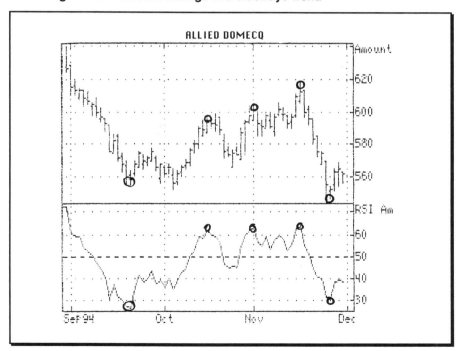

Figure 9.9

Chart by Reuters Technical Analysis

Overbought RSI readings around 70 and oversold readings around 30 imply rallies and reactions are prone to reversal.

However, the chart of Eastern Group in Figure 9.10 is clearly in a steady uptrend, as defined by the moving averages. Against this background, in that it is the nature of bull markets to allow overbought situations to get more overbought yet, readings over 70 can persist for some time before reactions set in. In addition, instead of RSI readings of 30 to suggest oversold, support tends to hold prices within the uptrend when the RSI is not registering levels much below 50. In other words, in persistent trends the readings shift; 70 and above in a strong uptrend can persist for some time, whilst relatively oversold readings come in well above the 30 level itself. The opposite effect can be noted in downtrends, as the chart of Fisons (Figure 9.11) shows. Rather like the price trends themselves, the previously horizontal 70 and 30 lines skew and develop an upward or downward tilt.

During the early stages of the chart the uptrend in price remains intact and prices are clearly overbought as the 70 area on the RSI is neared. Later, fol-

Overbought and oversold readings shift in a moving trend

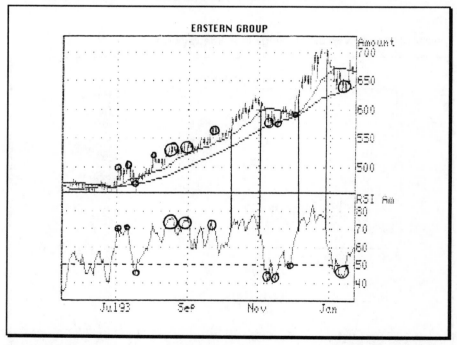

Figure 9.10   *Chart* by Reuters Technical Analysis

The RSI gives its best signals when the market is in a range or moving gently up or down. In a steady uptrend an overbought market can get more overbought yet and remain so for some time. Also, reactions rarely cause the RSI to go as low as 30 – levels just below 50 signal 'relatively' oversold. The same, but opposite, effect can be noted in downtrends.

Readings shifting during persistant trend and divergence

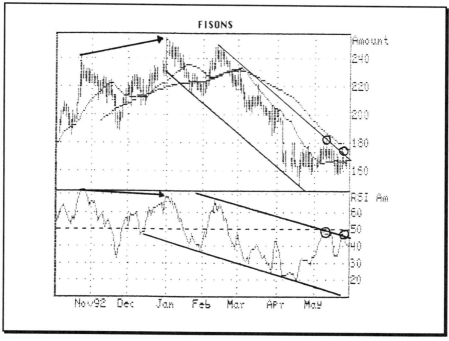

Figure 9.11   *Chart* by Reuters Technical Analysis

During the early stages of the chart Fisons' prices were in a steady uptrend and oversold readings were around 40 on the RSI. Later, when the trend was down, the RSI went to 20 and the subsequent rally left the market overbought at RSI levels around 50. The uptrend's reversal was signalled when the RSI failed to make new highs when prices did so in January. This is called 'divergence'; it is similar to a failure swing but occurs when the RSI is not signalling overextension – hence, it is a slightly weaker signal.

lowing the moving averages crossing into bearish sequence, the RSI spends a considerable amount of time below 30 and levels around 50 are highlighted as relatively overbought. But this chart shows something else too – divergence. The October peak in the RSI was well over 70 but, in January, when prices moved into new high ground, the RSI fell short of its earlier peak. It was a good warning of trend reversal.

Before leaving the subject of how to read overbought and oversold levels on the RSI it is worth examining the chart of BTR (Figure 9.12). During its early stages the price was in a steady uptrend, with the RSI registering overbought in the 70–80 region, and oversold around 40–50. However, in early November 1993 the uptrend was broken. For nearly a year prices moved within a broad sideways trend and levels around 70 and 30 on the RSI

Market background needs assessing before RSI readings are analysed

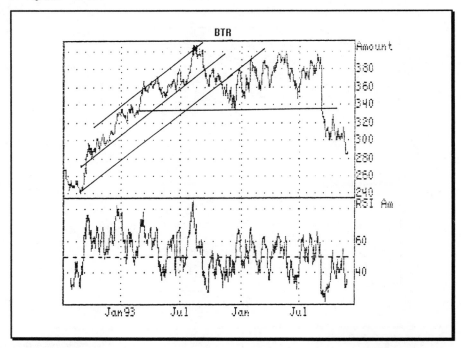

Figure 9.12   *Chart* by Reuters Technical Analysis

When using the RSI, and other momentum indicators, it is important to keep the market background in perspective. The early part of the chart shows a steady uptrend in the price; RSI readings are registering overbought around 80 and oversold in the 40-60 region. For the next year the trend is broadly sideways and the conventional overbought/oversold 70 and 30 levels on the RSI signal overextension. Then, when support is breached and a top forms and a severe downtrend sets in, the RSI goes to 20 and then signals relatively overbought on rallies just over 50.

signalled overbought and oversold. Then a very large top formed, and the fall was accompanied by an RSI reading which extended to 20 before a rally came in, and levels just over 50 then signalled overbought. This sort of behaviour from the RSI can be expected when a top is formed: the oversold condition just gets more oversold. At bottoms, when prices break the neckline, RSI readings will already be in overbought territory, but they are likely to go even higher yet. This serves as another reminder of how important it is to keep the market background in perspective when these indicator readings are analysed.

It can be noted that in the summary of Welles Wilder's suggested rules for analysing the RSI he did not mention monitoring the RSI's trends. However, after considerable research, I have found that this is a useful technique, not only for gauging relative overextension (as in Figure 9.11) but also as a warning of a possible reversal in the trend of the price. This is particularly true since, even though the RSI is traditionally used as a short-term indicator, sometimes these trends persist over many months.

The chart in Figure 9.13 shows a good example of a useful uptrend in the RSI; first the RSI readings come in at higher levels as the two lows at 180p on price are hit in August and September. After the uptrend in price formed, the uptrend in the RSI continued. It then gave a series of good warning signals. Firstly, at the end of December, the price made a new high and the RSI did

Monitoring an uptrend in the RSI

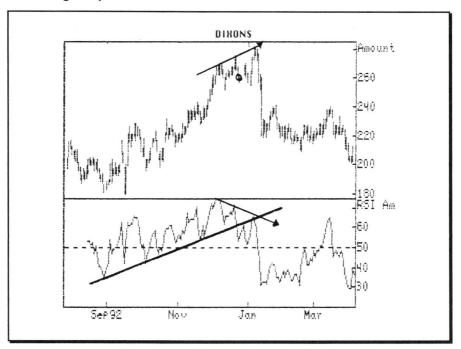

Figure 9.13   *Chart* by Reuters Technical Analysis

The technique of monitoring the trend in momentum indicators can be useful on the RSI too. This uptrend in the RSI began as Dixons scored its lows. It remained in place while prices rose but then, immediately after new highs were scored towards the year-end, the RSI's trend was breached. The danger to the price trend was increased by the fact the RSI had not confirmed the new high immediately before the trend break occurred. Serious alarm bells rang when further non-confirmation of new highs came through in January. This chart highlights the fact that it is frequently the second non-confirmation of new price extremes by the RSI that gives the final signal the trend is about to end.

not. Secondly, two days later, the RSI broke its uptrend. Finally, in January, the price moved into new high ground but the RSI, now in a downtrend, did not do so – the end was nigh. It is interesting to note that it is frequently the RSI's second failed attempt to confirm new highs (or lows) in price which actually signals the end.

However, whilst the trend break in the Dixons example was particularly timely, sometimes such a break can be premature. This happened twice on the chart of Forte in Figure 9.14.

First, the strict uptrend in the RSI was breached in December, long before the price's rise was arrested. Secondly, the RSI's downtrend was broken in May, only for prices to continue to fall at a slower pace. These signals can be very timely indeed but they should be used as warnings, as Welles Wilder himself implies, not as automatic reversal signals. Indeed, the reader with his own computer may find it worthwhile to experiment with different periodicities for the RSI on different shares for, although the default of 14 days has been used

Premature break in trend in the RSI

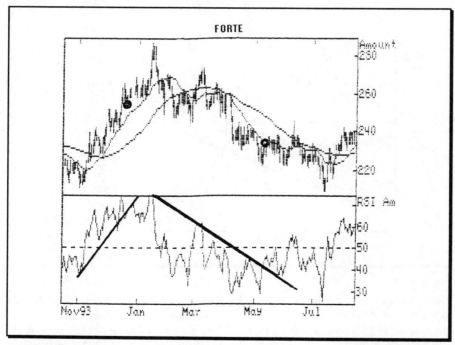

Figure 9.14

Chart by Reuters Technical Analysis

As with all momentum-based signals, a break in the trend in the RSI can be premature. They should be used as warnings, not signals to reverse positions automatically.

throughout the above examples, the analysis of some shares may well be improved if a slightly longer time period is used.

More space has been devoted to the RSI than will be given to other indicators. I have used it as the prime example of how to analyse oscillators in general since it is more flexible than many. It can be used during broadly sideways trends, as Welles Wilder recommended, or its trends can be monitored when the price itself is moving in an up or down trend. In these circumstances it can give early warning of the price trend's reversal. The interpretation of other oscillators cannot be adapted quite so easily, but the ground rules in most cases remain basically the same.

Another extremely popular indicator is called Stochastics. This was developed by George Lane and involves two lines – %K and %D, the latter being the moving average of the former. In the discussion on bar charts earlier it was stressed that the position of the close in relation to the high and low for the period is critical when a market is trending, and this indicator is based on the observation that, during the early stages of a trend, the close will be near the high of the range in an uptrend and the low of the range in a downtrend. When this is no longer the case, the early enthusiasm is waning and the indicator will begin to signal danger.

The calculation involves the ratio of the difference between the most recent close and the low for the period in question and the difference between the absolute high and low over the same time frame. If the price closes at the high for the period %K will be 100 and, were it to close at the low, it would be zero. Since this study is normally run over a relatively short time frame (periodicities of 5 and 3 are often recommended) these extremes on the oscillator's scale are hit quite often. The %D line is smoother – it is an average of %K – again the periodicity recommended is 3. The indicator tracks the price, rising strongly at the start of an uptrend and, when the trend slows, there is a strong likelihood the %K line will decline and the reverse will occur in a downtrend. The interrelationship between %K and %D at extremes is what is watched to give warning signals.

As with other momentum-based indicators, the interpretation of stochastics depends on its non-confirmation of new highs or lows in the price. The basic signal comes through when the price goes into new low ground and %D (the slower line of the two) is below 30 and does not do so (see Figure 9.15). Subsequently the actual signal is given when %K rises and crosses up over %D – as occurred on 2 June. The very strongest form of this signal is given if the cross over %D by %K comes when the former is below 15 and rising – but this was not the case on this occasion.

Figure 9.16 shows the stochastic indicator used on weekly data. Here the %K and %D lines first signalled the downtrend's reversal when, following new lows in price not confirmed by %D, %K rose through %D when it was rising and below 30. Then both the price and the stochastic lines rose and the latter

Stochastics Indicator

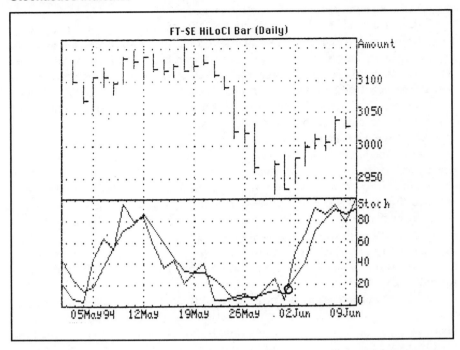

Figure 9.15

The stochastics indicator is a misnomer in that the word implies 'random' whilst the indicator does not. It appears in the bottom window and uses two lines – %K and its moving average, %D. Alerts come through when new highs or lows in price are not confirmed by %D. The chart shows a stochastic buy signal; prices are in new low ground and %D is below 30 and above its previous low. Then %K rallies and crosses %D from the right to give the actual signal; it is strengthened if %D is rising when crossed by %K.

remained in overbought territory above 70, consistently confirming new highs in price. However, the reaction in price at the beginning of January saw the stochastics fall and then recover; but the recovery did not take %D into new high ground (although the price achieved this) and, in due course, %K crossed down below %D, signalling the price trend's reversal.

Although, as has been said, %K can hit zero and 100 frequently, signals can sometimes come through when it does not do so. If, in an uptrend, %K hits 100 and then, having reacted by 20% or so, rallies back towards 100 – but fails to achieve the 100 level itself before turning down again – this is good warning the trend in price is tiring (doubly so if prices are at new highs as they are here). On the weekly chart of the FTSE in February 1994 this timely signal came through (see Figure 9.17). At the time of writing in June 1994 the

Stochastics Indicator used on weekly data

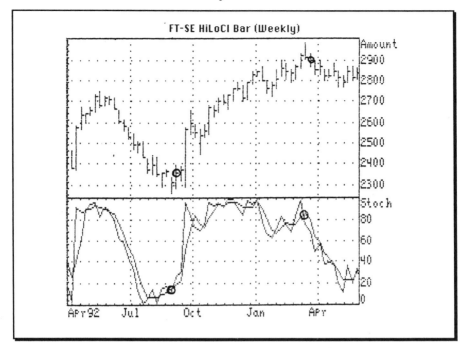

Figure 9.16   *Chart* by Reuters Technical Analysis

A strong buy signal came through on this weekly chart when the new lows were not con-
firmed by %D and then %K rose through the already rising %D below 30. The indicator
continued to confirm the new highs while the price rose and then, in March, following a
reaction in both, stochastics recovered from its reaction but failed to confirm the new high
in price. %K crossed %D over 70 and signalled the high.

opposite signal has come through; new lows in price have not been accompanied by further registrations of 0 on %K, even though it has seen a rally of 20
points or more, suggesting strongly the medium-term downtrend may be
prone to reversal soon.

There are a considerable number of finely-tuned signals that can additionally be used when interpreting stochastics but the ones mentioned above are
the main ones. Indeed, this indicator is more often used in its 'slow' form, as
seen in Figure 9.18.

Slow stochastics ignores the original %K; instead, it plots the original %D
and then a moving average of it. These, in turn, are called slow %K and slow
%D and are used in the same way. However, as they are both smoother, the signals are less sensitive and they are watched particularly for non-
confirmation, and subsequent crossovers at extremes, when prices reach

Stochastic levels of 100 and 0 can be significant

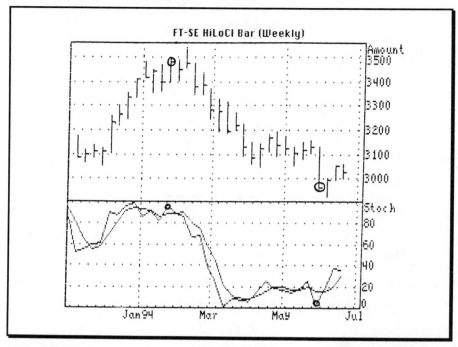

Figure 9.17

Chart by Reuters Technical Analysis

Although %K on the stochastic often hits 100 and 0, sometimes its failure to do so signals danger of reversal. If, having hit 100, %K reacts by 20 points or so and then prices make new highs but %K does not hit 100, a reversal could come through. The same warning comes through following %K hitting zero, rallying by 20 points, and then not reaching zero when the price makes new lows.

extremes and these lines fail to do so. This occurred in Figure 9.18 during the first week in February 1994. When this approach is employed the recommended time periods are 5 for the original %K (not shown), 3 for the original %D and then 3 for the slow %D (using the original %D as the slow %K).

The stochastic has a near-twin in the Williams %R, but this is a less well-known indicator. The formula is very similar, but it is upside down in relation to stochastics and the RSI and other indicators; the ratio of the highest high minus the most recent close for the period to the difference between the high and the low for the period is taken and this comes out with overbought conditions registering zero and oversold situations reading as 100. It, like %K (it does not employ a %D smoothing line) is extremely volatile and thus the overbought readings start at 20 and go up to zero and the oversold readings start

Slow stochastics

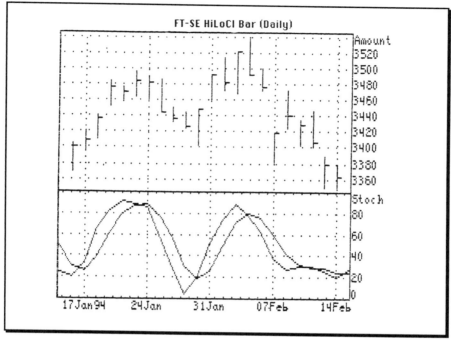

Figure 9.18

Chart by Reuters Technical Analysis

Slow stochastics is comprised of the original %D (which becomes slow %K) and its moving average. Less sensitive than fast stochastics, most people take signals when a crossover occurs below 30 or above 70.

at 80 and go down to 100. When tops form over 20 prices are likely to react and when base formations come through in the indicator below 80 price rises could well come through. The illustration in Figure 9.19 shows a timely base at the start of the chart and a useful top in early 1994. The signal that came through in the first quarter of 1993, however, merely led to consolidation in price, rather than trend reversal.

Although Larry Williams' %R is not a particularly popular indicator nowadays (its original fans have largely been converted to using stochastics) I keep an eye on it still, but not in the way it was originally intended. I use it on a longer-term basis (usually about 50 days) and find that it can give very good overbought and oversold signals when prices are moving within a medium-term trend – and can often signal that trend's reversal. These readings come through when the indicator moves to the mid-line on the scale i.e. 50. If the price is in a downtrend and the indicator rallies to 50 I read that as over-

Williams %R Indicator

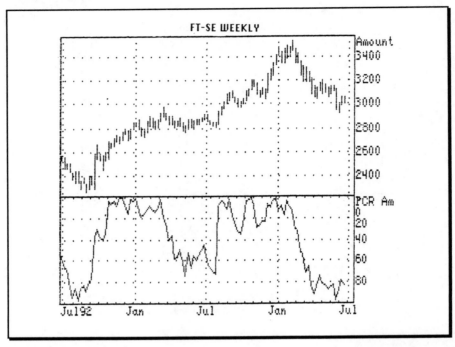

Figure 9.19   *Chart* by Reuters Technical Analysis

Williams %R is a similar calculation to stochastics but its readings come out 'upside down' – 0 is overbought and 100 oversold. It is a volatile indicator; trend reversal is implied when tops form over 20 and bottoms below 80.

bought. If, however, it goes further and crosses the 50 line – I usually allow for it to do this for two consecutive days as the indicator line is very volatile – this is a good signal the trend is about to reverse.

Figure 9.20 shows that, in October 1993 sterling met the downtrend and registered overbought. It retreated and then cleared the trendline, with the %R line clearing 50 with ease. The Williams %R formed a top over 20 at the end of January 1994 and the downtrend in price was confirmed by the %R five days later when levels below 50 were scored. Subsequently two rallies caused over-bought (50) readings on %R before the price reversed.

Another well-used indicator, particularly popular in stock market circles, is the Moving Average Convergence–Divergence (MACD). It comprises two lines: the first is the differential between two exponential moving averages of the price and the second is a moving average of the result. If you have a com-

Williams %R gives overextended readings around 50 on 0 medium-term basis

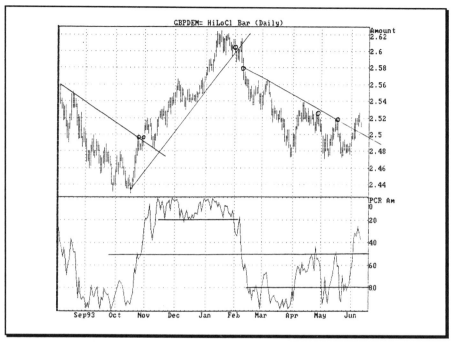

Figure 9.20   *Chart* by Reuters Technical Analysis

Through personal use I have found the Williams %R to be a useful trend reversal indicator over a slightly longer time frame. While the trend in price is in place moves by %R to 50 (or thereabouts) signal overextension, whilst conclusive clearance of the 50 level means trend reversal.

puter system that allows you to select the weightings of these averages it will probably default to 0.075 and 0.15 for the calculation of the first differential and 0.2 for the moving average of the original line itself. As with most moving average systems, the signals come through when the line and its average (called the 'trigger line') cross. A sell is signalled when the first line crosses down below its trigger, and a buy when the opposite occurs. In the example in Figure 9.21 the signals were timely but, as is known from the introduction to this chapter, this sort of indicator is particularly prone to false signals when the uptrend is merely losing speed.

Figure 9.22 shows a classic example of a good buy signal when the medium-term downtrend reversed, and a false sell signal when prices merely

Moving Average Convergence – Divergence (MACD)

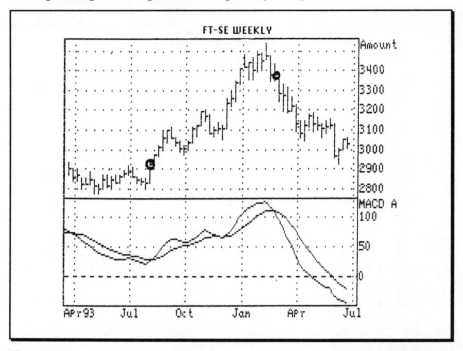

Figure 9.21   *Chart* by Reuters Technical Analysis

Momentum indicators fall into two categories: those that compare price today with price a certain period ago and those that effectively measure the distance between the price (or its moving average) and the core of the main trend. The MACD is one of the latter. It is another indicator which uses two lines crossing each other to give its signals. The first is the difference between two exponential moving averages of the price and the second is the moving average of the first; it is called the trigger line. It, like straightforward moving averages on price, is at its best when prices are trending, rather than moving broadly sideways. The crossovers in this example were timely.

consolidated the earlier gains and moved sideways at the start of 1992. Rather as with moving averages themselves, people have been tempted to try to overcome these false warnings by building in additional rules (filters).

One of the ways of confirming the cross from the MACD is to await a move (when prices are in an uptrend) below 0. It can be seen from Figure 9.23 this attitude would have averted sales when the summer reaction came through. Additionally, the differential between the MACD and its trigger line can be watched. In Figure 9.23 this appears as a series of vertical bars, often known as 'Forest'. While the differential between the two lines increases, then the signal is confirmed. But when these bars diverge from the direction of the two lines themselves, warnings not to take too aggressive a position come through.

Good buy signal and false sell signal from MACD

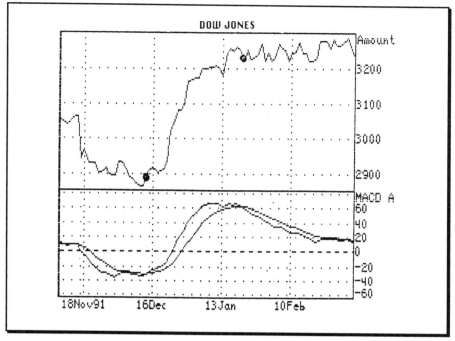

Figure 9.22

Chart by Reuters Technical Analysis

The first signal given by the MACD, a buy in December, was timely. But the January sell signal was premature and prices merely stopped rising, they did not reverse. However a momentum indicator is constructed, its role is to measure the speed of the trend. This means they can give very timely signals which lead to trend reversal; but equally, their signals can merely warn of the trend slowing.

It would be wrong to spend the whole of this chapter concentrating on 'modern' approaches to momentum without mention of the Coppock Indicator. Many years ago it was published on a regular basis in the *Investors Chronicle* by the now revered Harold Wincott. This was extraordinary since technical indicators were by no means a commonplace part of financial journalism in the 1960s. But the 'Coppock Indicator' was considered worthy of mention even then. It is an indicator which is based on long-term figures and is meant to give buy signals when it is likely the worst of the bear market is over and investors should re-commit monies to the market.

The version published in the *Investors Chronicle* is based on a ten month weighted momentum calculation. However, just before he died, I met Mr Coppock (a Texan who stood under 5 ft tall!) and he assured me his original calculation was based on twelve months. This was no coincidence, since he

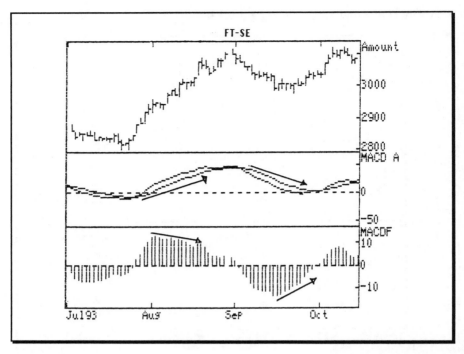

Figure 9.23   *Chart* by Reuters Technical Analysis

The histogram in the bottom window is the differential between the MACD line and its moving average – it is sometimes called the MACD Forest. When, as in August, Forest starts to fall while MACD lines are still rising, it warns of imminent reversal. The opposite signal came through in September.

equated a bear market in equities with a bereavement in the family and, on the advice of his priest, had determined the average period of mourning to be a year. Hence, he averaged the price of the index for each month over that period, calculated the difference from, say, November to November and, giving the first monthly differential in the calculation a weighting of one and the last a weighting of twelve, he summed the result. When it reversed its falls from below the mean line, a buy was given.

During periods when the stock market is enjoying cyclic behaviour, signals prove timely. But, as the long-term chart in Figure 9.24 shows, during secular trends very few signals come through. There is a good likelihood its time will come again. The one thing that should be noted is that Mr Coppock himself never intended the indicator to be used to give a sell signal.

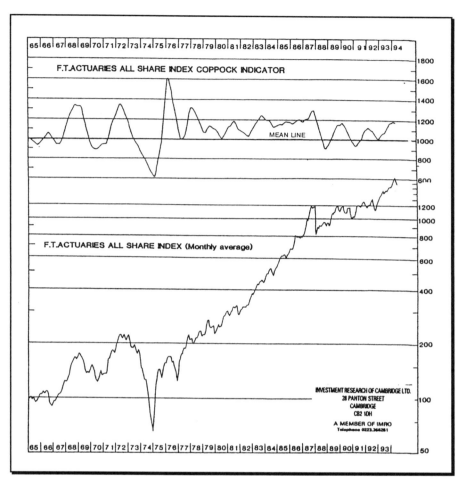

Figure 9.24   *Source:* Investment Research of Cambridge Ltd

Coppock Momentum is a long-term indicator, designed to mark times when it is safe to re-enter after a bear market. The buy signal comes through when the line turns up from below 1000. It is useful during periods when prices enjoy a regular cyclicality; when a secular trend is in force the signals are few and far between.

Much attention has been paid to the divergence aspect of indicators, rather than the overbought/oversold readings they can give. The indicator in Figure 9.25 pays no attention to speed and aims only to highlight overextension. It can be argued that life can be made too complicated (the American KISS principle – Keep It Simple Stupid – attests to this) and the indicator in Figure 9.25

Meisels Indicator

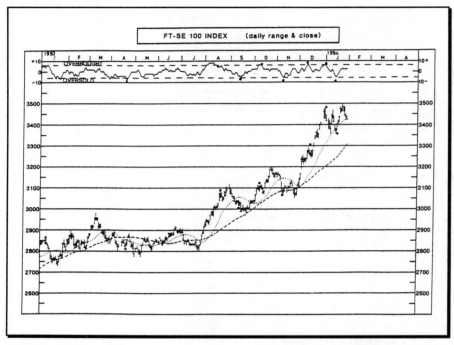

Figure 9.25

Source: Investment Research of Cambridge Ltd

The Meisels Indicator is simplistic in the extreme; it tallies the net number of times the market has closed up and down over the past 'n' periods (the default is ten). Readings of +/– 6 are considered overbought or oversold; it is more reliable when simultaneous RSI readings of 70 or 30 come through.

is seeking only to signal overbought or oversold. The concept is simplicity itself. Ron Meisels, a Canadian analyst, noted that it was extraordinary for prices to rise day-on-day for ten days. If they did so the market was over-bought and vice versa, if the market were falling. Thus, this indicator is merely the sum of the plus or minus observations day to day; no account of the size of the rise or fall is taken, just the fact the index in question was up or down on the previous day. Over time it becomes apparent that readings in excess of +/–6 are overextended. If the RSI is additionally over 70 or below 30 when such levels are registered, there is a high probability the market will reverse – near term at least.

A previously commonplace indicator on the trader's screen is called the Commodity Channel Index. It was developed by Donald Lambert and is also based on the relationship between a price and a moving average but it should be interpreted somewhat differently from other indicators.

The calculation involves the differential between the price and a moving average and the result is divided by the average differential between these two numbers over the period of the moving average used. It is based on the principle that really fast markets get overbought – only to get even more overbought. When the plot goes above 100 it is signalling the fact the market is trending upwards and should be bought. Long positions should be retained until the line crosses down below +100 – from which point on the market should be ignored (or traded with a short-term overbought/oversold indicator such as the RSI on the basis prices are in a sideways range). When the CCI goes below –100 it is signalling a short sale, a position which should be retained until the –100 level is crossed by the CCI on the upside again.

The signals that came through in Figure 9.26 on the FTSE using this approach were timely. Some argue it can be used to give buy signals when it crosses up through the –100 line and the sell signal would come through when it fell below the +100 level. In July 1992 the signal would have been timely but the early 1993 short signal would have been unfortunate.

Another indicator which monitors trend but does not attempt to identify overbought and oversold levels is called Accumulation/Distribution. It measures buying pressure (accumulation) and selling pressure (distribution) by comparing the difference between the two most recent closes. If it is a plus figure it is adjusted by the difference between the low and the previous close, whichever is the lower. If it is a minus figure it is adjusted by the difference between the high and the previous close, whichever is the higher. This forms a cumulative total whose plot should follow that of the price; if it fails to confirm new highs, as in February in Figure 9.27, this warns of trend reversal. The signal to sell comes when the trend in the ACD line is broken.

On one of the suites of software I use there is a very simplistic, and very useful, indicator called Rise and Fall. It too is a cumulative total; it starts at 100 and if the price closes up on the second day it becomes 101, and if it closes down it becomes 99, and so on. It is effectively expressing the balance between buying power and selling pressure and will usually look much the same as the price. But it can give some useful leads; in the chart of Brent Blend Oil in Figure 9.28 it first formed a base and then failed to confirm the price's move down to $13 at the end of March. It based and started moving strongly higher well before the base in the price – and then the uptrend – formed.

Figure 9.29 shows two indicators we have already seen in the previous chapter when addressing the analysis of the stock market itself – Volume/Price Trend and On Balance Volume. They are shown here on an individual stock. The analysis remains the same; when the indicator fails to confirm the price's new extremes a warning is given. The signal comes through when the indicator's trend is broken.

Considerable space has been given to some imaginative indicators developed by J. Welles Wilder, Jnr throughout this book. In this chapter the RSI

Commodity Channel Index

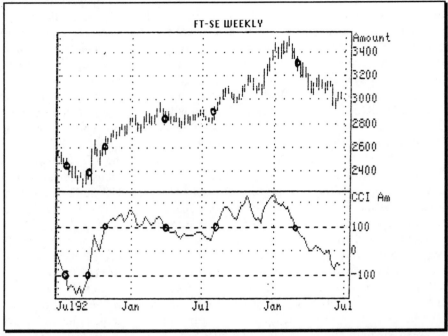

Figure 9.26

Chart by Reuters Technical Analysis

There are two views on the interpretation of the CCI. The main one is that buys are sig-nalled when it clears +100 and sells indicated when it falls below that level. Short sells come through when –100 is cleared, and closure indicated when the CCI moves above –100. Others argue clearance of –100 from below that point signals a buy and the stock remains a hold until the CCI falls below +100. The likelihood is that when the CCI is between +100 and –100 the market is in a sideways range.

has been looked at in detail and both the Parabolic Indicator and Volatility Index were touched on when trend monitoring was discussed. This is not to suggest all his ideas have found favour with market players – the Trend Balance Point and Reaction Trend Systems and the Commodity Selection and Swing Indices do not now appear on the popular software suites. But it seems fitting to end with one that does – the Directional Movement Index (see Figure 9.30).

The aim of Directional Movement is to rank all markets being traded on a scale of 0 to 100, with those in the upper part of the range enjoying a trend (up or down) and those in the lower section being in equilibrium (moving broadly sideways). Directional movement is gauged by comparing the range for the current period to that of the previous period; the basic increment of directional

Accumulation/Distribution

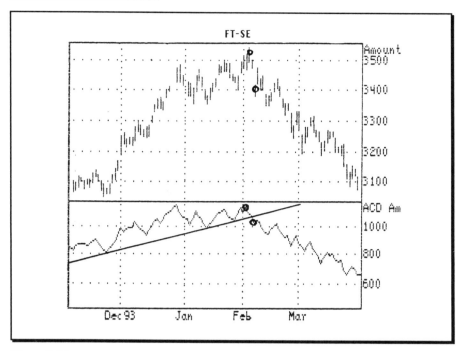

Figure 9.27   *Chart* by Reuters Technical Analysis

Accumulation/Distribution is a trend monitoring indicator. Its failure to confirm the FTSE's new highs in February gave an alarm. The break in the ACD's trend three days later signalled a sell.

movement is based on measuring the largest part of the current range that is outside the previous range, either on the upside or the downside. As with the RSI, the up directional movements are added together (as are the down ones) and a moving average (again, the default is 14) of each is taken. When the Plus DMI crosses the Minus DMI a buy signal is given and vice versa.

The chart in Figure 9.31 shows an average of the Directional Movement (ADX) – the result of amalgamating the DMI+ and the DMI– and its moving average, called the ADXR. It is the ADXR which gives the main signals; when it is above the 20–25 area it is said to denote a trending market and when it is below 20 the market can be considered to be trendless. Additionally, the ADXR can rise above the +DMI and –DMI; if it does so it is giving a profit-take signal on longs or shorts.

The ADXR shows up more clearly in Figure 9.32. From October through to the end of February it was above 20, identifying the Hong Kong market as being in a trending phase. Each time it peaked it was signalling the fact that

Rise and Fall

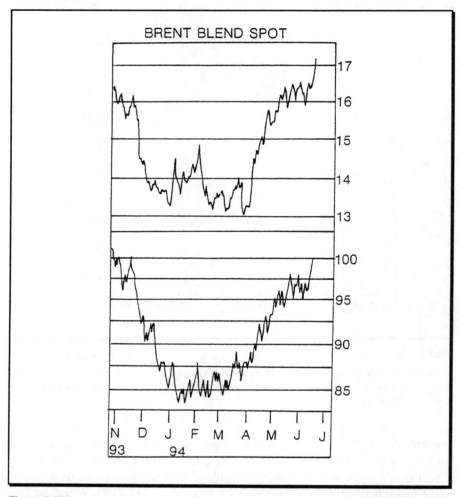

BRENT BLEND SPOT

Figure 9.28

Chart by Synergy Software's Technical Analyst

Another simple indicator which attempts to identify the buying power/selling pressure imbalance is Rise and Fall. It is the running total of the number of days (or period in question) a price closes up or down on the previous day, starting at 100. It formed a base in mid-March on this chart and its failure to go into new low ground when oil prices hit $13 gave another divergent signal. Since then it has confirmed the price's rise.

the trend was slowing and, in December, its rise highlighted the uptrend's re-acceleration. It can be a confusing indicator as a rising ADXR is signalling a trending market, but it is not stating that that trend is rising.

Volume indicators

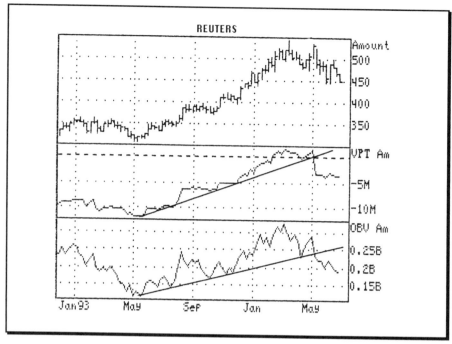

Figure 9.29

Chart by Reuters Technical Analysis

Both Volume/Price Trend and On Balance Volume amalgamate price and volume. Divergence from the price trend rings alarm bells and the signal comes through when the trend in either is broken.

The chart of the Treasury Bond and the ADXR in Figure 9.33 highlights this point. From June to October the ADXR was above 20, identifying the uptrend in the price. It peaked in September as the uptrend began to slow, giving good warning of the cross in the moving averages which came through in October. By late October it had fallen below 20, identifying a broadly sideways range in price. But it rose strongly through 20 again when the price broke down, this time confirming the existence of a downtrend. Its rise reversed towards the end of the chart as the downtrend, in its turn, began to slow.

The Directional Movement Index is popular with many but it is not always used as outlined above. Some find the comparison of the DMI+ and DMI– lines themselves most useful; they are usually a rough mirror image of each other but when they are not, and are at extremes, early warning of imminent trend reversal can come through. Others rely solely on the DMI, but however it is used, the concept is an interesting one. Throughout this book stress has

Directional Movement Indices

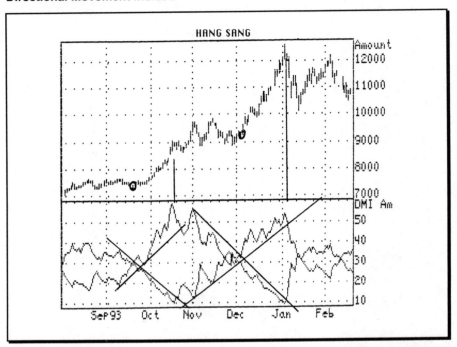

Figure 9.30   *Chart* by Reuters Technical Analysis

The Plus Directional Movement Index and the Minus Directional Movement Index can be used to initiate trades when they cross each other (the points are circled on the price chart) and profits can be booked if the trends in the +DMI or –DMI Indices are broken (marked with lines on the chart).

been laid on the fact that the market background should dictate the sort of discipline to be used and this indicator is useful as confirmation that the market is (or is not) likely to be trending.

ADX and ADXR

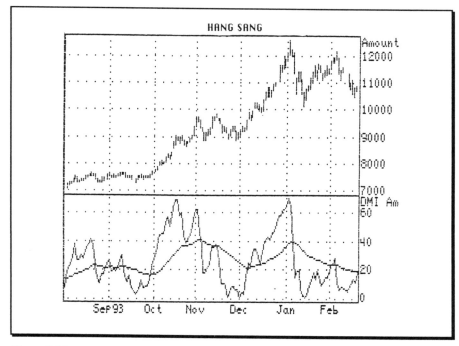

Figure 9.31

Chart by Reuters Technical Analysis

The Directional Movement Index is the result of combining the Plus DMI and Minus DMI. The ADX is a moving average of the DMI. The higher the ADX is on a scale of 0–100 the stronger is the market's directional movement, either up or down. The ADXR is a moving average of the ADX and when it is above the 20–25 range it identifies some trending activity. The higher its level, the stronger the trend so identified.

ADXR

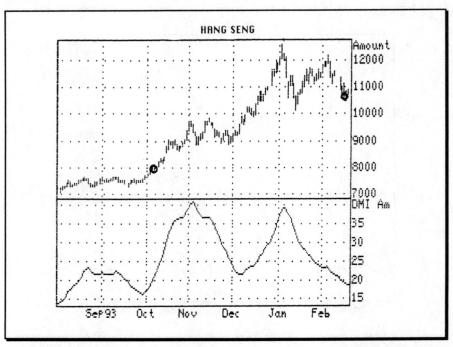

Figure 9.32

Chart by Reuters Technical Analysis

This chart shows the ADXR more clearly. While it is over 20 it is highlighting a trending situation, whether it is rising or falling.

ADXR rising whenever market is trending (either up or down)

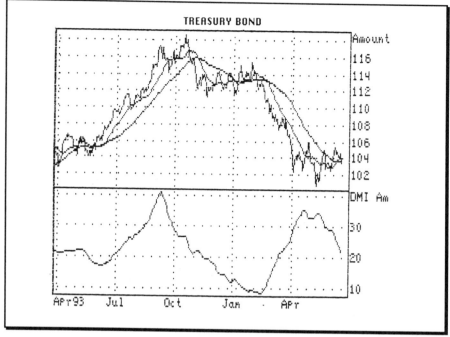

Figure 9.33

Chart by Reuters Technical Analysis

This chart of the Treasury Bond with the ADXR shows how the ADXR rises whenever the market is trending, either up or down. First it identifies the uptrend in prices. It then reverses, emphasising the fact the uptrend is slowing before the high is seen in October. It falls to a very low level as prices move broadly sideways over the turn of the year and then starts rising firmly, crossing the 20 line, to confirm the downtrend in the new year. Again, it tops out as the trend slows, this time emphasising the fact selling pressure is relenting.

10

APPLYING AND MONITORING DIFFERENT TECHNIQUES

- An investigation of the market background, using several price series and indicators to determine the likely outcome
- Methods for selection of the equity sector most likely to perform well against the already-defined market background
- The choice of a particular share for purchase and a programme for monitoring this investment
- What to do when the sell signals come through.

This book has now dealt with the basic techniques used by technicians to analyse the market and take investment decisions. This chapter is an attempt to pull them together and develop a discipline for use by a private investor selecting investments and monitoring his portfolio in a way which is timely, but allows for the fact that watching developments can only be a part-time commitment. It is not suggested this is the only way of using technical analysis to run a portfolio, nor is it suggested it is the 'right' way, and the variety of techniques available means there is room for individualistic approaches. However, this methodology should appeal to the cautious investor who has limited funds and wishes to trade reasonably actively, with the hope of utilising the rising trends in prices to make profits, but avoiding the periods when the risks of falls are greater. For practical purposes we will concentrate on only two investments here but the principles can obviously be applied to a fully diversified portfolio. More importantly, this section should give the new user of technical analysis confidence in his day-to-day role of monitoring his commitments.

The time is January 1991 and our notional investor has had a Christmas windfall; with all his financial commitments taken care of, he decides to consider an investment in the stock market. The technical situation of the market itself needs to be looked at first.

The long-term monthly range chart of the FT-SE Actuaries All Share Index in Figure 10.1 shows that the extremely strong uptrend in the UK stock market which had existed since the early 1980s has been broken. Indeed, following a challenge of the all-time highs, the late 1989 reaction low has now given way and it looks very much as though a large top has formed, signalling

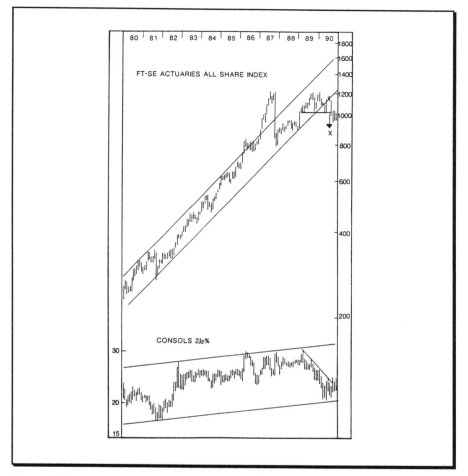

Figure 10.1

Source: Investment Research of Cambridge Ltd

The FT–SE Actuaries All Share Index has formed a top predicting further falls but Consols 2⅖% has broken its downtrend.

further falls. Measuring this top from the highs to the reaction low which has now been breached, and extrapolating that move, the falls could well extend to below 900 – a further 14 per cent from current levels. This suggests strongly that a stock market commitment now would be untimely to say the least. However, the chart of Consols 2½% seems to be telling a different story. Not only has the downtrend been broken, a base looks to have formed. In previous chapters historical comparison showed that a reversal in the gilt-edged market normally led, or accompanied, one in equities; against this conflicting background a closer look at the situation is needed.

Figure 10.2 shows daily plots and it can be seen that the monthly range chart of Consols somewhat blunted the exciting developments in the gilt-edged market over the end of the year. The chart of the Consols yield (the mirror image of the Consols stock itself) shows that, not only have recent falls breached the 200 day moving average, the last reaction low at 10.4 per cent has been broken and a double top has formed. There are two basic downside predictions which can be made for this yield – the major one is a fall of 1.6 per cent from 10.4 per cent (measuring from the 12 per cent high) and the other, more muted one, is of 1.2 per cent from the lower second peak at 11.6 per cent. Thus falls in long-term interest rates from the current levels around 10 per cent can be expected to extend by between 0.8 and 1.2 percentage points – more than adequate to support a rise in stock market prices. This analysis is supported by the base which has formed in the price Index of British Government Stocks Over 15 Years which completed at the beginning of December. Historic precedent suggests it is highly possible the apparent top formation in the All Share Index could prove to be an aberration.

The daily chart of the All Share Index shows clearly the large top formation and the resistance its neckline has subsequently offered to recent attempts at strength (see Figure 10.3). Additionally, however, it shows that, with recent falls holding over the autumn lows, two downtrends have been broken. Bearish factors are obviously diminishing, but they would only disappear if the

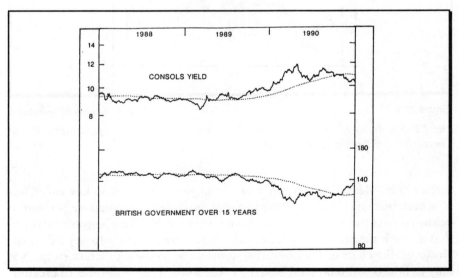

Figure 10.2　　　　　　　　　　　　*Source:* Investment Research of Cambridge Ltd

A top has formed in the Consols yield and a base has come through in the Index of British Government Stocks Over 15 Years.

Bearish factors diminishing but not disappearing

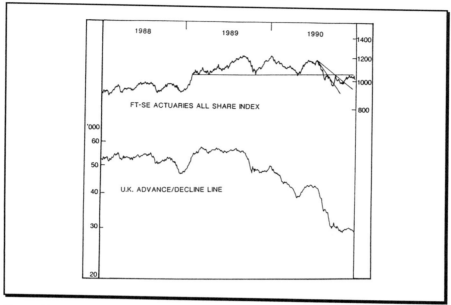

Figure 10.3

Source: Investment Research of Cambridge Ltd

Although the FT-SE All Share Index has broken two downtrends, rallies are still finding it impossible to clear the previous support level which is now offering resistance and the Advance/Decline Line is falling still.

critical resistance just over 1040 were to be cleared. But this is unlikely to happen now – the Advance/Decline Line has just hit new lows.

Whilst this indicator, as we know, has not put up a reliable performance over the past decade, it would seem unwise to ignore its message when it is so obviously highlighting the fact that large numbers of shares are still declining fast. Thus, although the gilt-edged market is hinting strongly that a recovery in equities is due, on the current evidence it would seem foolhardy to enter the market now, particularly as in the past the lead given by the gilt-edged market has, in some instances, been an exceedingly long one. Indeed, with short-term interest rates well over 10 per cent (the 3 months interbank rate is standing at 14 per cent) there is no need to move money off deposit yet. Meanwhile, the market needs watching closely and further analysis needs to be done now so that everything is in place to take action if and when the change of direction in the indices comes through.

In previous chapters we have looked at two other indicators which measure the health or otherwise of the market background. The first, the Yield Gap Ratio, is at a low level for the recent past, highlighting the fact the market is undervalued by historic comparison with gilts (see Figure 10.4). But so far its

Yield Gap Ratio and IRC new highs and lows

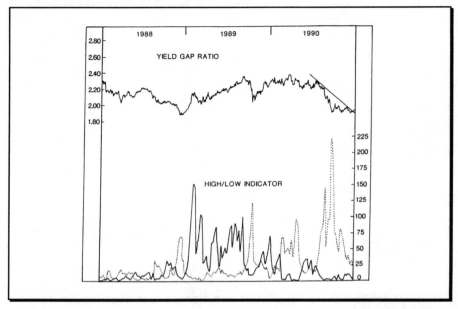

Figure 10.4   *Source:* Investment Research of Cambridge Ltd

The Yield Gap Ratio, already at a low level, has broken its downtrend but not reversed. The High/Low Indicator is falling from oversold readings.

downtrend, although broken, has not been reversed and, on a 'cheap is nasty' basis, there remains a danger it could get more undervalued yet. But the second indicator is showing more promise for the would-be bull; the IRC High/Low Indicator was registering very high numbers of shares in new low ground for the previous 12 months at the end of the year, but is not doing so now. Having become oversold, selling pressure on individual shares in the market has relented and they have stopped falling so fast; this is another strong intimation the picture could be set for recovery soon. The argument is becoming very finely balanced indeed.

By mid-January it is becoming clear that the decision to leave the money in the bank for now was a wise one. Selling pressure has increased and the All Share Index has fallen and is now testing its November lows for support (see Figure 10.5).

It is now early February; the November lows offered support and halted the All Share's decline. Indeed, a sharp rally has come through and it has proved energetic enough to break the third downtrend line – usually a strong signal of imminent reversal. The crucial resistance just over 1040 is being challenged

Resistance still in place

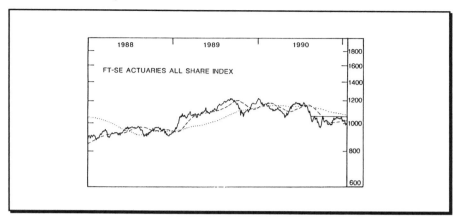

Figure 10.5   *Source:* Investment Research of Cambridge Ltd

The FT-SE Actuaries All Share Index is holding over its previous lows and the 50 day moving average has begun to rise. But the resistance remains in place.

and, since this is now the area where selling pressure from the declining 200 day moving average is likely to come into play, the situation is becoming ever-more critical. But other indicators are improving too and the challenge could soon be successful. The rally has been reflected in the Advance/Decline Line which has breached its immediate downtrend and there has been a sharp rise in the number of shares in new high ground for 12 months – the first such sign of strength since the All Share Index broke down. (See Figure 10.6.)

The indicators we have been monitoring closely give confirmatory signals. Now is the time to look at a leading indicator based on the speed of the trend, in this case the RSI (see Figure 10.7). A 13 week periodicity has been chosen as recent important lows have been roughly six months apart. Thus, half this cycle is a reasonable choice. The chart shows the FTSE Index, like the All Share, has broken its downtrends and is poised below 2200, the most recent rally peak. However, the RSI which has also broken its downtrend, has cleared its resistance, the recent highs around 51 which came through when the FTSE's 2200 highs were scored. This indicator is suggesting strongly the stage is set for the market indices to make an upside break.

Close monitoring has proved worthwhile (see Figure 10.8). The anticipated upside break has come through and a base has formed. This looks to negate the earlier downside prediction and, measuring from the lows below 2000, suggests a rise to the critical psychological resistance around 2400. Indeed, past experience has shown that if a pattern aborts – in this case the apparent top area – the scramble in the market to climb on board means that the subsequent predictions

All market indicators are becoming more positive

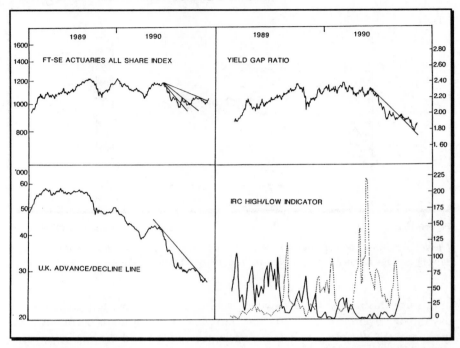

Figure 10.6   *Source:* Investment Research of Cambridge Ltd

The FT-SE Actuaries All Share Index has broken its third downtrend line, the Advance/Decline Line has breached its sharp downtrend, the Yield Gap Ratio has found support from the back of the previously breached downtrend and there has been a convincing increase in the number of new highs.

in the opposite direction can often be exceeded. If that were to happen in this case new all-time highs would be scored. The background should be checked again to ensure this potentially very bullish picture is confirmed.

With the All Share Index having cleared 1040, the charts of the other indices and the indicators suggest strongly the strength in the FTSE is genuine and should be followed through. A similar base has formed in the FT Ordinary and the sharp rise in the Yield Gap Ratio has cleared its previous rally peak. The A/D Line has behaved similarly and its rise is proof that this bout of strength is being enjoyed across the board. The fall in the Consols yield has extended, retaining the firm background from the gilt-edged market and, additionally, the interbank rate has now fallen through support, forming a top. This suggests that short-term interest rates are entering a long-term downtrend which should accomplish falls of at least another 2 per cent and

13 week RSI

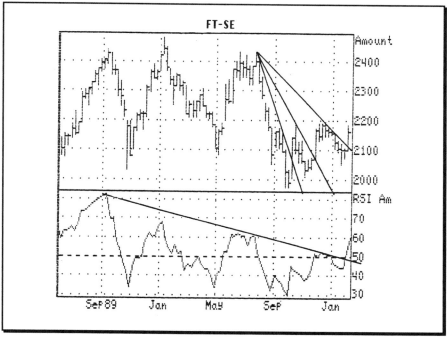

Figure 10.7

Chart by Reuters Technical Analysis

The FTSE Index has also broken its third downtrend line, as has the RSI which has also formed a base.

there is little reason to retain monies on deposit any more. Indeed, there is no technical reason not to enter the equity market now. (See Figure 10.9.)

The question of where to invest leads to an examination of the various market sectors. Were we attempting to build a balanced and diversified portfolio several areas would be selected in the normal course of events. However, on this occasion we are looking for one share alone, rather as though we were topping up an existing portfolio.

A close look at the F T Actuaries Sub Group Indices shows Brewers and Distillers have been extremely strong (see Figure 10.10). The ratio of this group to the market as a whole (the FT-SE Actuaries All Share Index is used for this purpose) is shown as the rising relative strength line below the price of the index itself; the uptrend has been in place for some time and emphasises this sector's consistent outperformance in the recent past. As can be seen, this is because this sector was not falling when the rest of the market was – not always a signal to buy at the start of a new bull trend. However, new highs in

Potentially very bullish chart

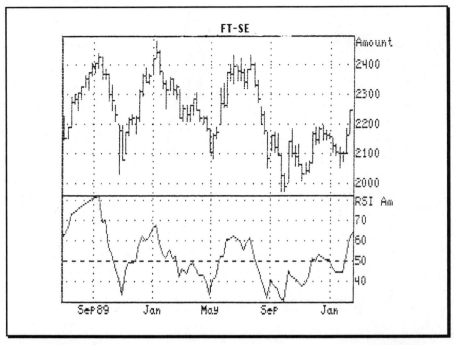

Figure 10.8

Chart by Reuters Technical Analysis

The FTSE Index has cleared its resistance and formed a base which should promote higher prices yet.

the index have been enjoyed during this current rise and, although they have not yet been confirmed by the relative strength, it remains in an aggressive uptrend, suggesting such confirmation could soon come through. Individual shares making up this index need to be examined now.

Looking at the major constituents alphabetically, Figure 10.11 shows Bass looking to hold good upside potential if new highs can be achieved. However, although attempts to move into new high ground are underway, they have not yet come through and this failure has forced a fall in the relative strength line which has allowed it to form a top. This is not conclusive evidence new highs will not be achieved but, with the monthly range chart highlighting the fact that the earlier aggressive uptrend has been breached, the overall picture lacks appeal right now.

The chart of Greene King in Figure 10.12 is very different from that of Bass. Over the past two years a serious downtrend has been in place but the recent bout of strength has taken out the rally peak, allowing a base to form.

Time to enter the equity market

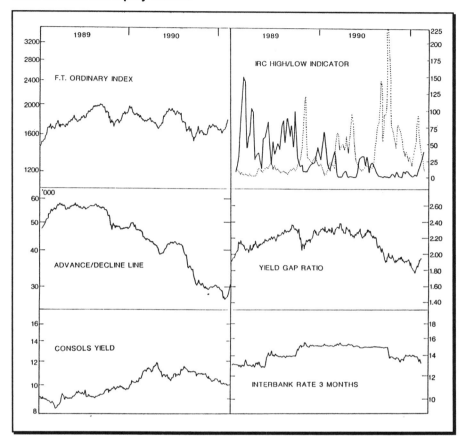

Figure 10.9

Source: Investment Reaserch of Cambridge Ltd

All the background indicators now look positive, particularly since the Interbank Rate has formed a top, implying short-term interest rates are likely to fall further.

Similar action in the relative strength line has also been seen. There is an implied move of 90p (measuring from 400p down to the lows around 310) which, from the point of breakout through the neckline, gives an objective of 460p, above which, as the monthly range chart shows, considerable resistance exists. But this is certainly an investment to be considered.

The picture of Guinness (in Figure 10.13) goes a long way towards explaining the sector's long-established outperformance. Whilst other shares, and the indices of the market as a whole, have been falling, Guinness merely stopped rising strongly and has, over the past nine months, enjoyed a bout of consolidation within its very well-established uptrend. Right now prices are

FT Actuaries index of Brewers and Distillers

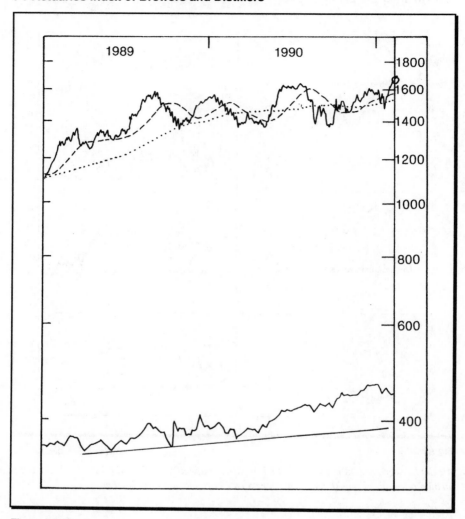

Figure 10.10

Source Investment Research of Cambridge Ltd

The rising line below the chart of the FT Actuaries Index of Brewers and Distillers is the relative strength line showing this sector to have been outperforming the market as a whole for over two years. The index itself has moved into new high ground.

poised to move into new high ground and, were they to do so, the current bout of sideways trading would look like a rectangle with an upside prediction of 90p (the chart's scale and this prediction have been adjusted to reflect an issue which has subsequently taken place). With both Greene King and

Bass monthly and daily range and relative strength

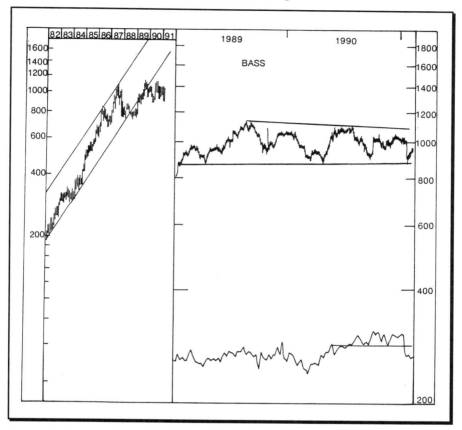

Figure 10.11

Source Investment Research of Cambridge Ltd

The monthly range chart of Bass shows a broadly sideways movement, as does the shorter-term chart. But the top formation in the relative strength line could prove ominous.

Guinness at similar levels and their upside predictions the same, the choice between the two is hard. However, the aggressive angle of Guinness' well-established uptrend in relative strength and the extraordinary pace of the advance in the monthly range chart must make it first choice if a clear move into new high ground is seen.

The charts of Highland Distilleries (Figure 10.14) and Guinness (Figure 10.13) are not entirely dissimilar in that strong rises in both have already been seen. However, whilst Highland Distilleries has just recovered strongly after severing support (and this could mean even greater rises are in store if new highs are seen), the picture is less dynamic than that of Guinness as far as the

Greene King monthly and daily range and relative strength

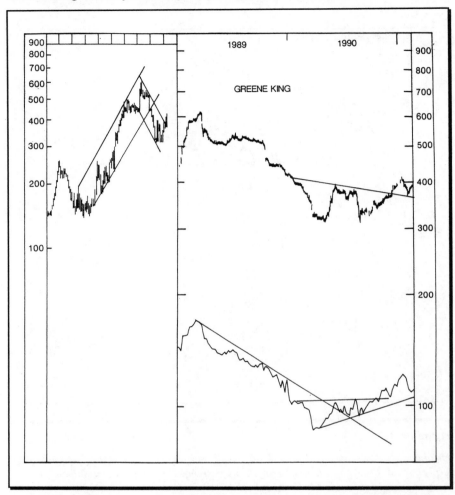

Figure 10.12   *Source:* Investment Research of Cambridge Ltd

Green King's downtrend has been broken and a base has formed. Additionally, an uptrend has formed in the relative strength line.

trends in the monthly range prices and the relative strength are concerned. It probably should rank as third choice among the front-runners right now.

Whitbread is another potentially strong picture (see Figure 10.15). Whilst its long-term rise has been accomplished at a somewhat slower pace than that of Guinness, its recent relative performance has been almost equally as good. However, the relative's uptrend is less well-established and looks to be stalling now. The trend has been breached, threatening the formation of a top.

Guinness monthly and daily range and relative strength

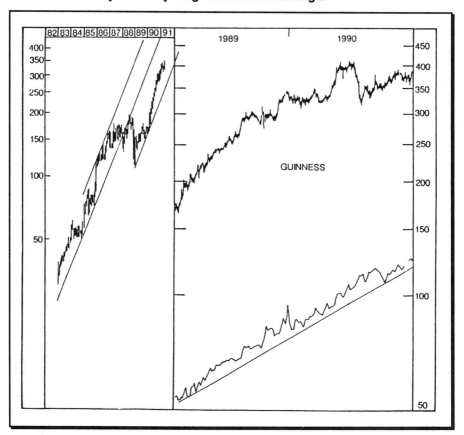

Figure 10.13   *Source:* Investment Reaserch of Cambridge Ltd

The rise in Guinness is continuing in an aggressive manner. The strong rise in the relative strength line suggests this share has been largely responsible for the sector's outperformance over the past two years. But the share is not yet in new high ground.

Wolverhampton and Dudley in Figure 10.16 offers a technical picture which falls between that of Greene King, where a reversal to the downtrend has been signalled, and Guinness where tight consolidation is underway, apparently prior to a move into new high ground. Wolverhampton and Dudley has seen a considerable correction but it by no means counts as a major downtrend. The upside break through the recent rally peak forms an intermediate base area which, measuring from the reaction low around 340p, gives an implied move of 90p, much the same in percentage terms to be looked for from Guinness. The choice is a hard one; however, the balance of the argument favours Guinness still as Wolverhampton and Dudley's upside

Highland Distilleries monthly and daily range and relative strength

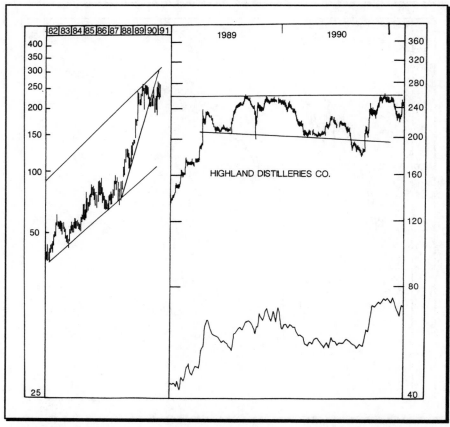

Figure 10.14

Source: Investment Research of Cambridge Ltd

Highland Distilleries shows an impressive long-term picture, but the picture is more mixed shorter term.

prediction can only be fulfilled if the previous highs are cleared. Since all-time highs are notorious as resistance areas, this could well mean the emerging strength could be delayed.

A close watch on the situation needs to be kept now and a daily range chart with the 20 and 50 day moving averages and the normal 14 day RSI can be employed for this purpose (see Figure 10.17).

Initially prices react from their challenge of the highs but bounce from the strongly rising 20 day moving average, which has just enjoyed a golden cross, up

Whitbread monthly and daily range and relative strength

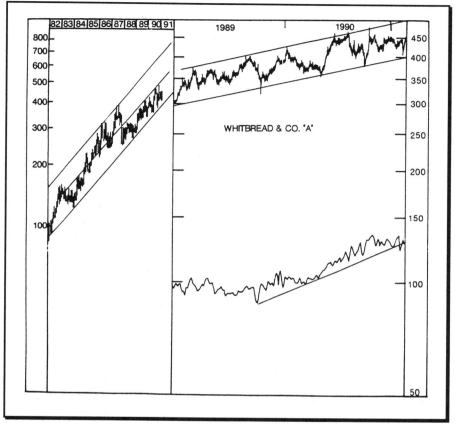

Figure 10.15   *Source:* Investment Research of Cambridge Ltd

Whitbread's picture is a basically positive one, but the uptrend in the relative strength line is looking vulnerable to reversal.

through the rising 50 day. Within a week new closing highs are scored against relatively high volume and a confirmatory move into new high ground by the RSI. Despite somewhat overbought readings near term, Guinness can be bought and watched now on a weekly basis unless danger signals suggest a closer look is needed. As momentum indicators lead on trend reversal the main monitoring will be done with the RSI, although relative strength will be watched too. Due to possible tedium (and space requirements) the illustrations are selected to show when changes occur, rather than publishing one every week over a rather long period.

Wolverhampton and Dudley Breweries monthly and daily range and relative strength

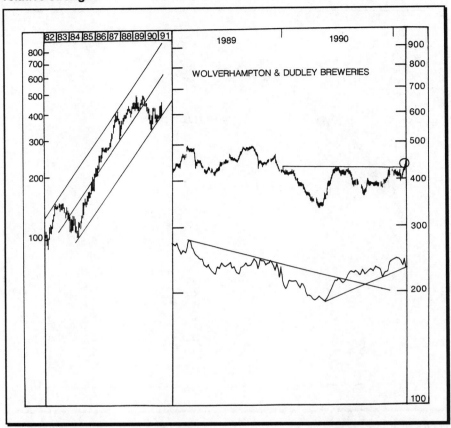

Figure 10.16   *Source:* Investment Research of Cambridge Ltd

Wolverhampton and Dudley's strong long-term uptrend looks capable of taking prices to challenge the highs. But the shorter-term picture is slightly less convincing.

Guinness daily range and RSI

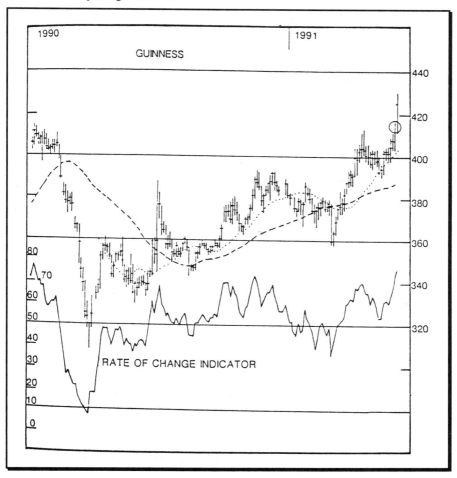

Figure 10.17

Source: Investment Reaserch of Cambridge Ltd

The daily chart of Guinness shows a clear break into new high ground, confirmed by the RSI.

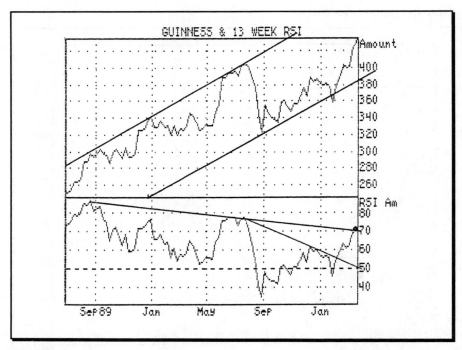

Figure 10.18

Chart by Reuters Technical Analysis

Figure 10.18: The rise has continued and the 13 week RSI has broken its downtrend, but not cleared the previous summer's highs. With readings over 70, the market is beginning to look a little overbought.

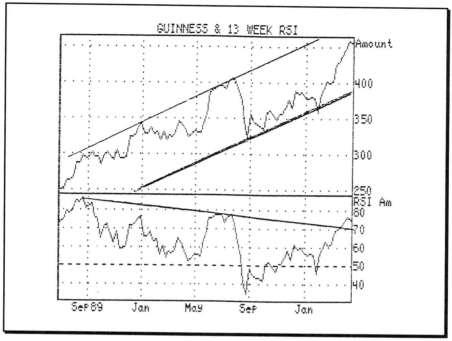

Figure 10.19

Chart by Reuters Technical Analysis

Figure 10.19: Despite earlier overbought considerations, the gains have extended and the RSI is now near 80. Some slight signs of hesitation look to be coming through.

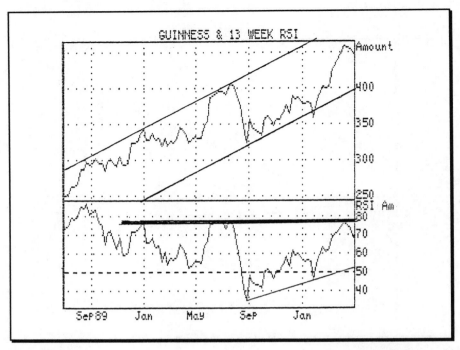

Figure 10.20

Chart by Reuters Technical Analysis

Figure 10.20: The RSI has failed to clear its earlier highs and a reaction has set in. This looks a normal development after a price rise of 50p and the uptrend should not be threatened.

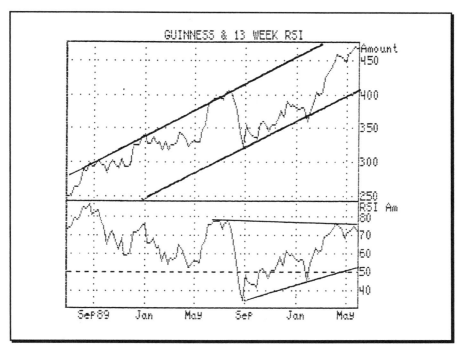

Figure 10.21

Chart by Reuters Technical Analysis

Figure 10.21: The reaction was short-lived and new highs have been scored. However, once again the RSI cannot clear its highs and, with the market again overbought, the rise in price is beginning to slow. But nothing serious is threatened yet.

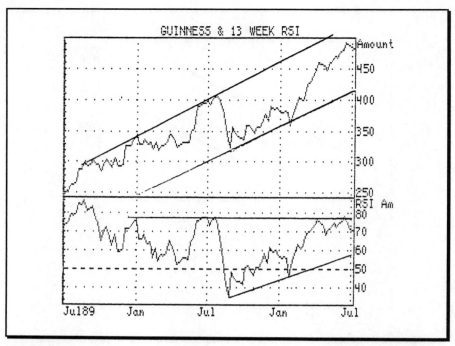

Figure 10.22

Chart by Reuters Technical Analysis

Figure 10.22: A reaction has come through again and the RSI has come back to test its previous reaction low just below 70. But it has not formed a top.

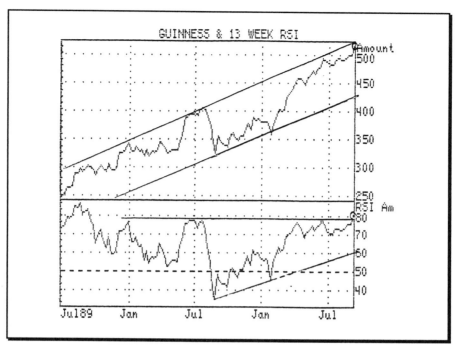

Figure 10.23

Chart by Reuters Technical Analysis

Figure 10.23: Our upside prediction has been fulfilled and there are two reasons to consider the market overbought. Firstly, the RSI is over 80 – a very high reading on a weekly chart. Secondly, the price is battling with resistance from the upper trend channel and a more sizeable reaction is becoming overdue.

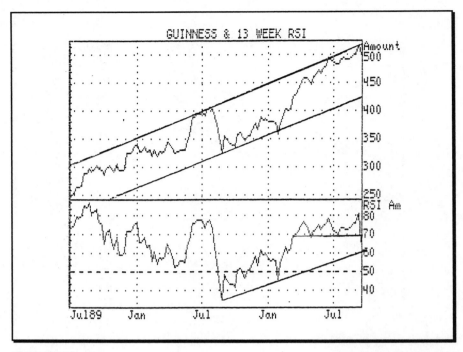

Figure 10.24   *Chart* by Reuters Technical Analysis

Figure 10.24: A rather sharp reaction has set in, causing the RSI to form a top. However, it remains in its uptrend and the likelihood is a bout of consolidation in price will come through.

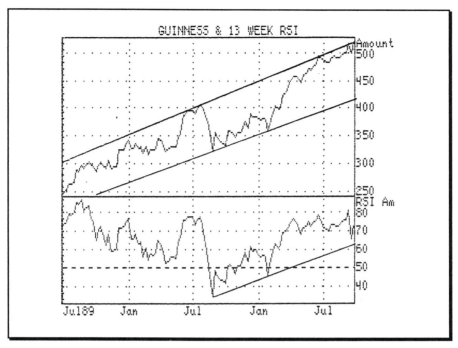

Figure 10.25

Chart by Reuters Technical Analysis

Figure 10.25: Extraordinary as it may seem, support has been established at 500p and new highs have again been scored. The RSI is back in its top area, giving no signals right now.

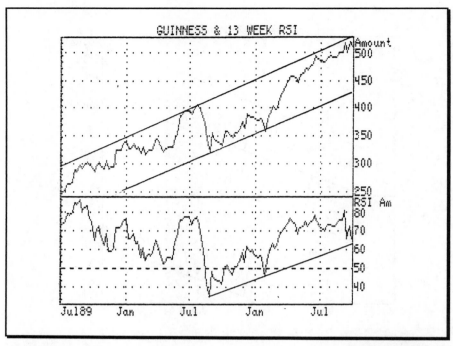

Figure 10.26

Chart by Reuters Technical Analysis

Figure 10.26: The price behaviour has now become very nervous, as selling pressure from the upper parallel to the trend channel continues to take its toll. The RSI has broken down once again and looks likely to test its uptrend for support.

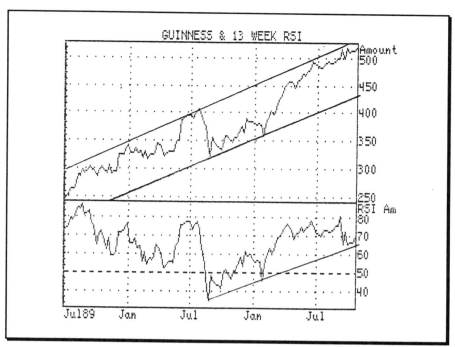

Figure 10.27

Chart by Reuters Technical Analysis

Figure 10.27: The RSI's uptrend has held and prices are, once again, in new high ground. But they are still faced with the barrier of the upper trend channel line.

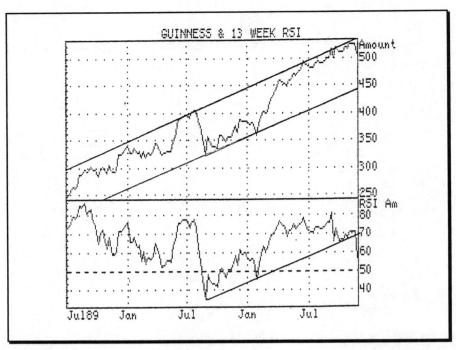

Figure 10.28   *Chart* by Reuters Technical Analysis

Figure 10.28: A more serious reaction is now likely. The RSI's trend has suffered breach and prices are, once again, testing the psychological support at 500. This is the initial support. The more important support is at 475 – the July reaction low. With upside targets achieved, nervous holders may wish to dispose of their shares but a glance at the relative strength looks worthwhile first.

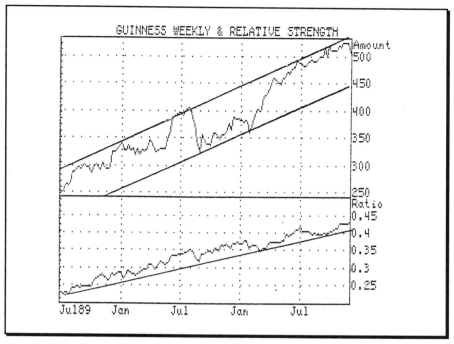

Figure 10.29

Chart by Reuters Technical Analysis

Figure 10.29: The very healthy uptrend in the relative strength line and its confirmation of new highs suggests supports for Guinness should hold. With the gilt-edged market still firm, only the most nervous holders should sell Guinness now.

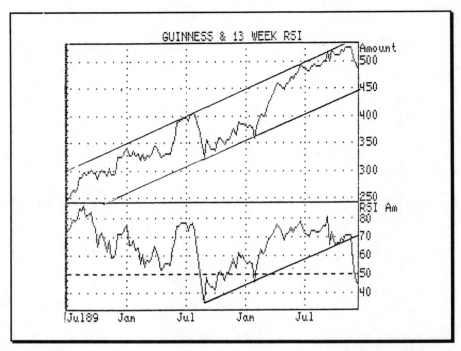

Figure 10.30   *Chart* by Reuters Technical Analysis

Figure 10.30: The RSI is below 50 suggesting that Guinness, in its strong uptrend, is becoming relatively oversold.

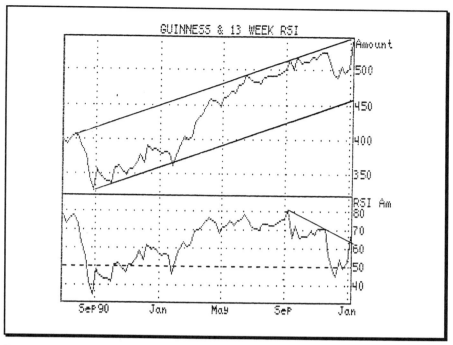

Figure 10.31

Chart by Reuters Technical Analysis

Figure 10.31: Supports have held and a strong rise has come through. Prices are in new high ground and the RSI has broken its downtrend. The new highs make the recent sideways trending look like a rectangle with an upside prediction to 590p (the distance between the 490p reaction low and the 540p previous high, extrapolated from the break through 540).

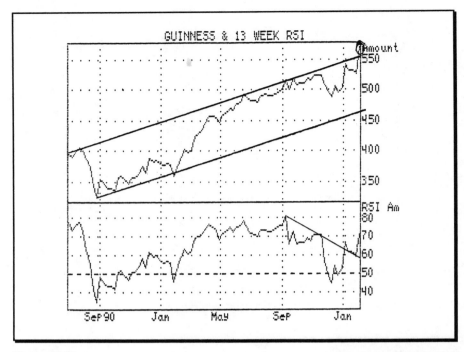

Figure 10.32

Chart by Reuters Technical Analysis

Figure 10.32: Once again the start of the year is bringing strength. After a reaction (when the RSI found support on the back of its broken downtrend) prices have not only gone into new high ground, but cleared the resistance from the original uptrend channel that had held them back for so long. Re-acceleration of an uptrend at a late stage in its development can rarely be sustained but it can carry prices higher short term. The new target could yet be met.

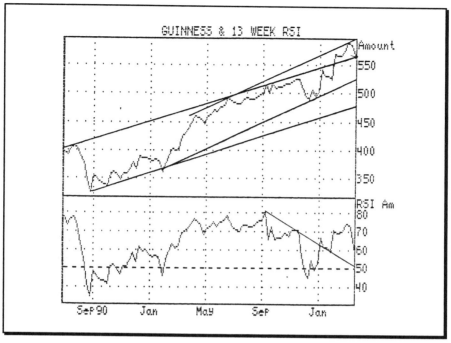

Figure 10.33

Chart by Reuters Technical Analysis

Figure 10.33: A sharper angled uptrend channel has been defined. Prices are reacting but the previous upper trend channel line which was consistent resistance, now it has been broken, should offer support

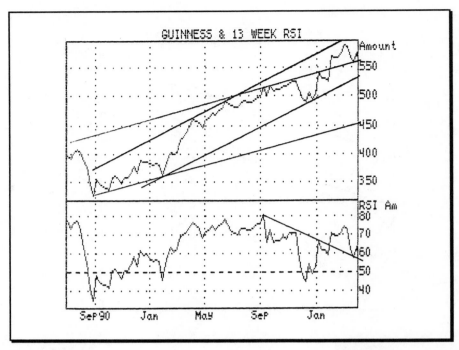

Figure 10.34

Chart by Reuters Technical Analysis

Figure 10.34: The trend channel line has offered support and the price has bounced. The RSI has bounced from its newly defined downtrend but needs to rally sharply if warning bells are not to sound loudly as its recent peak not only failed to confirm new highs, but it was also far short of that seen in September.

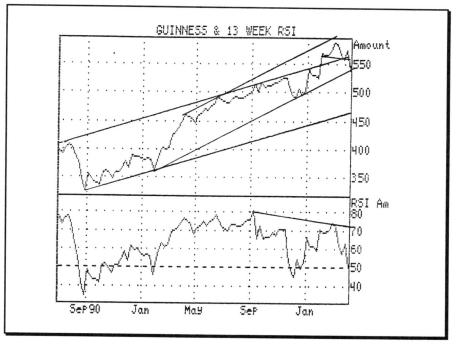

Figure 10.35

Chart by Reuters Technical Analysis

Figure 10.35: Alarm bells are ringing now. A small head and shoulders top has formed, predicting falls to around 520p – coincident with the January reaction low. But the uptrend remains intact. Relative strength should be examined again.

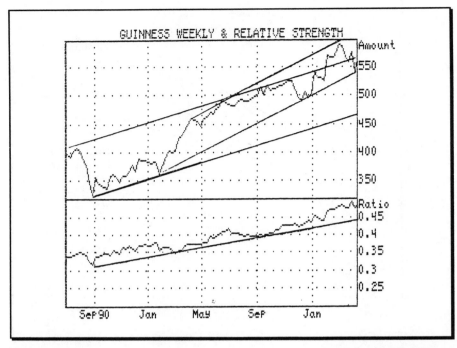

Figure 10.36   *Chart* by Reuters Technical Analysis

Figure 10.36: The rising relative line shows no sign of reversing yet. With the gilt-edged background still firm, this outperforming share looks less vulnerable than others. It will remain a hold while 520p holds.

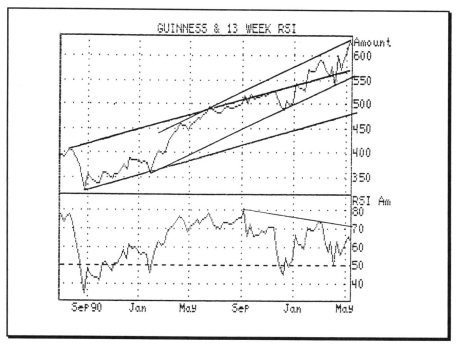

Figure 10.37

Chart by Reuters Technical Analysis

Figure 10.37: Prices bounced sharply from the uptrend line, not quite reaching the 520p downside prediction and previous reaction low support. New highs have now been scored (and the upside prediction fulfilled) but the RSI is in a downtrend still and, with prices up against the upper channel to the recently introduced sharply angle uptrend, Guinness is looking very vulnerable. Some sales at least should be considered seriously now.

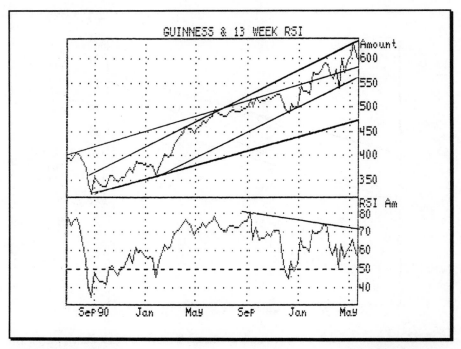

Figure 10.38   *Chart* by Reuters Technical Analysis

Figure 10.38: Prices are retreating but, near term, look well underpinned by support from the recent reaction low and the trend channel lines.

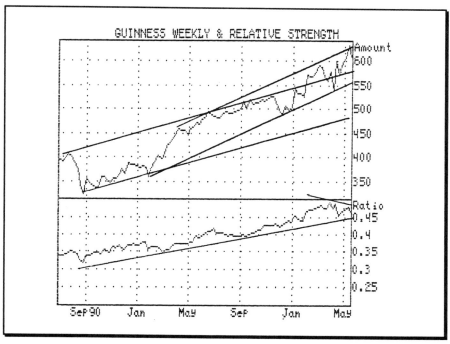

Figure 10.39

Chart by Reuters Technical Analysis

Figure 10.39: The relative strength line has not confirmed new highs. As we know, this is not the first time this has happened but, with no further upside predictions to go for and momentum declining (as highlighted by the RSI's downtrend) it could be signalling mounting danger now.

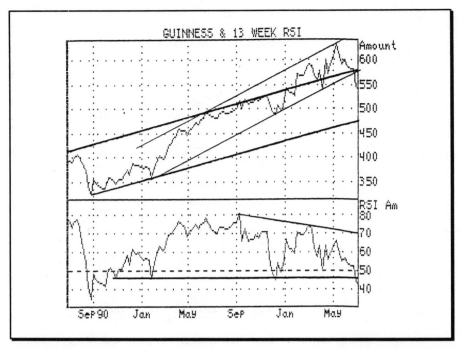

Figure 10.40

Chart by Reuters Technical Analysis

Figure 10.40: Support from the sharp uptrend has been breached. The reversal to this trend will be signalled if the 540p reaction low seen in April is broken. Falls could then be as large as 85p (measuring from the 625 highs) and support from the lower line defining the original trend channel would then be liable to test. An additional bear factor has come through; the RSI has broken support, implying the price is likely to do so too. Only those emotionally committed to Guinness, which has served them so well, would be willing to retain the shares then.

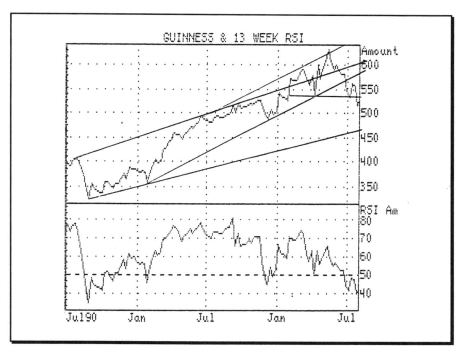

Figure 10.41

Chart by Reuters Technical Analysis

Figure 10.41: The top has formed. On this chart there is no reason for large falls not to come through.

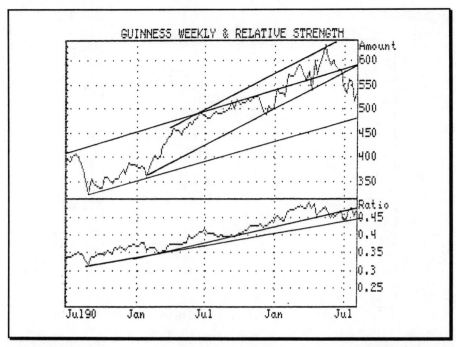

Figure 10.42

Chart by Reuters Technical Analysis

Figure 10.42: The most recent uptrend in the relative strength line has been broken, although the gentler one remains intact and it has not formed a top.

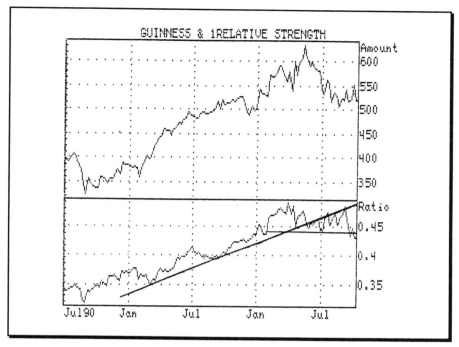

Figure 10.43

Chart by Reuters Technical Analysis

Figure 10.43: Eight weeks later a top in the relative does form.

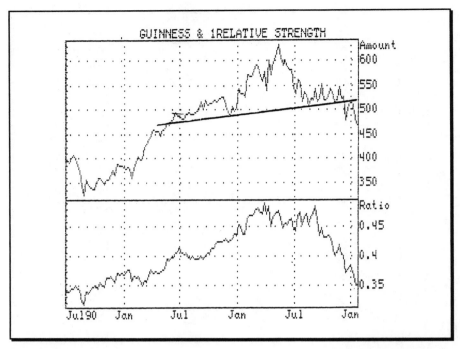

Figure 10.44

Chart by Reuters Technical Analysis

Figure 10.44: Six months later a major breakdown occurs.

It cannot be argued that my choice of Guinness was not without the benefit of hindsight; this useful indicator is of course very difficult to ignore! The charts in Figure 10.45 show the fortunes of the shares looked at earlier.

Bass eventually managed a gain of 16 per cent but its upside break did not come through for a year – the breakdown in relative strength in early 1991 gave genuinely good warning of poor performance ahead. Greene King's rise was 26 per cent to its high. Its upside prediction was exceeded but the earlier highs proved a barrier to more aggressive strength. The fortunes of Guinness we know only too well; here the strongly rising trends in the monthly range and relative strength charts served us well, highlighting the fact that strong performers frequently get even stronger yet. Highland Distilleries rose by 19 per cent but failed to fulfil its upside prediction. The rather ragged perfor-mance of its relative strength line warned of this eventuality. In the case of Whitbread, the breach of the uptrend in the relative strength line was a saving grace. Little else warned that, having exceeded previous highs, its upside pre-diction would not only fail, money could of have been lost. This leaves Wolverhampton and Dudley where our fears that the earlier all-time highs would prove a barrier were unfounded (at least in the long term). The original

Montage of all six shares

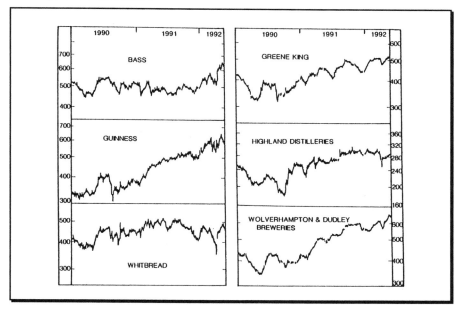

Figure 10.45   *Source:* Investment Reaserch of Cambridge Ltd

The updated picture of the Brewery shares seen earlier shows that Guinness was a good choice as would have been Wolverhampton and Dudley.

highs, 500p, held the advance for some weeks but, once they were cleared, steady gains came through. The maximum upside prediction was exceeded and gains from the point of breakout to the high measured 42 per cent.

Our notional investor's first foray into the stock market has served him well. He bought Guinness around 415p and should have averaged around 550p for his sales if he started unloading his position around 580p when the real danger signals came through, even if he left his final sales until the 520p support was breached. His capital should have appreciated by at least 30 per cent, enough to entice anyone to consider further investments now.

It is time to look at the overall market position again. Indeed, it should be kept under constant review, but in the background only, since the primary stress should be placed on the technical situation regarding the individual shares. Providing this includes the monitoring of trend and relative strength, major signals should not be missed. The All Share Index has achieved new highs but is reversing fast (see Figure 10.46). Once again, the background indicators need to be checked.

As Figure 10.47 shows, the falls in the All Share have been reflected in the FT Ordinary Index too, but the downtrend in the Consols yield remains intact. Once again the long-term interest rate background is conflicting with appar-

FT–SE Actuaries All Share Index reversing fast

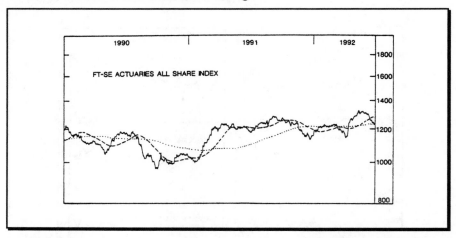

Figure 10.46   *Source:* Investment Research of Cambridge Ltd

The FT-SE Actuaries All Share Index, having scored new highs, is now reversing fast.

ently bearish stock market developments. In addition, short-term interest rates are falling still – the interbank rate has just nudged below 10 per cent. The Yield Gap Ratio is once again suggesting shares are relatively cheap and the IRC High/Low Indicator shows the number of new lows is highlighting a reasonably oversold condition. The Advance/Decline Line is, however, falling still. Despite somewhat lower returns on bank deposits than he enjoyed at the start of 1991, our investor might be best served to place his money in the bank for the time being at least and keep an eye on the market as developments come through.

The fall in the FT-SE Actuaries All Share Index has continued and intermediate supports at 1140 and 1120 have been breached (see Figure 10.48). This action, following the apparently abortive move into new high ground, shows that market analysis over recent months has been difficult to say the least. Additionally, it highlights the danger of relying on pattern analysis alone. However, the newly defined parallel uptrend channel (put in place since the strong long-term uptrend seen in Figure 10.1 was broken) has proved of consistent use and it looks very much as though this support has allowed a small reversal to be effected now. Upside predictions from this little reversed head and shoulders pattern cannot be considered large, and they have already been fulfilled, but the four month downtrend has been broken and, with the long-term uptrend intact, the picture could develop more positively yet. Once again the background indicators need to be researched.

Mixed picture

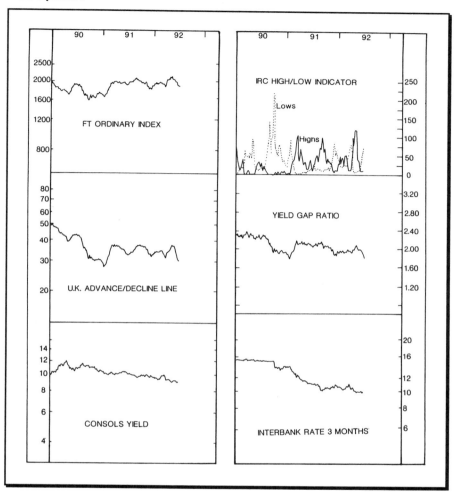

Figure 10.47

Source: Investment Research of Cambridge Ltd

The picture is mixed; although the Index is falling fast, the Consols yield is still in its downtrend and short-term interest rates are falling too. The Yield Gap Ratio is low. Readings on the IRC High/Low Indicator show a large number of highs having been scored in the recent past but new lows are increasing fast. The Advance/Decline Line is falling.

Figure 10.49 shows the latest situation. The past weeks have seen dramatic developments in the interest rate background as at first steps were taken to protect sterling's position within the ERM and then this attempt was abandoned. The 3 months interbank rate shot up to 14 per cent, only to reverse this

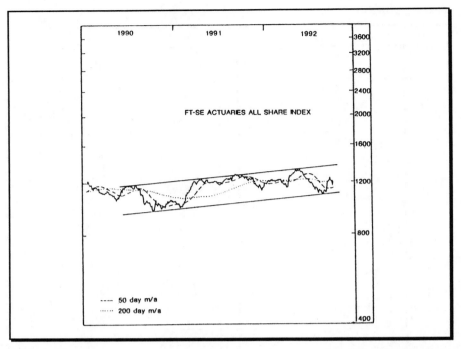

Figure 10.48   *Source:* Investment Research of Cambridge Ltd

Following the apparently abortive move into new high ground, the FT-SE Actuaries All Share Index has fallen fast. But it is now recognising support from the uptrend channel and has broken its four month downtrend.

move the following day and head straight down into new low ground. Meanwhile, the chart of the British Government Stocks Index Over 15 Years also suffered ill-effects from this drama; however, it has held over its critical support at 140, offered by the Spring lows. The Yield Gap Ratio, having achieved new lows, has recovered fast and the IRC High/Low Indicator, having scored high oversold readings, has effected a reversal. Also a small base in the Advance/Decline Line looks to be forming.

Among the various stock market sectors the banks appeal most (see Figure 10.50); the Index is edging into new high ground and the relative strength is rising fast. This attitude has served our investor well and, although he could take a different approach and look for recovery situations, he is not tempted to do so at this late stage in the bull market. After all, the reversal in the trend in long-term interest rates was two years ago. Historic comparison suggests this is the latter phase of the bull trend.

Going through a process of comparison similar to that employed on Brewery shares, the investor chooses National Westminster. The monthly

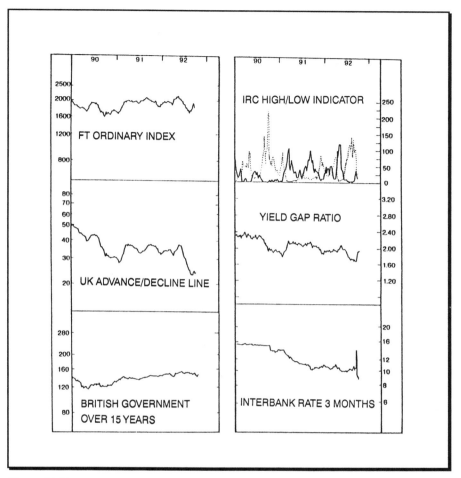

Figure 10.49

Source: Investment Research of Cambridge Ltd

The ERM crisis has unsettled all the price series, with the interbank rate in particular being forced to first move dramatically higher and then reverse the move by falling into new low ground. The Index of British Government Stocks has held its support and the Yield Gap Ratio looks to be recovering fast. The High/Low Indicator has scored a large number of new lows and there is a good chance the Advance/Decline Line could be effecting a reversal.

range chart shows a stodgy performance over the past four years, with prices still stuck below the 1987 highs (see Figure 10.51). However, efforts to make new highs seem to be increasing and, with the relative strength line rising strongly, they have a good chance of success. This time, instead of using the RSI as the primary monitor of the state of the trend, On Balance Volume is

FT–SE Actuaries index of banks

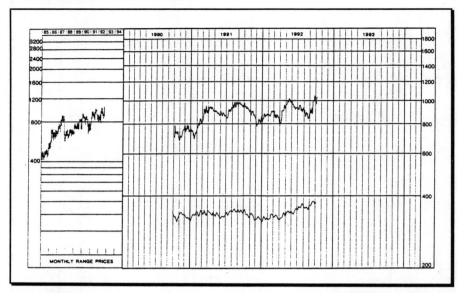

Figure 10.50

Source: Investment Research of Cambridge Ltd
Chart design by NNIF

The FT-SE Actuaries Banks Index shows a good relative performance and a move into new high ground.

used. It measures the difference between the cumulative volume for periods when the price goes up and when it goes down and it gives warning signals when it diverges from action in the price. When its uptrend is broken a sell signal is given and vice versa. Additionally, 13 and 21 week moving averages will be used to define the trend.

National Westminster Bank – monthly and daily range chart

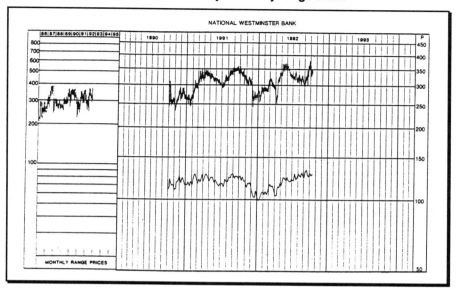

Figure 10.51

Source: Investment Research of Cambridge Ltd
Chart design by NNIF

Against a background of strong relative strength National Westminster Bank prices are attempting a conclusive move into new high ground.

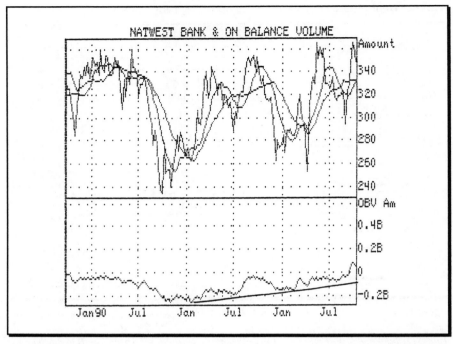

Figure 10.52

Chart by Reuters Technical Analysis

Figure 10.52: Prices are trapped below the recent 360 highs but the OBV line has managed a break into new high ground. It could be leading the market up.

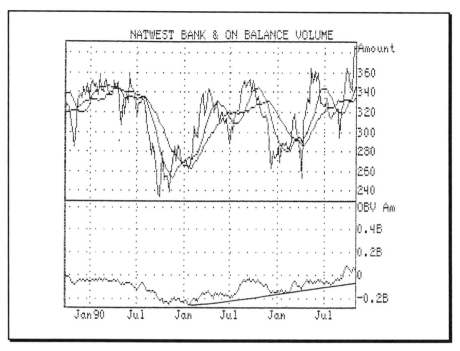

Figure 10.53   *Chart* by Reuters Technical Analysis

Figure 10.53: New highs in price have been scored. It is the signal to buy. The minimum upside prediction is 100p from the 360p point of breakout – the depth of the pattern stretching down to the most recent 260p low.

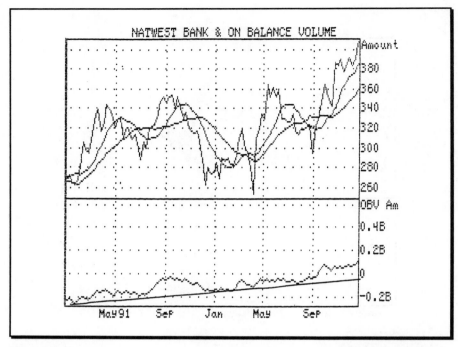

Figure 10.54

Chart by Reuters Technical Analysis

Figure 10.54: After a short bout of consolidation around 380p, new highs are again seen. These are confirmed by OBV moving higher yet. If it is argued this upside break from the short consolidation forms a flag, then the 460p target is confirmed as this can be considered a halfway hesitation and the move can be expected to extend by the same amount it has covered already i.e. 80p.

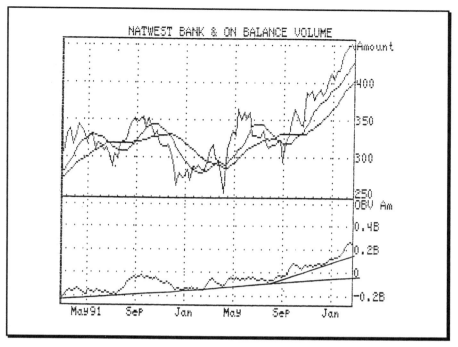

Figure 10.55

Chart by Reuters Technical Analysis

Figure 10.55: Prices are virtually on target now and, with the uptrend in the OBV accelerating, the pace of increase may not be maintained.

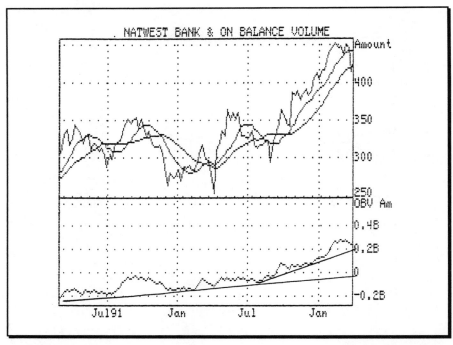

Figure 10.56

Chart by Reuters Technical Analysis

Figure 10.56: A small top area has been formed by prices breaching the reaction low at 440p. Its downside prediction has already been fulfilled, however, and against this background there is good reason for the longer-term moving average to offer support. This is particularly the case since the accelerated uptrend in the OBV remains intact.

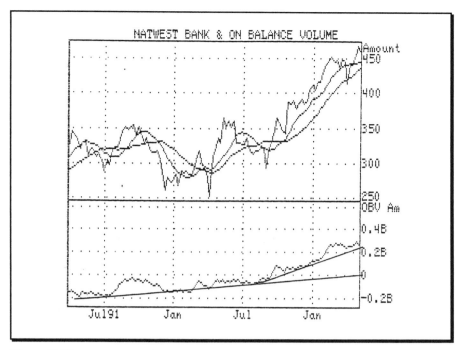

Figure 10.57

Chart by Reuters Technical Analysis

Figure 10.57: Prices have bounced from support offered by the moving average and achieved new highs. These have been confirmed by the OBV. We can now consider the consolidation between 455 and 415 (the reaction low) a rectangle and estimate another upside target of 495p.

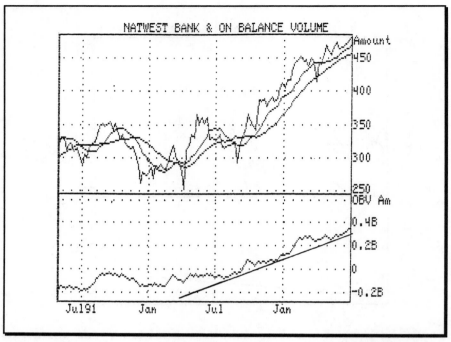

Figure 10.58

Chart by Reuters Technical Analysis

Figure 10.58: Further gains have been made but the two moving averages are drawing together, highlighting the fact the uptrend is slowing somewhat. However, the strong trend in the OBV continues – trend reversal is not likely yet.

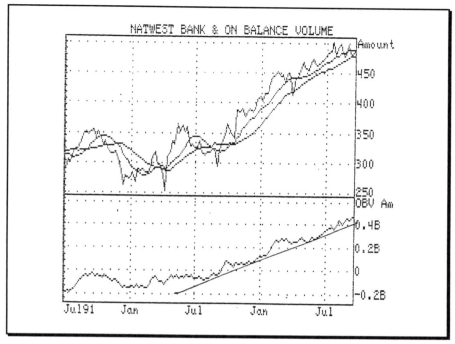

Figure 10.59

Chart by Reuters Technical Analysis

Figure 10.59: Our recently introduced upside target of 495p has been fulfilled and prices are consolidating, once again testing the longer-term moving average for support. However, OBV is rising strongly still, suggesting this support should hold.

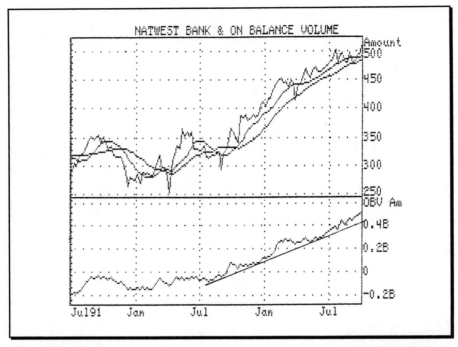

Figure 10.60   *Chart* by Reuters Technical Analysis

Figure 10.60: New highs in price are again confirmed by OBV. This means another upside prediction can be put in place; measuring from the 510 original high down to the 470 reaction low gives an implied move of 40p – to 550.

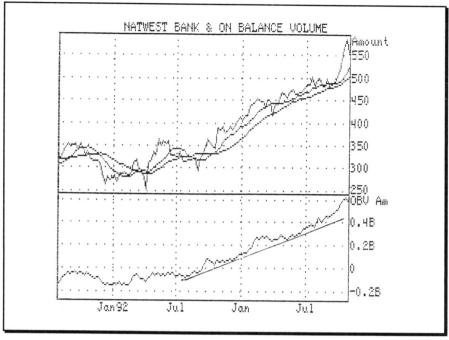

Figure 10.61

Chart by Reuters Technical Analysis

Figure 10.61: The upside prediction has been exceeded and, with prices well above the moving averages and looking overbought, the reaction which has set in could extend. But the OBV picture remains positive and the uptrend should hold.

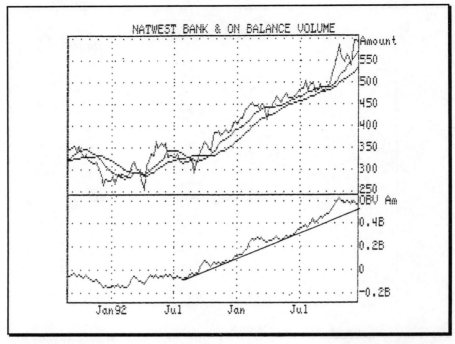

Figure 10.62

Figure 10.62: Prices have bounced from support offered by the shorter-term moving average and have achieved new highs. However, these have not been confirmed by the OBV – this should serve as a warning signal the trend could be tiring. Certainly, it would be unwise to come up with further upside targets now.

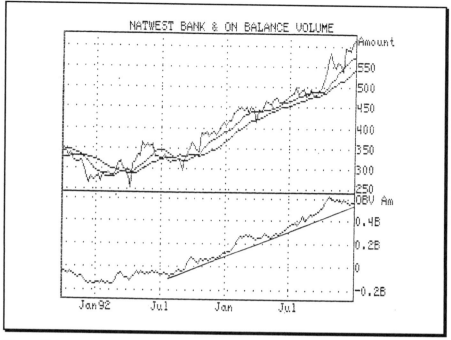

Figure 10.63

Chart by Reuters Technical Analysis

Figure 10.63: Further new highs, but still the OBV does not confirm.

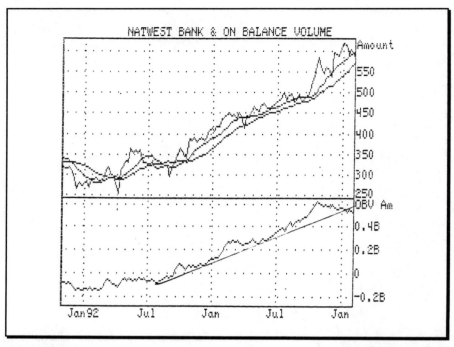

Figure 10.64

Chart by Reuters Technical Analysis

Figure 10.64: A small head and shoulders top with a neckline at 580p looks to be forming; its downside prediction would be to below 550p, i.e. the late 1992 reaction low. But, more importantly, the uptrend in the OBV has at last been broken. This looks a strong sell signal now.

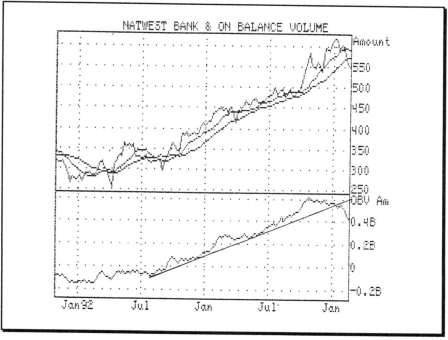

Figure 10.65

Chart by Reuters Technical Analysis

Figure 10.65: The head and shoulders has formed and prices are in the targeted region. If this support is broken a major reversal will be signalled.

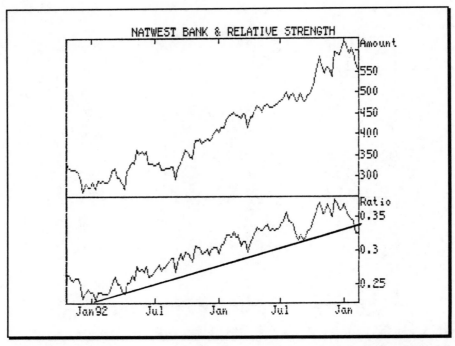

Figure 10.66   *Chart* by Reuters Technical Analysis

Figure 10.66: This is the first time we have published the relative strength line because, as can be seen, it has only just formed a top and broken its uptrend. In this example the OBV has proved a more timely indicator.

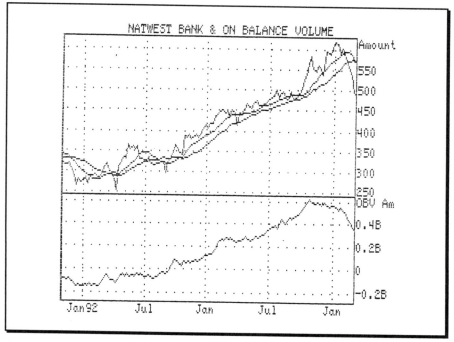

Figure 10.67

Chart by Reuters Technical Analysis

Figure 10.67: Support has been severed and the moving averages have moved into bearish sequence. Trend reversal has been confirmed.

These two examples of monitoring trends have taken us through to early 1994. By the time the signal to sell NatWest came through, the downtrend in Consols yield had been reversed and the IRC High/Low Indicator was registering extremely high readings of nearly 200 new highs. The All Share Index had risen to levels above its upper parallel to the uptrend channel (as we saw in earlier chapters in this book) and the somewhat unreliable Advance/Decline Line was consistently scoring new highs. The Yield Gap Ratio was at relatively high levels – over 2.2. All the signs of an overheated market were in place and our investor wisely decided that, despite low short-term interest rates still, he would put his money in the bank and stand aside.

These practical examples have, of course, benefited considerably from hindsight. For instance, I freely admit the choice of the OBV rather than the Volume/Price Trend Indicator was no coincidence – it put up a much more timely performance. Obviously, it is not possible to achieve such consistent success at timing investments every time. However, I have sketched out what I believe to be a sensible approach, incorporating checks and balances which should enable the basic rules of technical analysis to be put to good use. As I have said before, the many aspects of this art allow each individual to design a system that suits his or her attitude to investment best. But all should incorporate the core benefit of using charts – discipline. This way even an inexperienced analyst should be able to avoid the more serious mistakes which can be made when vision is distorted by the emotions of the crowd and, hopefully, over time he should achieve above average returns.

11

THEORIES

- Cycle theory is summarised – and mention is made of the famous cycles
- The Dow Theory – upon which Technical Analysis as it is used today is based – is summarised
- The Elliot Wave Theory – a sophisticated form of price/motion analysis applied to charts – is looked at. Elliott believed price action was part of a natural law of the universe and could be broken down into pattern, ratio and time. These concepts are addressed.
- Gann similarly believed the behaviour of price was a function of a natural law which responded to certain price levels – and time. His Theory is summarised and emphasis is placed on his view that 'when price meets time a change is imminent'.

The previous chapters have been devoted to an explanation of the basic concepts of technical analysis with the patterns, trends and their reversals explained by investor psychology. There are, additionally, some well-known theories that take this basic concept and address market analysis in a more scientifically rigorous manner, believing that the actions and reactions of investors are part of a larger pattern of things which affect all aspects of life. This, the final chapter, is devoted to a brief summary of these concepts.

Some mention of price cycles has already been made but they need re-addressing now as it is upon their recognition that the major theories are based. Cycles and their analysis are by no means associated only with the financial world. Natural cycles such as the seasons, night and day and the ebb and flow of the tide are obvious ones. Even in Biblical times, cycles in crop yields were evident – Joseph's seven fat years leading to seven lean ones. Cycles and their analysis are well accepted in the modern world; it is recognised that patterns, or waves, enjoy a rhythm and repeat and such repetition results in the recurrence of events and, hence, predictability. Thus, major research projects abound and the results are given total reliance in many spheres. As part of our day-to-day lives we accept without question the time for lighting up, high tide, etc.

It is the basic concept of cycles that underlies the theories of the three famous Americans, Dow, Gann and Elliott. The normal illustration of a cycle will look like a sine wave (see Figure 11.1).

The y axis is devoted to price (or variation) and the x axis represents time. Cycle terminology denotes the lows as 'troughs', the highs as 'peaks' or 'crests'

Illustration of a cyclic wave

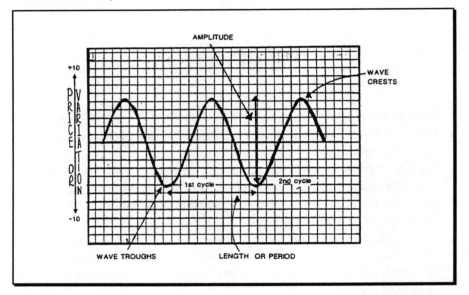

Figure 11.1   Source: Investment Research of Cambridge Ltd

and the depth of the waves is called the 'amplitude'. The length or 'period' of the cycle is measured from trough to trough; purists argue that a minimum of five observations of troughs an almost equal distance apart are necessary before the cycle can be recognised. This is fine if short-term cycles are being defined but cycles co-exist on all timescales and sometimes very long-term data is not available, meaning three observations have to suffice until more data is collated.

There are many famous cycles of varying periodicity which have been recognised in a variety of financial price series. A Russian economist, Kondratieff, published a work in 1926 showing a 54 year cycle in the US economy and others have found a similar cycle in the UK economy stretching over several hundred years. Similarly, Lord Beveridge found evidence of the same cycle in wheat prices over several hundred years up to the publication of his work in 1869. The Kitchen cycle (40 months) can commonly be found operating in commodity prices and interest rates and commodity traders can often be found using a periodicity of 28 days in their analyses, reflecting the lunar cycle.

One of the most easily recognised cycles is the four year cycle on Wall Street whose regularity is no doubt at least partially influenced by the four year Presidential term. Figure 11.2 shows over 30 years' history of the Dow Jones Industrial Average and it can be seen that the lows in the price falls are roughly four years apart during this long history. It is interesting to note that the sharp falls in the crash of 1987 were 'overdue' on a cyclical basis – the bull market was so strong the turning point was missed by a year! Although the

Long-term US stock market cycle

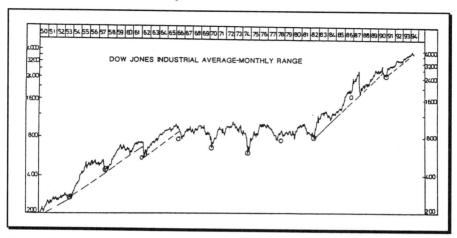

Figure 11.2   *Source:* Investment Research of Cambridge Ltd

lows were, overall, regular occurrences roughly four years apart, the highs enjoyed 'right translation' during the major upward phases, emphasising the fact that prices during these periods spent more time rising than falling. 'Left translation' can also occur, often in commodity price series, and it is for this reason cycle lengths are measured from trough to trough.

The recognition of these cycles in price led Dow, Gann and Elliott to examine the movements closely and their Theories, used rigorously, should assist investors in discovering where in the cycle they are and what to expect next.

DOW THEORY

Dow's name has cropped up on many previous occasions in this book since his Theory's basic principles are very much at the heart of technical analysis as it is used today. Although the ground has, to a great extent, been covered already, the Theory is outlined formally here since it also formed the basis of Elliott's later work.

Charles Dow was editor of the *Wall Street Journal* and, towards the end of the last century, he devised two market averages – the Industrials and Rails. His Theory is based on the closing prices of these Averages alone.

The basic principles of the Dow Theory state:

(1) The Averages Discount Everything (except Acts of God)

Dow believed the movements of his two Averages reflected the sum of all known factors likely to influence the economy, including the investors' hopes and fears. Events likely to take the market completely by surprise (Acts of

God, such as earthquakes, floods and frosts) would not be discounted in the price. However, once they had occurred he believed their effect would be factored in quickly.

(2) The Trends

Dow defined three types of trend. The primary trend was the one he considered of greatest interest to investors and estimated it would likely last for a year or more. An uptrend should have successively higher peaks and troughs and, while this remained the case, it would be considered intact. The opposite set of circumstances – falling peaks and troughs – would define a downtrend. He likened these major trends to the tide; the tide would remain in (and the trend up) as long as the waves continued to cover new sand. Dow's signal that the primary uptrend had reversed was when new highs were no longer scored and the reaction breached the previous reaction low.

Dow's second trend definition concerned the reactions against the main trend. These he likened to the waves and estimated they should last between three weeks and three months, correcting between one-third and two-thirds (often 50 per cent) of the previous move. He called them intermediate or secondary trends.

The third definition concerns the near term fluctuations, usually lasting less than three weeks, which make up the secondary trends. These he called minor or tertiary trends and likened them to the ripples.

(3) Bull and Bear Markets

The primary bull trend should break down into three phases of advance, interrupted by secondary corrections. The initial rise is one of accumulation where bargain hunting in the depressed stock market causes prices to stop declining and then advance steadily. It most likely will take out the last rally peak in the downtrend, giving Dow's reversal signal. The next stage of strength is likely to be more vigorous as the news improves and more investors come on board. The third, and last, advance is usually enthusiastic, but often short, as bullish headlines become common and late-comers rush to get in on the ride. However, volume is often poor.

The bear market enjoys three main phases of weakness. There is the initial distribution which comes through once the top forms and volume is usually high. After a relatively short pause, the next phase of weakness extends quickly as news deteriorates and investors rush to get out. The third stage, usually preceded by a secondary correction, is a steady decline as news worsens. Volume is usually low, with prices sinking due to lack of buyers more than a rush of late selling, although sometimes a selling climax can come through.

(4) Lines

Dow noted that secondary corrections did not always occur. Sometimes, instead, prices would trade tightly sideways, often within a band as narrow as 5% of the price. The line is a version of a rectangle and is more likely to occur in a bull, rather than a bear, market. It highlights strength and the breakout, when it occurs, is likely to be faster than when a secondary trend is reversed.

(5) The Averages Must Confirm

Dow believed that if the economy was liable to turn then both his Averages should reflect this since a pick-up in demand would favour industrial companies and railroads alike. Thus, a bull market would only be signalled once both Averages had cleared their last rally peak in the downtrend; and a bear market would only come in when both had broken their previous reaction lows. Until such time as the lagging Average confirmed the other's break, the previous trend could be considered ongoing. Additionally, Dow considered new all-time highs were important, arguing that if investors were prepared to pay more than had ever been paid before, then they must have reason to believe prospects were particularly good. But only if both Averages hit new highs would the signal that the rise would extend significantly be confirmed.

(6) A Trend Continues Until it is Reversed

Whilst Dow estimated the length of a primary trend as a year or more, the Theory emphasises it is not reversed until the series of rising peaks or declining troughs comes to an end. The main signal comes through when the last reaction low in an uptrend or the last rally peak in a downtrend is broken.

There is some confusion among Dow Theorists as to how to weight the two possible signals. Some argue that if prices move into new high ground and then reverse and break the reaction low, that is less bearish – because one of Dow's bull market tenets, the move into new high ground, is there – than if they first fail to make new highs and then break the reaction low. I personally do not go along with this view since I would argue that if prices first fail to maintain their new highs and then breach both the previous rally peak and the reaction low, something has unsettled investors badly. But the Dow Theory itself does not amplify. Equally, the argument can be applied to a downtrend's reversal following a fall into new low ground.

(7) Volume Goes With Trend

Dow placed the greatest emphasis on price but believed volume was a good confirmatory indicator. In a rising market it should expand on strong days and contract if reactions set in, and vice versa in a falling trend.

Those are the main tenets of the Dow Theory and, as has already been seen, most have been adopted in one way or another to form the core of technical analysis as we know it today. The part of the Theory that links it to the more rigorous, mathematically-based, Elliot Wave Principle is Dow's observation that trends have three main phases of advance which are likely to be corrected by certain percentage movements. Elliott, previously completely unconnected with the stock market, devised his Theory after studying the Dow Theory and Averages while convalescing from a serious illness in the 1930s. Many believe that Elliott's mathematically-based retracements and objectives enhance the wave examinations immensely since they overcome the main criticism of the Dow Theory, i.e. the relatively late entry and exit points. Elliott himself believed his Theory was part of a larger law established throughout the universe. He called his major work (published in 1945) 'Natures Law – The Secret of the Universe'.

ELLIOT WAVE PRINCIPLE

The Elliot Wave Theory is a sophisticated form of price motion analysis applied to price charts. Elliott devoted his attention to the movements of the Dow Jones Industrial Average and, because he believed if trading conditions were narrow it could mean the expected patterns caused by mass psychology might not occur, he did not intend it to be used in individual shares. Many today concur, believing the Principle is only appropriate to stock market prices representing economies enjoying continual growth because, as will be seen, the cycle is in a continual uptrend. However, the Elliott Wave Theory is increasingly popular and is in use in shares, bonds, commodity and currency markets alike today.

There are three aspects to the Elliott Wave Principle – Pattern, Ratio and Time. Elliott believed Pattern carried the greatest import and the majority of the Theory is devoted to it.

Pattern

The pattern (or cycle) that dominates the Theory is the major bull market advance developed in five waves and corrected by a three wave decline.

Elliott analysis can be applied to any timescale. The eight waves pictured in Figure 11.3 (1, 2, 3, 4, 5, a, b, c) could represent 200 years or 15 minutes. Elliott himself classified nine different magnitudes of cycle, starting with the Grand Supercycle, continuing through the Cycle and on to the last, the Subminuette. The smaller waves function as subwaves of the larger waves which, in turn, are subwaves of still larger formations. The Elliott Wave Principle has attracted much study in recent years and an Elliottician for whom I have immense respect (and gratitude, since he has helped greatly with this synopsis) is Alasdair Macleod of Shaw & Co Ltd. He breaks down the movements in the stock market as follows:

Elliotts 5 upwaves and 3 wave correction

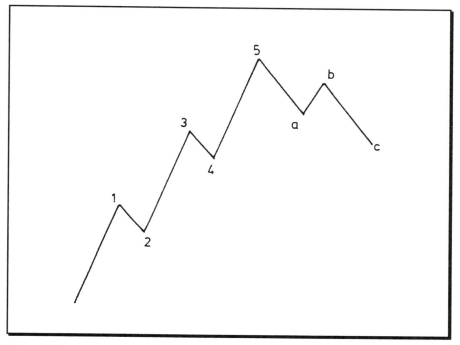

Figure 11.3

Source: Investment Research of Cambridge Ltd

'1 Grand Supercycle equating to 150 to 200 years, consisting of five supercycles.
2 Supercycle, which equates to the bull market from 1932 to the present day, and consists of five cycles.
3 Cycle, which equates to the bull market from 1975 to the present day, and consists of five primaries.
4 Primary, which equates to the bull market from 1981 to 1987, and consists five intermediates.
5 Intermediate, which equates to a bull market of lesser degree, being about one or two years in duration, consisting of five minors.
6 Minor, which can be expected to last three to nine months, consisting of five minutes.
7 Minute, consisting of five minuettes.
8 Minuette, consisting of five sub-minuettes.
9 Sub-minuette, which may span less than a day.'

Alasdair goes on to say:

'Thus, in theory, a bull market can be dissected into the smallest components, all working to a common pattern, or it can be regarded as a component of a bigger picture. It is this big picture aspect which allows the theory to do something that no other technical analysis does: to look beyond the accepted bull or bear market dimension and make accurate longer term predictions.'

It must be understood that the application of the Elliott Wave Theory is an art, and a scientific approach usually fails in practice. The Theory is a disappointment to those who seek a guaranteed formula for predicting markets. Its application can leave room for doubt, particularly in corrections (the second and fourth waves), which can be complex and difficult to dissect. The theory's rules are therefore a theoretical framework which has to be applied to a practical situation.

Notwithstanding this artistic element, the predictive powers of the theory have impressed the technical analysis community to the point where the theory has been extended by it and applied beyond its original purpose; that purpose being specifically the prediction of the course of the Dow Jones Averages.'

Thus, the simple cycle pictured above, when looked at more closely, will subdivide further and cycles within cycles will be revealed (see Figure 11.4).

Waves 1, 2, 3, 4 and 5 make up wave (1) of the longer-term cycle, whilst waves a, b and c form wave (2) of that larger cycle. Waves (1), (3) and (5), i.e. those going in the direction of the next major trend, wave 1, subdivide into five separate, smaller waves and are called impulse waves. Waves (2) and (4) are corrective waves and subdivide into three. The downwaves (a) and (c) which form part of the (a), (b), (c) correction to major wave 1 break down into five, whilst wave (b) breaks down into three. The basic rule is that five wave moves favour the direction of the wave of the next larger degree – in the case of this

Elliotts waves broken down into subwaves

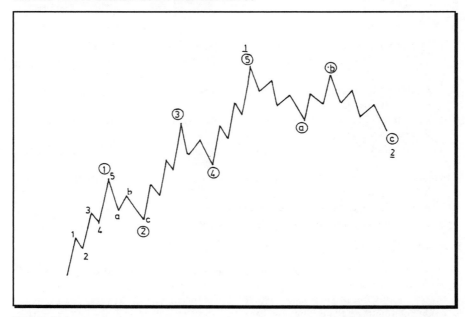

Figure 11.4

Source: Investment Research of Cambridge Ltd

a,b,c correction, wave 2. This is a useful rule of thumb as the Theory, and corrections in particular, can be very complex with waves of one cycle building the waves of the next cycle (into infinity) and the correct perspective can, from time to time, be lost.

The five wave advance

The bull market's three advancing waves (1, 3 and 5) are called impulse waves and waves 2 and 4, which move against the main trend, are called corrective waves. As has been said, the impulse waves break down into five subwaves whilst the corrections break down into three.

Within longer-term trend analysis impulse wave 1 can be likened to Dow's initial phase of accumulation which can result in the previous downtrend's reversal. It is, in any case, likely to be part of that pattern but often proves to be the shortest, least aggressive, of the impulse waves.

The next wave, corrective wave 2, may well give back most of the upmove in wave 1 but it should hold over the low of wave 1. The next wave is an impulse wave (3) and this is the one which can, as Dow said, be expected to be more vigorous as the news improves and volume increases. Indeed, Elliott argues this wave is the one most likely to be the largest. If wave 1 did not clear the previous rally peak in the downtrend, this one does so and trend followers get on board. The Elliott Wave Principle states this wave will never be the shortest of the impulse waves, and it should be the longest. Alasdair's comment reflects the fervour of the true Elliott expert:

> 'Wave 3 is often a strong broad-based affair, exceeding by far the targets thought to be reasonable by non-Elliott analysts. Elliott analysts adore third waves, because of their potential for profit, and because they often follow the Theory closely in their structure and, if you miss the top of the wave, the fifth wave will give you an opportunity to sell later on.'

Corrective wave 4 is often a complicated reaction and will take on a different form from wave 2, the previous corrective wave. However, it should reverse before support from the top of wave 1 is penetrated.

Impulse wave 5 is likely to make new highs, but it may be short-lived. This is the wave that, in a conventional Dow-style primary trend, will occur against a background of bullish news and somewhat late public participation. It is frequently shorter than wave 3 and often equates to wave 1. Volume and other technical indicators will likely fail to confirm its gains.

Whilst it would be nice to believe that impulse waves (numbered 1, 3 and 5) always behave in the same way, letting us know exactly where we are, this is not always the case. There are variations, and the most common is the extension. This is an elongated impulse wave that accentuates a bull or bear market. In equities an extension will most often occur in wave 3; it can form an 'unidentified extension', allowing the normal five waves to extend so that the original four gain another five waves so there are nine in total (see Figure 11.5). This carries the same significance as a five wave advance.

Extensions are relatively unusual and normally only one wave will extend. The other two (again, usually 1 and 5) will tend towards equality in both time and extent.

Other 'non-classic' shapes can, and do, form. Figure 11.6 shows something called a 'truncated fifth' which can be classified as a 'failure'. The fifth wave fails to clear the peak of the third; however, it can still be identified as a fifth wave – a truncated fifth in this case – because it subdivides into five. Its failure to move into new high ground highlights weakness and its action will usually lead to the formation of a double top in conventional charting.

Another 'non-classic' shape which is prone to appear in wave 5 is the diagonal triangle (see Figure 11.7). The pattern breaks down into five waves; wave 1 is the longest and wave 5 is shorter than wave 3. This is the only time an impulse wave breaks down into a 3-3-3-3-3 formation. The lines defining it converge, as they do on a rising wedge – a bearish pattern in a bull market in traditional pattern analysis. Again, it is highlighting weakness and the ensuing reaction can be large.

The three wave correction

Corrective waves are akin to Dow's secondary or intermediate trends and tend to be complex in their development. Whilst wave a (the first of these three

Unidentified extension

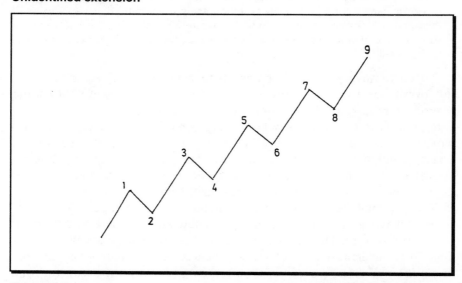

Figure 11.5 *Source:* Investment Research of Cambridge Ltd

Truncated fifth

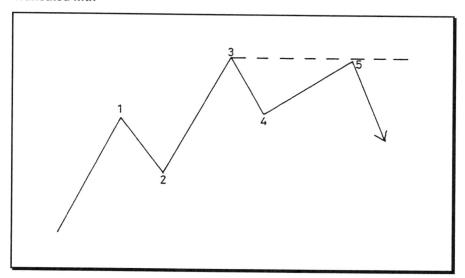

Figure 11.6   *Source:* Investment Research of Cambridge Ltd

Diagonal triangle

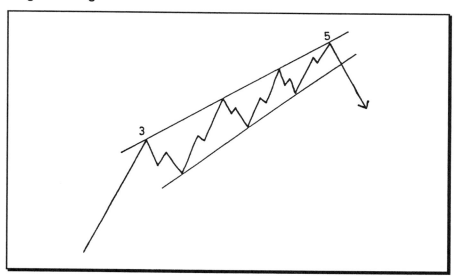

Figure 11.7   *Source:* Investment Research of Cambridge Ltd

corrective waves) may initially look like a minor correction in an uptrend, the clue that it could be the start of a more serious bear trend comes through if it breaks down into five subwaves.

Wave b will come through as a rally in the downtrend. It may test, and even exceed, the earlier highs before turning down again. It is usually accompanied by relatively low volume.

Wave c is likely to fall below the bottom of wave a; it could even go below the bottom of wave 4, making traditional double tops, etc. appear on the chart. However, it should always hold over the bottom of wave 2, leaving the major bull trend intact.

These waves are prone to complication and can come through in several different ways. The standard shape is called a zigzag and is most common in wave 2 (see Figure 11.8).

Wave a breaks down into 5 waves. Wave b breaks down into 3 and ends below the high of wave 5. Wave c breaks down into five and ends below the low of wave a. Occasionally a double zigzag forms, although this is relatively unusual.

Whereas the zigzag is a classic 5-3-5 pattern, the flat takes on a 3-3-5 formation. It is associated with a strong bull market since it is effectively a sideways consolidation rather than a reaction against the bull trend – rather like a rectangle or a Dow Line. Wave a breaks down into three waves, as does wave b which ends below the peak of wave 5. Wave c breaks down into five subwaves

Zigzag and double zigzag

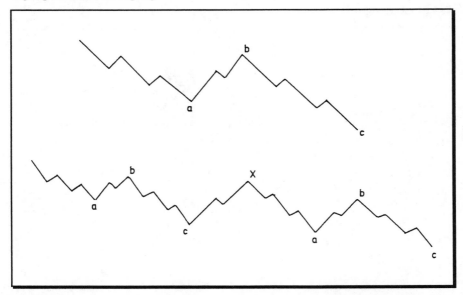

Figure 11.8   *Source:* Investment Research of Cambridge Ltd

and its low should be at or just below the low of wave a. If it is above the end of wave a it indicates the subsequent move will be strong. A rarer version of this pattern is the irregular flat where the high of wave b exceeds the top of wave 5 and the low of wave c tends to fall below the low of wave a. (See Figure 11.9.)

The third pattern typical of a corrective wave is the triangle. It is almost always associated with wave 4 and can also develop during wave b. Elliott's triangles are defined in the same manner as conventional triangles.

The triangles break down into five waves, each of which subdivides into three. Whilst Elliott regarded them as continuation patterns, as is usually the case in conventional pattern analysis, he did not believe that they carried a predictive ability. Additionally, as Figure 11.10 shows, he included the expanding triangle as a potential continuation pattern whilst this formation is considered more likely to prove to be an expanding top in traditional pattern analysis. However, some writers imply Elliott himself was not convinced of its role by the time he came to his later works.

Elliott made two further observations concerning triangles. Firstly, in that they frequently come through in wave 4 they may be considered bullish ini-

Flat and irregular flat

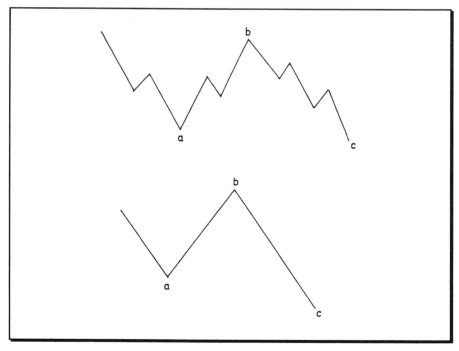

Figure 11.9   *Source:* Investment Research of Cambridge Ltd

Four triangles

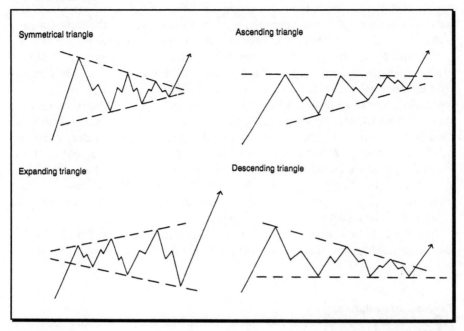

Figure 11.10

Source: Investment Research of Cambridge Ltd

tially but, once the breakout comes, the last bout of strength (wave 5) has been signalled and may not prove enduring. This is emphasised by his second observation, that the point on the timescale at which the apex of the triangle falls is often the point at which the high of wave 5 is seen.

Corrective waves will occasionally form complex patterns called double and triple threes (see Figure 11.11).

A double three develops where two simple a-b-c patterns join together to give a total of seven waves and a triple three – the result of combining three a-b-c patterns – has a total of eleven waves. Alasdair comments:

> 'These corrections can be extremely complex, and often slope upwards or downwards, sometimes appearing to the inexperienced eye as an impulse wave that is impossible to count. They are indicative of a market that needs to spend a disproportionate amount of time moving sideways. Subsequent market action tends to be strong.'

Trend channels

A further form of pattern analysis incorporated in the Elliott Wave Theory is the definition of the trend by channel analysis (see Figure 11.12). This is another part of the Theory in use in conventional charting techniques.

Double and triple three's

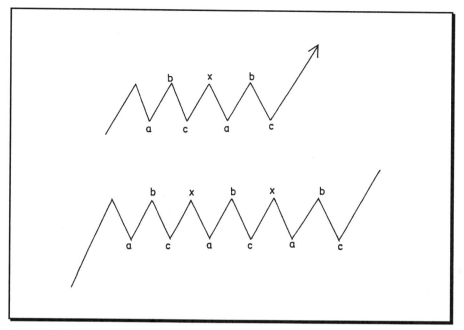

Figure 11.11   *Source:* Investment Research of Cambridge Ltd

Trend channels

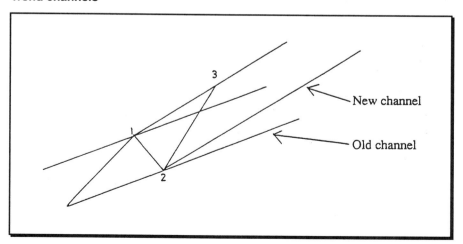

Figure 11.12   *Source:* Investment Research of Cambridge Ltd

Once wave 2 has completed the channel can be drawn in. If wave 3 exceeds the upper channel line – which will often happen if wave 3, as it is wont to do do, extends – the channel needs to be redrawn, joining the peaks of waves 1 and 3. The most reliable points for drawing in the final channel are the lows of waves 2 and 4. These channels can be used for estimating price objectives within the waves and it is often found the top of wave 5 falls just short of the upper channel line.

Rule of alternation

The last item to be mentioned in this section on pattern analysis is the Rule of Alternation. Elliott believed that the market would behave differently two times in a row. Thus, if wave 2 formed a simple pattern such as a flat, wave 4 (the next corrective wave) would be complex, such as a triangle. In other words, the Rule of Alternation does not tell us what to expect, but what not to expect.

Before going further into the mathematical properties of pattern within the Elliott Wave Principle, a recap might be helpful:

1 The main pattern is the five wave advance followed by the three wave decline. This occurs over all timescales, with cycles forming within cycles infinitely.
2 The waves going in the direction of the main trend are called impulse waves and normally subdivide into five.
3 The waves going against the trend are called corrective waves and subdivide into three.
4 The second wave never ends below the start of the first wave.
5 Wave 3 is usually the longest of the impulse waves, it is never the shortest. Impulse waves can extend and break down into nine subwaves, instead of five; such extensions are most likely to be found in wave 3. The other two impulse waves (usually 1 and 5) tend towards equality in both time and extent.
6 The fourth wave should end above the top of wave 1.
7 Corrective waves are often complex; they break down into three with these three breaking down into a 5-3-5 zigzag or a 3-3-5 flat. Triangles are particularly complex and are usually seen in wave 4; they break down into five waves, each of which breaks down into three.
8 Wave 5 will usually make new highs but it is frequently shorter than wave 3, often equating to wave 1. This is the impulse wave most prone to non-classic shapes, signalling the failing health of the trend. One such shape is the diagonal triangle consisting of five waves which break down into three – and the fourth wave can often end below the top of wave 1.
9 The Rule of Alternation states the market will act differently two times in a row, telling you what not to expect next.

Ratios: Price objectives using Fibonacci numbers

Fibonacci of Pisa was a medieval mathematician who introduced the decimal system to Europe and, when presented with the problem of calculating how many pairs of rabbits one pair could produce in a year, devised the series of numbers which carries his name today. To tackle the problem he made several assumptions (none died, for instance): in the first month the original pair (1) gave birth to another pair (1+1=2). The following month the same pair gave birth to another pair (3). The next month the original pair and their firstborn pair both gave birth to a pair each (5). With it being assumed that each new pair can reproduce another pair once they are in their second month, if the first births were in January, by April eight pairs of rabbits would be alive and, by May, 13. Thus the sequence goes 1, 1, 2, 3, 5, 8, 13. It can be seen that, after the first two numbers the next number is the product of the previous two. This recursive sequence can be continued – 21, 34, 55, 89 – and so on, into infinity. It is interesting to note that, despite the goal of infinity, 144 is the only square number in the series.

This number sequence has considerable properties. It can be found throughout nature and the universe; the leaf arrangements of plants (the Spiral Phyllotaxis) follows it and branches develop round the trunk of a tree in a spiral with the number of branches between one branch and the one immediately above it being a Fibonacci number. Each arm of a galactic spiral has a logarithmic shape. The spiral's constant form is maintained from the smallest to the largest elements of nature and Elliott followers believe the stock market's growth pattern is merely part of this natural phenomenon, with Fibonacci numbers and logarithmic spirals being the automatic product of a simple growth system, with success breeding its own success. Indeed, whilst this series carries Fibonacci's name, it is evident he rediscovered it since the ratios between one Fibonacci number and the next (both its predecessor and successor) form the Golden Numbers used by the Ancient Greeks and Egyptians in their building structures.

The Elliott Theory breaks down into pattern, ratio and time and it is the ratios and interrelationships between two Fibonacci numbers which form the mathematical basis for the Principle. The two most important ratios are 0.618 and 1.618, gained by dividing one Fibonacci number by that succeeding it and by the one preceding it as follows: it can be seen that, after the first few calculations, all subsequent ratios tend to 0.618 or 1.618 – 1:1=1. 1:2=0.5, 2:3=0.67, 3:5=0.6, 5:8=0.625, 8:13=0.615, 13:21=0.619, 21:34=0.6176. And, again after the first few calculations, 1.618 is the result of dividing one Fibonacci number by the one preceding it – 13/8=1.625, 21:13=1.615, 34:21=1.619, 55:34=1.617, 89:55=1.618.

The ratios of alternate numbers approach 2.618 or its inverse, 0.382. If the procedure is repeated using numbers even further away from each other 4.236 (and its inverse, 0.236) and 6.853 and 0.146 come through, and so on.

Elliott's waves (the cycles) break down into Fibonacci numbers. Going back to the basic pattern of the Elliott cycle there are five waves up and three waves down, totalling eight. The five waves in the advancing phase will break down into 21 (5+3+5+3+5) whilst the three waves down will break down into 13 (5+3+5); together this adds up to 34. This can be continued, with the result remaining a Fibonacci number.

Fibonacci ratios are used to calculate price objectives and retracements. The top of wave 3 can be calculated by multiplying the height of wave 1 by 1.618 and adding this to the bottom of wave 2. The top of wave 5 is estimated by multiplying the height of wave 1 by 3.236 (2×1.618) and adding that to wave 1's low for a minimum target and to the top of wave 1 for a maximum objective. If wave 1 and wave 3 are equal, then wave 5 may extend; the target could be calculated by measuring the distance between the top of wave 3 and the low of wave 1, multiplying this by 1.618 and adding the result to the low of wave 4. In a 5-3-5 zigzag the length of c is often the length of a (the ratio being 1:1) and in a 3-3-5 flat correction, if b exceeds the top of a, c will be roughly 1.618 times the length of a. In the case of a symmetrical triangle, each wave should approximate 0.618 of its predecessor.

The ratios are a very popular method of calculating likely retracements among market traders, with 61.8 per cent (0.618×100), 38.2 per cent (100−61.8) and 50 per cent (1:2) being the most commonly used. Indeed, they are often watched by many who have no knowledge of the Wave Principle at all. It is interesting to note that these numbers are very similar to the 2:3, 1:3 and 1:2 retracements Dow estimated were likely. If one of these retracement levels gives way, prices are projected to the next.

These retracement points are also used to construct Fibonacci fanlines – very similar to speedlines calculated by using the 1:3 and 2:3 retracement levels (see Figure 11.13). Again, if support from a fanline is eroded, the fall should extend to the next one.

The Elliott Wave Theory addresses pattern, ratio and time and the latter (although considered the least important) creeps in when Fibonacci arcs are constructed. Arcs are drawn through the percentage retracement levels and give an estimate of the timeliness of the support (see Figure 11.14). The fanlines and arcs are frequently used together and, like trendlines and speedlines, should offer support or resistance and, if they do not, will change their roles and resist subsequent rallies or support later declines.

The Fibonacci numbers themselves can also be used to estimate future market turning points. Once an important turn has occurred, the days, weeks or months (depending on which sort of chart is being analysed) can be counted

Fibonacci fanlines

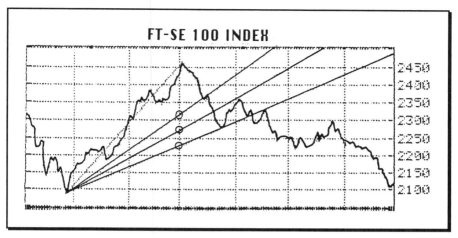

Figure 11.13   *Chart* by Synergy Software's Technical Analyst

ahead to estimate the timing of the next important turn. However, these implied turning points are not necessarily lining up a turn in the opposite direction to the first. In other words, if the first turn is from up to down, the next may prove to be another turn from up to down, after a corrective rally has aborted. Thus, it is usually recommended that very much less emphasis is placed on the timing element of the Theory than on pattern and ratio.

Fibonacci arcs

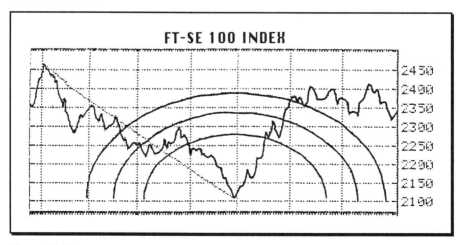

Figure 11.14   *Source:* Synergy Software's Technical Analyst

It seems appropriate to conclude this section on Elliot with the words of Alasdair Macleod who makes the following interesting and practical observations:

'Quite why Fibonacci is so important is a mystery. Gann works on a different series of numbers, 100%, 50%, 25%, 75%, 33% and 66%. But the application of Gann seems to be considerably better suited to individual stocks than Elliott, which was designed specifically for the Dow Jones Indices.

More recent research seems to have uncovered the importance of Fibonacci ratios determining the relationship limits between, for example A and C waves, rather than insisting that A=C times 0.618. As with so much of the Wave Theory, insistence on absolutes is counter-productive; the Theory is an art in its application, and not a science.

Not surprisingly, perfectionists try to pursue the application of Fibonacci to the furthest limits. They draw logarithmic spirals to show where the market is likely to move to, and, with the benefit of hindsight, they find lots of obtuse relationships. This flies in the face of advice from the older practitioners, such as Hamilton Bolton: "keep it simple." Above all, the simpler Fibonacci ratios (1.618, 2.618, 0.618 and 0.382), together with the simplest ratios between the lowest numbers in the series (notably 1, 2 and 0.5) can be used, perhaps more confirming wave counts and their proportions, rather than trying to double guess the markets too much.

An excellent example is provided by the 1987 crash. The following time relationships were noted with respect to Wall Street:

- 1932 supercycle low to 1987 was 55 years.
- 1966 cycle top to 1987 was 21 years.
- 1974 cycle low to 1987 was 13 years.
- 1982 primary low to 1987 was 5 years.

This recurrence of Fibonacci numbers was why followers of Elliott knew that 1987 was going to be important. They knew that it would be either an important peak or a major bottom: it in fact turned out to be both. But those analysts who pursued the Fibonacci relationships to their logical extent would have been unlikely to have forecast the subsequent rise in global stock markets.

Elliott devised his Wave Theory with stock markets or, more specifically the US stock market, in mind. The success of the Theory in this regard has encouraged technicians to apply it to non-equity markets; but to work properly these other markets have to possess certain characteristics.

At the heart of the Theory, there are two important propositions:

1 Equity markets are in a perpetual long term bull market. Wave 2 never retraces all of wave 1, and wave 4 never transgresses the top of wave 1, so a bear market of any magnitude is limited to the constraints of the next larger magnitude of cycle. A Grand Supercycle lasts between 150–200 years and itself appears to be a component of a larger bull market cycle.
2. Markets rise in fives and fall in threes.

These two propositions immediately create a problem for two applications which have spawned erudite literature: bonds and currencies.

Fortunately, bond yields are not in a constant bull market and, unforunately neither are bond prices. The idea that bond markets can satisfy an Elliott count cannot be true. It may be that one market movement bears a Fibonacci relationship to other, but that is not Elliott.

The same applies to currencies: their movement depends on macro-economic policy, and not Elliott Waves. Then there is the conundrum: if one currency is in a bull market against another, then it must be rising in fives, while the other is going down in threes; it is just not possible.

Commodities in theory should not respond, except possibly gold. At least the value of gold can be proxy for the long term tendency for man to improve his lot, in the same fashion as equities, but gold is generally measured in dollars, and it is not generally true that dollars will go down accordingly. So, even here, some caution is required.

Other metals are driven by market forces over the long term, and are not subject to the same conditions as equities. Soft commodities are worse, being prey to the vagaries of the weather.

So, in conclusion, the only markets that can be said to truly respond in an Elliott Wave fashion are equities and the application has to be an index, so as to neutralise the distortions inherent in individual companies.'

GANN THEORY

The last major Theory summarised here is that of W. D. Gann, a renowned market trader (of both stocks and commodities) at the beginning of the century who combined mathematics with the mystical elements of the market as the basis for his trading rules, with great emphasis placed on rigorous capital management.

His basic rules rest on a combination of precise mathematical and geometric principles, and time and space. Taking the basics of cycle theory to heart, he found the duration of a move of great significance and believed the longer the cycle, the greater the amplitude. In traditional charting techniques, this often means the larger the base pattern, the more significant the subsequent bull market.

In his works he frequently referred to the importance of support and resistance and 'lost motion' (the equivalent of momentum studies today); when this occurred he anticipated a failure to reach the target. Like Elliott, he believed bull markets lasted longer than bear markets and he, too, used Fibonacci numbers and ratios. But, being a successful commodity trader (where price swings are wide), he did not base his work on the theory of a continuing bull trend. He did, however, believe that price moves were part of a greater order of things, the natural law of the universe. His Theory is based very heavily on cycles and he had a huge respect for 'anniversary dates' for cyclic turns and the relationships he believed existed between price and time – the 'time/price squared' part of his theory is perhaps the best-known. He believed that 'when price meets time, a change is imminent'.

Gann and Price

Gann placed great stress on using long-term charts and one of the most significant points from which to predict future tops and resistance areas was the all-time low. He believed there are certain natural divisions expressed as percentages, with 0 per cent and 100 per cent the most important. Thus a move upwards would very likely complete once the price had doubled (+100%) from the all-time low. And subsequent falls would stop at the original low (0%), as would be expected in traditional technical analysis, based on Dow's view that all-time highs and lows force investors to reconsider their value judgements.

Gann also believed round numbers had a considerable psychological effect on traders, especially the eighths. Retracements of 75 per cent (6:8), 50 per cent (4:8), 25 per cent (2:8), 12.5 per cent (1:8) and so on are also important in Gann Theory (as are 33.333% and 66.666%) with 50 per cent (the number that crops up in Dow and Elliott too) the next most important percentage after 100. Whilst the all-time low price is the more important, Gann also placed significance on the all-time high and the same percentage retracements from it. Thus, if prices first retraced 50 per cent of a previous rise before rallying and breaking down again, he would look for the next move to fall to half of the 50 per cent point – 25%, and so on.

Gann took a similar attitude to time cycles. He was a great believer in the geometric circle and likened the year's 365 (or 366) days to the circle's 360°. Half a year (26 weeks), a quarter (13 weeks), 45 days and 22.5 days etc. from a previous turning point were critical turning points in time. He also used divisions and multiples of the circle as actual prices (45 pence, 90 pence, 360 pence, 720 pence) as resistance and support points, calling them 'natural levels'.

Another original method used by Gann for predicting important price levels at which prices could turn was the Cardinal Square.

The example in Figure 11.15 is constructed starting with the figure 1 in the middle and with 2 in the box to the left and 3 in the box immediately above it. The next figure, 4, is placed to the right of 3, and so on, in an ever-increasing circle, with price increments moving from square to square in a clockwise manner. Gann used the approach of putting the all-time low (or high, in which case the subsequent numbers decline) price in the centre square (instead of 1 in the above example) and sometimes the square can be seen constructed with prices moving anti-clockwise. Whichever approach is used in constructing the square, the most important area containing numbers which are likely to offer price resistance and support are to be found in the 'Cardinal Cross' formed by the squares immediately above and below the central number, and those immediately to its left and right. Additional support and resistance numbers are those that fall on the diagonal lines.

Gann attempted a form of systematic trend analyser called Trend Indicator Lines (TILs) (see Figure 11.16). This line is plotted on the same chart as the price as a reminder of the direction of the main trend, but it does not recognise the same timescale.

This approach is usually used with weekly data, a favourite with Gann. When a price has a higher high and a higher low in the second week than in the first, the TIL moves up on the price scale to the new high. The horizontal

Cardinal Square

5 7	5 8	5 9	6 0	6 1	6 2	6 3	6 4	6 5
5 6	3 1	3 2	3 3	3 4	3 5	3 6	3 7	6 6
5 5	3 0	1 3	1 4	1 5	1 6	1 7	3 8	6 7
5 4	2 9	1 2	3	4	5	1 8	3 9	6 8
5 3	2 8	1 1	2	1	6	1 9	4 0	6 9
5 2	2 7	1 0	9	8	7	2 0	4 1	7 0
5 1	2 6	2 5	2 4	2 3	2 2	2 1	4 2	7 1
5 0	4 9	4 8	4 7	4 6	4 5	4 4	4 3	7 2
8 1	8 0	7 9	7 8	7 7	7 6	7 5	7 4	7 3

Figure 11.15   *Source:* Investment Research of Cambridge Ltd

plot is always the same width, ignoring the passage of time. When the price has two consecutive weeks of lower prices (both highs and lows) the TIL moves down to the low on the price scale. Thus the TIL is usually squashed into the left-hand side of the chart.

It can be seen that Gann came up with a very considerable number of prices which were useful potential support or resistance points. However, unlike

Trend Indicator Lines

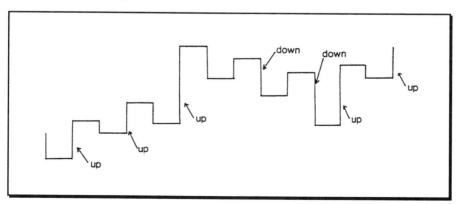

Figure 11.16   *Source:* Investment Research of Cambridge Ltd

Elliott, Gann placed the greatest emphasis on time, rather than price. Indeed, if there were to be a conflict as to where or when the price move would change direction, Gann would give precedence to his cyclical turning point, rather than the price level. It was his belief that not until the 'time was up' would the price move begin.

Gann and time

Gann believed actual dates could be pinpointed for future turning points by extrapolating from those that had occurred in the past. One year, two years, 18 months ahead, etc. with one year being the most significant, could be critical. Again, however, rather like Elliott, the direction from and to which the price might turn could not be predetermined.

Gann believed some individual dates are of special importance. January 2–7 and 15–21 are considered critical. The highs and lows made during these periods should be noted and, until they are exceeded, the original trend will remain in place. Sometimes these extremes can contain prices for the rest of the year.

Gann also believed the number seven to be of considerable significance in price cycles, based on the seven-day week. The most important number is 49 – seven weeks of seven days. If an important turning point comes through, look for another 49 days ahead; 49 to 52 weeks ahead could prove very significant since it virtually coincides with the one year anniversary date already mentioned.

Gann's fascination with geometry was by no means confined to price (see Figure 11.17).

In time analysis the Gann Emblem is used when a major top or bottom has occurred. The turning point in time is placed at zero degrees. So, if that turn occurred on 10 January 1992, the emblem would look like it does in Figure 11.18.

Another turn, in the same direction, will be indicated at the 90, 120, 240 and 270 positions – those numbers of days in the future. The 180° point is considered the point of opposition. Thus, if the other turning points were implied to be from down to up, this would be from up to down.

Gann: Price and Time

The most popular aspect of Gann analysis in use on most computer systems today is referred to as 'The Squaring of Price and Time'. Gann saw a proportional relationship between the two and this is most clearly expressed when the time taken to reach a price is in direct proportion to the price distance moved. The example in Figure 11.19 shows a price moving by 200 points over 200 days.

In practice, to draw in his 1:1 line, he used chart paper which, when this line was extended from the low or high, it crossed through the intersections of the

Gann Emblem

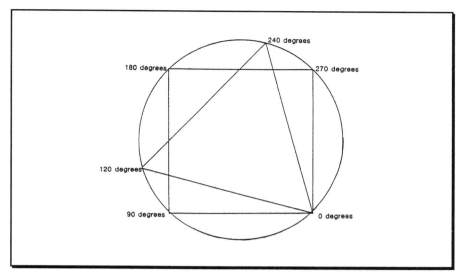

Figure 11.17   *Source:* Investment Research of Cambridge Ltd

Gann Emblem dated

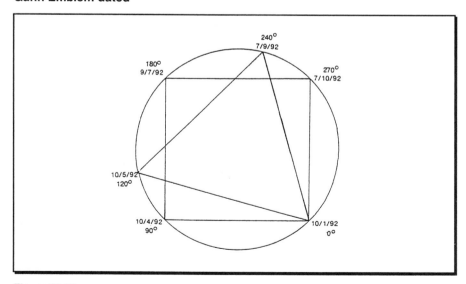

Figure 11.18   *Source:* Investment Research of Cambridge Ltd

Price/Time Squared

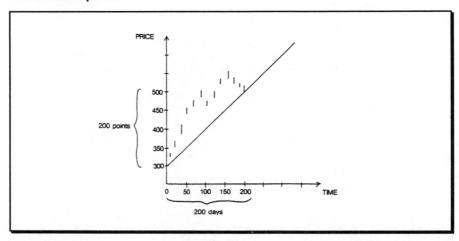

Figure 11.19   *Source:* Investment Research of Cambridge Ltd

squares at an angle of 45°, forming a trendline. This has already been seen in the section on point and figure but, with point and figure charts totally ignoring the passage of time, it may be considered a coincidence to a Gann analyst if the trendline proves effective. This line forms the main trend definition; if prices are rising above it there is a bull market in place; if they fall below it, the bull market is being reversed. But other lines are used too; Gann angle lines can reflect two units of price to one of time, three units of price to one of time, and so on. Additionally, lines can reflect one unit of price per two units of time and, again, one unit of price per three units of time, etc. This can be continued 2:3, 3:2, 4:3 and so on.

Gann fanlines are used in the same manner as speedlines and Fibonacci arcs where, it will be remembered, they are looked to to offer support and, if broken, should subsequently offer resistance. Once broken, the implication is the price should extend its move to the next speedline or arc. The reverse is true in downtrends. (See Figure 11.20.)

The Theories of Dow, Elliott and Gann all give methodologies for defining the cyclical structure of the market. It is interesting to note there are many similarities in their individual approaches and that Elliott and Gann were convinced that the natural law of the universe was responsible for this cyclical structure and functioned as a measure of human psychology which led, in turn, to predictable patterns of behaviour and, hence, price.

Unsurprisingly, these Theories are complex and I have done little but scratch the surface in presenting the summaries here. Whilst there are a considerable number of people in the market doing the rigorous hard work necessary

Gann fanlines

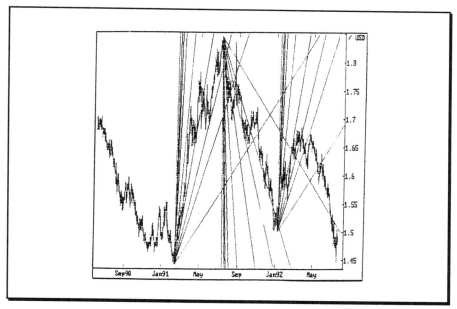

Figure 11.20

Chart by Reuters Technical Analysis

for their implementation in full, their most popular use is in gauging likely retracements and turning points in price and time, with the most popular numbers being those which are coincident (or virtually so) in all three Theories.

GLOSSARY

Accumulation: A period of sideways trading during which buyers accumulate shares.

ACD: The Accumulation/Distribution Indicator which measures the buying and selling pressure and forms a cumulative plot which should look like the shape formed by the price. If it does not, warning signals sound. A breach of its trend argues in favour of closing positions.

Acts of God: A phrase used in the Dow Theory to describe surprise events which have not been factored into the price.

Advance/Decline Line: The cumulative net total of the number of shares which close up or down on the previous day. Its shape is analysed in comparison to market indices to show what shares across the market as a whole are doing. When it fails to confirm the indices' trend, warning bells sound.

Amplitude: The height of a cyclic wave.

Angle (45°): The angle of a trendline of major importance in the Gann Theory and used by some point and figure analysts.

Anniversary Dates: Gann Theory anticipates critical market turning points recurring on the Anniversaries of previous turns. The most important is the one year anniversary – but eighteen months, two years, etc., are important too. It should be noted that the turn which occurs on the anniversary may not be in the same direction as the original.

Arithmetic Scale: (The English equivalent of the American Linear Scale.) A method of scaling charts where the distance between each scaling line is the same. It allows considerable flexibility in displaying plots and is very popular for short term price analysis.

Bar Charts: Probably the most popular plot which forms vertical bars by joining the highest price for the period to the lowest traded over the same period. Traditionally such charts would also have either a horizontal bar to indicate where the price closed for that period (European style) or two such horizontal bars showing the opening price (plotted to the left of the vertical bar) and the close (plotted to the right) – this is the American convention.

Bear Market: A period during which prices are falling; it is used in reference to any length of trend, depending on the time perspective of the investor using the term. Traditionally, a bear market in shares lasts between nine months and two years.

Bollinger Bands: Named after John Bollinger, these are two lines plotted above and below the moving average used to define the trend and their placement relates to the volatility of price change. Thus, as the volatility varies, so does their distance from the moving average, allowing a trend channel of variable width to form.

Box Size: The value give to a square on the price scale of a point and figure chart.

Broadening Formation: Traditionally considered to be a top formation which displays volatile rallies and reactions which break support and resistance levels but, unconventionally, fail to follow through. Over time, the formation takes on the appearance of a megaphone. It is an unusual pattern nowadays – highlighting considerable confusion in an overbought market. It does not have a bottom reversal equivalent. It apparently proliferated on Wall Street during 1929. Confusingly, there is an Elliott Wave pattern which takes the same shape and is called an expanding triangle and is a corrective wave during the five wave advance. However, Elliott's later writings did not mention it.

Bull Market: A period during which prices rise. As with the definition of a Bear Market (above) it is used to describe variable periods, depending on the time horizons of the trader concerned. Traditionally, in post-War stockmarket analysis, it refers to a period lasting between eighteen months and three years.

Candlesticks (interchangeable with Candles): A Japanese method of plotting open/high/low/close prices so they can take the appearance of a candle (or 'candlestick' in American parlance). These charts have considerable visual impact since they employ colours; if a price opens low and closes high the candle is white. If the reverse occurs, the candle is black. Hence, even an uninitiated chart watcher can see immediately if, during a long trend, buyers or sellers are in control. The technique is famed for near term reversal patterns.

Cardinal Square: A methodology used in Gann Analysis to give future support or resistance levels by constructing a square which, in the centre, has a number reflecting a previous high or low. In the next square to the left (or right, it makes no difference as long as the sequence is consistent) is the next number up – or down – and the series continues in a clockwise (or anticlockwise) manner. The various numbers so displayed across horizontal, vertical or diagonal lines, offer support or resistance to subsequent moves.

Chartism: The analysis of price movements by the reading of price charts – considered by many to be subjective and thus an art, rather than a science.

Charts: The graphic representation of price movements, usually plotted at regular intervals – such as monthly, weekly, daily, hourly, every five minutes – and so on. Some charts represent irregular plots; tick charts (those reflecting every single trade) develop as trading occurs and point and figure charts are plotted only when a significant price change occurs.

Closing price: The final price of a predetermined trading period. The most common is the daily close.

Commodity Channel Index (CCI): Designed by Donald Lambert, this is an indicator based on the relationship between a price and its moving average and the average differential between these two numbers. It gives buy signals when it rises over 100 and sell signals when it falls below –100. The rest of the time it is indicating a ranging market – although some people follow the trends of the indicator once it reverses, whatever the numbers.

Confirmation: Action by another price, index or indicator which is effectively closely related or very similar to the price itself. Such action adds validity to signals given by the price and is at the core of the Dow Theory. In this instance the requirement was that when the Dow Industrials (for instance) moved into new high ground, it was only considered significant if the Dow Rails did so too. Otherwise no major renewed buy signal was given.

Consolidation: A band of virtually motionless price trading which follows a rise or fall. It reflects a period of profit-taking and reassessment and provides an opportunity for overextension to unwind – before the trend resumes. The term is a neutral one, whilst 'accumulation' is used to represent a period when prices are consolidating whilst shares are bought (or accumulated) and 'distribution' describes a period of consolidation whilst shares are being sold (or distributed).

Coppock Momentum: One of the oldest measures of the speed of the trend, developed by Sedge Coppock in the 1950s. It is based on a twelve (sometimes ten) month weighted momentum of a stock market index and was designed to trigger re-entry to the market after a bear market. Mr. Coppock drew an analogy between the effect of a bear market on an investor and a family bereavement and, on his priest's advice, used the period of one year.

Correction: A movement in the opposite direction to the main trend – a rally in a downtrend or a reaction in an uptrend.

Crest: The top (or peak) or a cyclic wave.

Crossover Signals: The buy and sell signals that come from a short term moving average moving up or down through a longer term moving average. The assumption is all signals are obeyed – so the operator is always in the market, long or short.

Cycles: The regular occurrence of turning points in price (and other) series based on time. Their representation normally looks like a sine wave.

Dark Cloud Cover: A Japanese Candlestick pattern which warns the highs in an uptrend have been seen. It forms over two trading periods: the first is a large white candle and the second is a black candle which opens above the previous candle's high but closes within its real body.

Diagonal Triangle: An Elliott Wave pattern which often appears in Wave 5 and breaks down into five. The lines defining it converge. It is warning the highs are nigh.

Diamond: A four-sided diamond-shaped pattern that forms as a top reversal pattern – like a head and shoulders top where the shoulders are 'shrugged'. Occasionally it will appear as a continuation pattern in an uptrend. It is not recognised as a reversal pattern to a bear trend.

Directional Movement Index (DMI): Welles Wilders' attempt to define up or down trending markets as against those which are caught in ranges. The trending characteristics ranked on a scale of 0–100 – with the higher numbers showing the stronger trending conditions. The directional movement is gauged by comparing the range of the current period to that of the previous one. Two indices, Up DMI and Down DMI, give the basic buy/sell signals when they cross over. Other signals come from the amalgamation of the two and its moving average.

Distribution: A period of consolidation within a downtrend which reflects sellers – on balance – disposing of their holdings. The downtrend is resumed in due course.

Divergence: Effectively the opposite of Confirmation. Usually used in indicator analysis, it refers to occasions when the indicator does not do what the price does – for instance, move into new high ground. This warns that the trend is tiring and could be vulnerable to reversal.

Doji: A Japanese Candlestick formation which looks like a European high/low/close bar chart as the opening and closing prices come through at the same level. This highlights market confusion – and a doji often forms part of a more important reversal pattern.

Double (and Triple) Threes: An Elliott Wave pattern – one of the shapes a corrective wave can take.

Double Tops and Bottoms: The top pattern causes the reversal of an uptrend in price. First twin peaks are formed, followed by the breach of support (the neckline) offered by the reaction low which occurred between them. The base reversal pattern is its opposite: a pattern formed by twin lows which is resolved when the neckline (at the level of the intervening rally peak) is cleared.

Dow (Charles, H.), died 1902: Editor of the Wall Street Journal at the end of the 1800s and devisor of the Dow Averages and the Dow Theory which is at the core of Western technical analysis as it is used today. Dow's original thinking was put into theoretical form by Hamilton, his successor. Whilst the Dow Theory per se is little used today, its tenets have spawned much other work and its basic concepts are still very much in use.

Downtrend: A series of falling peaks and troughs.

Elliott, Ralph N. (1871-1948): Influenced by the Dow Theory, Elliott – a non-market person, devised his sophisticated theory of time motion analysis based on price charts. He believed price movements were part of a larger law, established throughout the universe which involves pattern, ratio and time.

Engulfing Pattern: Japanese Candlestick pattern which comes through over two trading periods and warns of trend reversal. The bullish engulfing pattern follows a series of price falls and is formed by first, a small black candle which is followed by a large white candlestick whose real body completely engulfs the black one. The bearish engulfing pattern follows a series of rising prices and its first candle is a small white one; this is followed by a candle with a large black body that entirely engulfs the white one.

Enveloped Moving Averages: The plotting of points a certain percentage above and below a moving average which forms a band operating as a trend channel, denoting areas of potential support and resistance to the price.

Evening Star and Evening Doji Star: An important Japanese Candlestick bearish reversal pattern which develops over three periods in an uptrend. The first candle is long and white; the second is a star and the third is long and black and closes well into the first candle's real body. The Evening Doji Star has a Doji as the second candle and carries more bearish connotations.

Exponential Moving Averages: Moving averages which never discard early data, but give greater weight to recent data. The calculation involves taking its last value and adjusting it by a percentage of the difference between the most recent price and the previous moving average value.

Extension: The name given to an elongated impulse wave in the Elliott Wave Theory.

Failure: An Elliott Wave term describing a fifth wave failing to clear the peak of the third.

Fibonacci, Leonardo: A medieval mathematician who described a recursive sequence of numbers with interesting properties. These numbers and their ratios are used to predict market moves and define fanlines and arcs which should offer support and resistance to prices.

Five Wave Advance: The main part of the Elliott Wave Pattern; the five waves are numbered 1 to 5 and are followed by a three wave correction, labelled a, b and c.

Flags: A short term rally or reaction in a fast trend which forms a parallel trend and is occasioned by profit-taking. Once over, the price is predicted to move by the same amount enjoyed prior to the flag's formation. In other words, it is a halfway hesitation.

Flat (& Irregular Flat): An Elliott Wave pattern that forms a corrective wave in a 3-3-5 wave format. It has bullish connotations. An irregular flat is not dissimilar to the early stages of the broadening formation.

Fundamental Analysis: The study of the 'value' of an item traded (via balance sheet analysis, supply/demand balance, etc.) as opposed to the study of its price – Technical Analysis.

Gann, W. D. (1878-1955): A very successful trader famed for his Theory based on mathematical and geometric principles.

Gann Emblem: Part of the Gann Theory; the emblem is a combination of geometric shapes and is used to forecast future turning points in price in terms of time.

Gann Fanlines: Part of the Gann Theory. The lines progress in a time/price ratio (e.g. two units of price to one of time, three units of price to one of time, one unit of price to two of time – etc.). The lines are drawn up from an important low or down from a significant high. If breached, the price is anticipated to move to the next one.

Gaps (Common, Breakaway, Running, Measuring): The space that appears on a chart when a price move is completely above or below – by a margin – the previous plot. In certain circumstances such spaces signal immense energy and add to the likelihood of the price move extending.

Grand Sypercycle: Elliott's very long term cycle – equating to 150–200 years.

Halfway Hesitation: A short term pattern indicating profit-taking after a fast move – e.g. a flag or a pennant. Once over, the price is indicated to move by the same distance already travelled.

Hammer: A Japanese Candlestick pattern which occurs over one trading period and signals the possible end to a downtrend. It has a long lower shadow which should be at least twice the length of the small real body near the top of the trading range.

Hanging Man: A Japanese Candlestick formation which occurs at tops and warns of retreats. It forms over one trading period and has a small real body and a long lower shadow – at least twice the length of the real body. It is the 'brother' pattern to the Hammer, occurring in the opposite circumstances.

Harami: A Japanese Candlestick formation which warns of a possible change of trend. A small real body forms, well within the body of the previous candle's real body.

Head and Shoulders Reversal (& Inverted and Inverse): A pattern which takes on the shape of someone's shoulders and head in silhouette. It identifies a dynamic market argument and usually signals an important trend reversal. The signal is given when the line joining the two reaction lows (neckline) is broken. The reversed head and shoulders is the opposite and signals the reversal to a downtrend when the line joining the two rally peaks (neckline) is broken. There is a slight confusion in that the American term for this formation is 'inverse' rather than 'reversed'. Occasionally a pattern taking on this shape occurs within an uptrend and is a continuation pattern – referred to as inverse; this is very rare in a downtrend.

High/Low Indicator (IRC): An indicator which, on a weekly basis, plots the number of shares in the Investment Research of Cambridge's library scoring new highs or lows for the past twelve months. High numbers denote overbought or oversold conditions.

High/Low/Close Charts: Known also as range or bar charts, the plot joins the highest price traded to the lowest price traded over the period with a vertical line and the closing price is represented by a horizontal bar.

High Price: The highest price traded over the period in question.

Impulse Waves: The Elliott Wave Theory's bull market's three advancing waves (1, 3 and 5) within the five wave advance.

Indicators: Plots of calculations based on price movements (and other related statistics) whose purpose is to confirm the significance of a price move and highlight over extended market conditions. Some are based on the speed of a price move and often reverse their trend before the price does. Also referred to as 'studies', they are frequently oscillators within 0–100 parameters.

Intermediate Trend: Dow's name for reactions against the primary trend, lasting between three weeks to three months and often retracing one third, half or two-thirds of the previous move. Also called a 'secondary' trend. Confusingly, in Elliott Wave terminology it means a trend lasting one or two years – equivalent to Dow's Primary trend.

Inverted Hammer: A Japanese Candlestick pattern which forms over one trading period and warns of the end of a downtrend. It takes on the same shape as the Shooting Star – it has a long upper shadow and a small real body near the low.

Island Reversal: A price (or, sometimes, a few prices) at the high or the low of a fast-moving up or down trend which is isolated from the previous and subsequent trading by gaps.

Key Reversal: A one period pattern which occurs after a sharp move up or down. In an uptrend the price will make new highs but then fall to a low lower than that of the previous period and close below that period's low. The reverse occurs in a downtrend. Short term it warns of reversal. Longer term it can often be seen to be part of a large reversal pattern.

Length: The distance in time between cycle troughs.

Line Chart: A plot formed by joining the price for the period in question to the previous equivalent one. The closing price for the period is the one most frequently used.

Linear Regression Line (Line of Best Fit): Normally calculated by the method of least squares, it is a straight line computed to cut through the core of past data points – and extrapolate the trend into the future.

Linear Scale: See Arithmetic scale.

Lines: Mentioned in the Dow Theory, a narrow sideways trend with a range of less than 5% of the price which substitutes for a rally or reaction.

Log Scale: Short for Semi-Logarithmic – and also known as a Ratio scale – this is a method of scaling whereby price change is expressed visually in percentage terms so that the horizontal lines on the y (price) axis get closer together as the price increases. These distances are calculated so that the distance between numbers representing the same percentage change is the same; thus the scale lines representing a move from ten to twenty would be the same distance apart as those representing a move from twenty to forty – both increases of 100%.

Long: A term used mainly in the futures markets to describe a purchase of a contract with the anticipation of a price rise which should allow the position to be closed out at a higher price.

Low Price: The lowest price traded over the period in question.

MACD (Moving Average Convergence/Divergence): An indicator developed by Gerald Appel. Two lines which oscillate above and below zero are employed. The first represents the differential between two exponential moving averages of the price and the second – called the Trigger Line – is a moving average of the first. Buy and sell signals are generated when the two lines cross; trend reversal itself is warned of when these lines fail to confirm the price's new highs or lows.

MACD Forest: A plot representing the differential between the MACD Line and the Trigger; when it diverges from the MACD it warns of an imminent cross.

Meisels Indicator: A simple overbought/oversold indicator devised by Ron Meisels and based on the net total of the number of days in the past set period (10 is the default) the price closed up or down. Using 10 days, +/–6 indicates overbought or oversold.

Minor Trend: A Dow Theory term describing the trends of a lower degree which make up the secondary/intermediate trend which lasts between three weeks and three months. Again there is a conflict in terminology between Dow and Elliott Wave Theory as in the latter Minor refers to a trend which can be expected to last between three and nine months.

Minuette: An Elliott Wave Theory term describing a trend lasting only a few days.

Minute: An Elliott Wave term describing a trend lasting a matter of weeks.

Momentum: A generic term for the study of the speed of a trend – its rate of change. There is also a specific indicator which bears the name Momentum. It is the differential between the price today and that n periods ago.

Morning Star: An important Japanese Candlestick bullish reversal pattern which comes at the end of a decline. It is formed by three candles; the first has a relatively long black body. The second has a small real body and the third has a relatively long white real body which closes well into the first candle's real body.

Moving Averages: Calculations involving the smoothing of a price series by summing the prices and dividing the result by the number of prices used; the term 'moving' refers to the fact that calculation is redone on a regular basis.

Multiple Tops and Bottoms: Reversal patterns which involve a series of rallies and reactions within a broad sideways range whilst a major market argument occurs. The pattern forms when either the line joining the reaction lows (neckline) gives way and an uptrend is reversed or the line joining the rally peaks (neckline) is breached and the downtrend is reversed.

Neckline: The line defining the critical support or resistance which, when broken, signals the reversal of a trend.

On-Balance Volume: An indicator devised by Joseph Granville, it is a running cumulative total reflecting the amalgamation of price and volume. Its plot should take on the same shape as that of the price. When it does not do so a trend reversal is warned of. When its trend is broken, that of the price is likely to follow suit.

Open Price: The first traded price during a pre-defined period. It can also refer to the first quoted price.

Oscillator: The generic description of various indicators which move up and down around a mean line which is usually either zero or, more likely, 50. These indicators reach highs and lows which identify overbought or oversold conditions which have forced price moves to reverse in the past. When their action diverges from that of the price trend reversal is warned of. It is also the name given to a specific overbought/oversold indicator which reflects the differential between two moving averages used to monitor the trend in price.

Overbought: A description of the state of the market when a price rise has gone 'too far' and profit-taking is attracted, causing either price reversal or consolidation.

Overextension: Overbought or oversold.

Oversold: A description of the state of the market when a price fall has gone 'too far' and profit-taking is attracted, causing either price reversal or consolidation.

Parabolic: The name given to an indicator developed by J. Welles Wilder, Jnr. It is a time/price reversal system which uses SARs which take on the shape of a parabola as a fast trend progresses since the calculation involves acceleration factors.

Parallels: The parallel lines drawn in to define up and downtrend channels, encompassing the vast majority of data points in that trend. Conventionally such lines are drawn parallel to a line rising or falling to the right of the price.

Pattern: The shapes that develop time and again in price charts as market arguments occur. Continuation patterns reflect a pause in a market advance or decline prior to the trend's resumption. Reversal patterns reflect major market arguments which are eventually resolved in the opposite direction to that which had pertained previously. It is also the name given to the part of the Elliott Wave Theory that maintains markets advance in five waves and then enjoy a three wave correction.

Pennants: A short term continuation pattern which takes on the shape of a pennant – a tiny triangle – and reflects profit-taking after a fast move. The trend then reasserts itself and, when it does, prices are expected to move by the same extent to that already enjoyed.

Percentage Retracements: Once a market advance or decline has attracted profit-taking prices are anticipated to react by an amount which reverses a certain percentage of the previous advance or decline. The most popular is 50%, with 33%, 38.2%, 66% and 61.8% also looked for.

Period: The length of a cycle, measured in terms of time between cycle troughs.

Periodicity: The number of time periods used for calculating moving averages and momentum-based indicators, etc.

Phasing: The practice of placing a moving average on the x axis so that its most recent calculated value is plotted half the periodicity in the past. Thus a 20 day moving average would be plotted 10 days back. This allows the average to fit the price curve, rather than follow it, and is used to take the differential between the price and the phased average to reveal underlying cycles of a lower degree to that of the average used.

Piercing Pattern: A Japanese Candlestick pattern which occurs over two trading periods and signals the likely reversal of a downtrend. A large black candle is succeeded by a white candle that opens in new low ground but closes well into the black candle's real body.

Point & Figure Charts: Charts constructed from price change alone – time factors are ignored. Rising prices are represented traditionally by a column of crosses and falling prices by a column of noughts. In the case of a one box reversal point and figure chart both noughts and crosses can appear in the same column.

Prediction: Price forecasts made when a pattern is resolved.

Price/Time: Gann's geometric angles form fanlines which offer support or resistance. The most important is the 45° line when perfect balance is said to be achieved – price and time are 'squared'.

Primary Trend: Dow Theory gives this name to the main bull or bear market, lasting a year or more. Elliott Theory ranks the primary trend below the Cycle (which lasts roughly twenty years) and above the intermediate, which lasts one or two years – further conflicting terminology between these two Theories.

Rally: An upmove in price; the term is usually used within the context of a countertrend rise in a downtrend.

Range Charts: Bar charts, made up of vertical lines joining the high price to the low price for the period in question.

Rate of Change: A generic term for the measurement of the speed at which price change is occurring. Also the name given to a specific indicator which computes the ratio of the price today to that n periods ago.

Ratio Scale: See Log scale.

Reaction: A downmove in price, usually used to refer to a fall in an uptrend.

Real Bodies: A Japanese Candlestick term describing the vertical rectangular shapes formed when the bars representing the open price and close price are joined by vertical lines at their left and right extremities. These rectangles are coloured white when the open is lower than the close and black when the close is lower than the open.

Rectangle: A continuation pattern within an up or downtrend. It is effectively a sideways trend with the upper and lower parameters roughly horizontal. The pattern reflects a period of equilibrium in the market and is resolved by the original price trend being resumed.

Relative Strength: A popular stockmarket indicator used to measure the performance of an individual share against the market as a whole. It is a ratio of the share price to an appropriate market index and its rising plot will highlight an overperforming share and its falling plot an underperforming issue. The trends in these plots can be used as indicators to foretell what the price is most likely to do next.

Resistance: A price area where sellers are likely to come out in adequate quantity to thwart – or resist – the rise. Typically resistance will be found around earlier highs or when a price rallies to a level which had previously offered support.

Return Lines: The name given to the upper parallel in an uptrend channel or the lower parallel line in a downtrend channel.

Reversal Factor: The amount by which a price has to fall or rise before the plot of a point and figure chart moves from the column representing rising or falling prices to the next one, representing falling or rising prices.

Rise and Fall: A simple indicator whose plot is constructed by measuring the number of times a price closes up or down over the period in question. Its shape should confirm that of the price chart.

Round Numbers: These are prices such as 10, 100, 1000, etc. Others are 20, 200, 50, 500 – etc. They are likely to offer support or resistance since they force market participants to reconsider sales or purchases – as any shopkeeper knows!

RSI (Welles Wilder Jnr.'s Relative Strength Index): An indicator which, using a ratio of the amount by which a price has closed up over a period to the amount by which the price has closed down over the same period, measures the strength of the price now to that n periods ago. The plot oscillates between 0 and 100 and 30 registers oversold and 70 overbought. It is not to be confused with the stockmarket concept of relative strength.

Rule of Alternation: Part of the Elliott Wave Theory which states that the market is likely to behave differently two times in a row. Thus, if wave 2 – the first corrective wave in an uptrend – is a simple formation, wave 4 – the next corrective wave in the uptrend – will be complex. The rule does not tell you what to expect, but tells you what not to expect.

SARs: Stop and Reverse Points: calculated stop loss levels which, when broken, signal not only closing the original position, but reversing it and entering the market in the opposite direction.

Saucers: Reversal patterns which form rounding tops and bottoms, evidencing a gradual shift from buying pressure to selling power – and vice versa.

Secondary Trend: See Intermediate.

Shadows: The 'spikes' which extend above and below the real bodies of candle charts, showing the distance of the highs and lows above and below the real bodies.

Shooting Star: A Japanese Candlestick pattern which warns of an impending top. It occurs in an uptrend when prices open near their lows and rally strongly. But the gains are not maintained and prices close near the open, leaving a long upper shadow and a small real body near the low.

Short: Going short is a practice used by hedgers and speculators in the futures markets; a contract, not already owned, is sold in anticipation of its price falling so that a purchase – to close the position – can be made at a lower price.

Simple Moving Average: A moving average calculation which affords the same weight to each price in the data series.

Speedlines: Trendlines drawn through the one-third and two-third retracement points measured from a significant high to the most recent low or from a significant low to the most recent high. The lines are drawn from the high or the low, through the retracement levels, and should give resistance or support. When breached, the price is indicated to rise or fall to the next speedline; once the second speedline has been broken, the price is implied to rise to the significant high used for its construction – or fall to the significant low. They often look unusual as they can, like fanlines, pass through (rather than to the right of) previous data.

Spikes: The pattern formed when a fast-moving price reverses direction 'on a sixpence'. Also known as Vee reversals.

Stars: Japanese Candlestick patterns which have small real bodies which gap away from the previous candle which has a long real body.

Stochastics (Fast & Slow): An indicator devised by George Lane which employs two lines called %K and %D. %K is calculated involving the ratio of the difference between the most recent close and the low for the period and the difference between the high and the low for the period. %D is its moving average. The plots oscillate between 0 and 100 and signals to buy and sell come through when the two lines cross at overbought or oversold extremes. Slow Stochastics uses %D from the fast calculation as Slow %K and then further smoothing gives us Slow %D.

Sub-Minuette: An Elliott Wave term describing a trend which lasts for less than a day.

Super Cycle: An Elliott Wave term describing a trend which lasts over fifty years and consists of five cycles.

Support: A price area where buyers can be expected to come in in sufficient quantity to stem – support – declines, such as previous lows or previous highs which have subsequently been overcome.

Tasuki Gap: A relatively uncommon Japanese Candlestick continuation pattern which occurs when a fast moving trend (up or down) is underway. The upside Tasuki Gap shows a white candle gapping higher followed by a black candle of similar size which opens within the white real body and closes below it. The opposite occurs with a Downside Tasuki Gap.

Technical Analysis: The analysis of price behaviour using patterns, trends and indicators based on price and related factors. Computerised trading systems are often based on these factors and remove the judgemental element evident in charting.

Tertiary Trend: The minor, very short term trends referred to in the Dow Theory.

Thirds – One and Two: The amount by which prices are popularly expected to retrace a previous price move.

Three Methods – Rising & Falling: A Japanese Candlestick pattern which implies the price trend will continue in the same direction. It occurs over five trading periods. In an uptrend a tall white candle is followed by three candles with small real bodies within the white candle's range. The fifth candle is white and closes at a new high. The Falling Three Methods occurs in a downtrend and has first a large black candle, followed by three small real bodies within its range. The fifth is a tall black candle which closes at a new low.

Three Soldiers: A Japanese Candlestick pattern which implies further strength is due. Three strong white candles which start around the lows, each showing a higher close, give the probability of further gains.

Three Wave Correction: An Elliott Wave pattern which follows a five wave advance; the three waves are number a, b and c.

Three: An important number in technical analysis. Long term analysis requires support or resistance to be broken by 3% to confirm a major reversal. Trends frequently only finally reverse after the third trendline is broken. The three box reversal is the most popular form of point and figure chart. Three is a Fibonacci number. One-third and two-third retracements are popularly anticipated and used to draw in speedlines. Three points of contact are needed to confirm the validity of a trendline. Bull and bear markets enjoy three principal phases.

TILS: Gann's Trend Indicator Lines which appear at the left hand side of a chart, denoting the trend's direction.

Trend Channels: Upper and lower parallel lines that define the upper and lower reaches of a trend.

Trendlines: Straight lines joining reaction lows in an uptrend or rally highs in a downtrend.

Triangles: A pattern showing increasing anxiety as the market argument develops with falling rally peaks and rising reaction lows. Usually a continuation pattern, it can sometimes form as a reversal pattern.

Triple Tops & Bottoms: Reversal patterns showing triple peaks or troughs which complete when the necklines joining the reaction lows or rally peaks are broken.

Troughs: Cycle lows.

Truncated Fifth: An Elliott Wave term for a failure – when the fifth impulse wave fails to clear the peak of the third.

Uptrend: A series of rising peaks and troughs.

Volatility Index: A system of stop losses (SARs), devised by J. Welles Wilder, Jnr., which move away from the price when volatility increases and move back towards the price when volatility dies down. It aims to avoid whipsaws in fast markets.

Volume: A generic term for the amount of trading done. Specifically, it refers to the number of shares traded and, in the futures markets, the number of lots.

Volume/Price Trend: A plot formed by amalgamation of price and volume whose shape should follow that of the price. When it does not, the price trend could be vulnerable to reversal. When the volume/price trend is broken a buy or sell signal is given.

Waves: The up and down moves seen from cycle troughs to peaks – and back to troughs again.

Wedges (Rising & Falling): A rally across an uptrend – or a reaction within a downtrend – which does not enjoy definition by parallel lines but, instead, the lines defining it converge. Such convergence emphasises the loss of upward or downward impetus and warns of imminent reversal.

Weighted Moving Average: A moving average whose calculation weights the most recent price in the calculation heavily and the first lightly. In a five day moving average, for example, the first day's value would be multiplied by 1, the second by 2, the third by 3, the fourth by 4 and the fifth by 5. The result is summed and divided by the sum of the multipliers.

Williams' % R: An indicator devised by Larry Williams and based on the ratio between the difference between the most recent close and the high of the period and the differential between the highest and lowest price of the period. Unusually it has 0 at the top of the scale and 100 at the bottom: levels between 20 and 0 are overbought and between 80 and 100 are oversold.

Window: A Japanese Candlestick term for a Western 'gap' – the empty space which appears on the y axis of the chart when a price moves up or down and fails to trade within the previous period's range.

X Axis: The horizontal timescale on a chart.

Y Axis: The vertical price scale on a chart.

Yield Gap Ratio: The ratio between the yield on gilt edged stocks and the yield on equities, its number reflecting the relative dearness or cheapness of equities.

Zigzag (and Double Zigzag): An Elliott Wave formation for a corrective wave which breaks down into a 5-3-5 pattern.

INDEX

abandoned baby pattern 137–8

acceleration 34, *36*, 45, *46*, 76, 76–7, 101–2, *104*, 107, 181, 210, 319

accumulation 20–1, 293, 314

ACD (Accumulation/Distribution) indicator 207, *209*, 312

A-D (Advance/Decline) Line 146–8, 146–9, *147–9* 148–9, *150*, 219, *219*, 221–4, *222*, *224–5*, 262, *263*, 264, *265*, 283,312
   and trend reversal 146–8, *148, 150*, 312

ADX *see under* Directional Movement Index

ADXR *see under* Directional Movement Index

Amstrad *5*, 5–6

angles *see under* Gann Theory, trendlines

Anglia Television 89–90, *93*

anniversary dates *see under* Gann Theory

Appel, G 317

arbitrage 150

Argyll Group 118, *121*

arithmetic scale
   application 17–23, *19–23*, 23, *26*, 26–8, *28*, 31, 48, 50–1, *52*, 312
   see also under short-term analysis
   comparison with logarithmic scale 17–18, 25, *26*, 50, 100

ASDA 113, *116*, 184, *185*

Australia 165

Australia and New Zealand Banking Group 109, *110*

Babcock International Group 6–7, *6–7*

Bank of Scotland 110, *112*

banks 262, 264, *266*

bar charts *see* High/Low Close charts

Barclays Bank 45–7, *46*, 101–2, *103*

base formations 38, *39*, 89–90, *93*, 171, *173*, 221, *224*, 224, *228*, 305, 308
   in Advance/Decline line 264, *265*
   and oscillators 192, *192*, 207, *210*, 218

Bass 224, 227, 260, *261*

BAT Industries 3–4, *4*, 35

bear markets 8, 32–3, *34*, 44, 146–7, 152, 163, 168, 172, 203–4, *205*, 304, 312, 314
   in commodities 165, 167–8, *169*
   duration 32, 161, 304–5
   moving averages 55, *55*, 59, *61*, *283*
   necklines *86*, 86–7, 89, 218–19, *219*
   signals of 47, *48*, 109, 111, 132, 136, *138*, 288–9, 294, *295*
   and volume 173, *176*, 288

Beveridge cycle 286

Body Shop *87*, 87–8

Bollinger Bands 69, *73*, 81, 312

Bolton, H 304

bonds 57, 157–8, 304

Boots 105, *106*

bottoms *see* base formations, broadening formations, double bottoms, multiple bottoms

boxes 29–30, 312

breakaway gaps 122–6, *124–125*, *127*, 316

breakouts 33–8, *35*, *38–9*, 49, 50,

FINANCIAL TIMES
Magazines

IT'S LIKE HINDSIGHT IN ADVANCE.

INVESTORS
CHRONICLE
THE CITY INSIDE OUT

At your newsagent every Friday

Dear Pitman Publishing Customer

IMPORTANT – Please Read This Now!

We are delighted to announce a special free service for all of our customers.

Simply complete this form and return it to the FREEPOST address overleaf to receive:

A Free Customer Newsletter
B Free Information Service
C Exclusive Customer Offers – which have included free software, videos and relevant products
D Opportunity to take part in product development sessions
E The chance for you to write about your own business experience and become one of our respected authors

Fill this in now and return it to us (no stamp needed in the UK) to join our customer information service.

Name: Position:

Company/Organisation:

Address (including postcode):

                                                         Country:

Telephone: Fax:

Nature of business:

Title of book purchased:

ISBN (printed on back cover): [0] [2] [7] [3] [ ] [ ] [ ] [ ]   [ ]

Comments:

--------------------------- Fold Here Then Staple Once ---------------------------

We would be very grateful if you could answer these questions to help us with market research.

1 Where/How did you hear of this book?
[ ] in a bookshop
[ ] in a magazine/newspaper
(please state which):

[ ] information through the post
[ ] recommendation from a colleague
[ ] other (please state which):

2 Where did you buy this book
[ ] Direct from Pitman Publishing
[ ] From a bookclub
[ ] From a bookshop (state which)

3 Which newspaper(s)/magazine(s) do you read regularly?:

4 When buying a business book which factors influence you most?
(Please rank in order)
[ ] recommendation from a colleague
[ ] price
[ ] content
[ ] recommendation in a bookshop
[ ] author
[ ] publisher
[ ] title
[ ] other(s):

5 Is this book a
[ ] personal purchase?
[ ] company purchase?

6 Would you be prepared to spend a few minutes talking to our customer services staff to help with product development? YES/NO

The Business Publisher

Written for managers competing in today's tough business world, our books will give you a competitive edge by showing you how to:

● increase quality, efficiency and productivity throughout your organisation
● use both proven and innovative management techniques
● improve your management skills and those of your staff
● implement winning customer strategies

In short they provide concise, practical information that you can use every